SERMONS.

BY

REV. CHARLES HENRY PLATT, A. M.
LATE RECTOR OF CHRIST CHURCH, BINGHAMTON, N. Y.

TO WHICH IS ADDED

AN ADDRESS,

DELIVERED AT WATERLOO, N. Y., JUNE 24, 1867.

EDITED BY

REV. JOHN G. WEBSTER,
Rector of Zion Church, Palmyra.

NEW YORK:
MASONIC FURNISHING COMPANY,
52 BLEECKER STREET.
1872.

EDWARD O. JENKINS,
PRINTER AND STEREOTYPER,
20 North William Street, N. Y.

ADVERTISEMENT.

IT may appear inconsistent for a Society which specially eschews theological discussions, and professes to have no creed in religion nor party in politics, to become the herald of a work like the present, in which religious views are presented from the stand-point of a particular church; and we therefore esteem it a duty to correct at the outset any misapprehension on this subject. When the hand of death was laid upon the author, and his career of usefulness checked at its meridian splendor, his friends and brethren felt that they had lost one whose earnest and devoted zeal for every good work had given him a place in their affections not easily to be filled by another, and they especially desired to have some token of remembrance that should incite them to imitate his virtues and lead them to emulate his unselfish devotion to the right. Under these circumstances, it appeared that nothing could be more appropriate than a volume expressing the best feelings of his heart in a service to which he had freely devoted his life. In no other way could it have been so truly said of him that, "being dead he yet speaketh."

While many will find comfort in perusing the sentiments of the following pages, which else had not seen the light, no one need see in them any attempt to make Freemasonry further responsible than a desire to pay the most fitting tribute to the memory of one who served the Craft with fervent zeal, yet never forgot his higher obligations to the Divine Master whose servant he proclaimed himself to be.

The press has been aptly described as a means whereby thought is made immortal; and in assisting thus to rescue from oblivion the thoughts of our departed friend and brother, we do not feel that we are derogating from our often announced conviction that Freemasonry knows no sectarianism.

We may be further permitted to add, that, whatever a brother's religious preferences may be, he will find nothing in these sermons to disturb them, but only, it is to be hoped, to increase his reverence to the Deity, and his kind remembrance of one who can "no longer extenuate for himself."

And so we commend this Memorial to the brethren as the most fitting monument to commemorate the pure life and loving fraternal walk of our lamented brother.

Fraternally,

JOHN W. SIMONS.

CONTENTS.

PREFACE.

THE publishing of the following Discourses is briefly explained. On the 25th day of February, A. D., 1869, at his residence in the City of Binghamton, the reverend author entered into the rest of the faithful departed in the Lord, leaving as many warm friends as he had acquaintances, besides an afflicted family, which consisted of a devoted wife and four children, three of whom were within the legal age of infancy, and all were dependent upon his labors for their maintenance.

As the first prompting of love for an honored *Frater*, Central City Commandery, No. 25, K. T., of which order the deceased was a member in high standing, determined to initiate a movement for the erection of a monument to his memory.

A committee was raised by that Commandery, to solicit, from the Fraternity within the State of New York, the means for carrying that resolution out.

It resulted in the prompt collection of a handsome sum. But before anything was done towards the execution of the work, it was suggested that it would be in better accord with the character of the deceased, the circumstances of the case, and the spirit of Masonry, to use a sufficient amount of the moneys collected for the erection of an appropriate, substantial, monument, every way in harmony with the character of the man, and with the balance or so much of it as would be necessary, publish "a memorial volume of his Sermons, the copyright, plates and volumes, to be the property of the widow and family of our lamented friend."

The suggestion met with the unanimous approval of those who expressed themselves upon the subject. At the session of the Grand Commandery held in Albany in October, 1871, the matter of publication of such volume was confided to a committee, consisting of John G. Webster, John W. Simons and Orrin Welch.

To the undersigned the task was given of selecting and arranging the MSS. for the book. It has been a labor of love to him. He confesses to have had a melancholy pleasure and to have derived much profit in following the glowing and sententious utterances of his departed friend, still instinct with eloquence and wisdom, although the hand that traced them, and the tongue that uttered them, are in the grave.

The Editor would not intrude himself between the reader and the following pages further than to add, that these Discourses have been selected from about one hundred placed at his disposal for the purpose. His difficulty has been not to get a sufficient number to make the book, but rather to determine which to take and which to leave, when all are of such equal merit. They are published just as first writen by the author, in first draught, not having been revised or copied. The Address is embodied at the request of several ot the author's clerical brethren, (not Masons) who listened to its delivery. With these "words of explanation" the volume is sent forth, companion of sincere trust that its perusal may benefit many readers, and that its product may help to lighten a widow's sorrows, and to supply the orphans' needs.

J. G. W.

PALMYRA, N. Y., *February*, 1872.

I.

THE LABORERS AND THEIR HIRE.

St. Matthew xx. 6, 7.

"And about the eleventh hour he went out, and found others standing idle, and saith unto them, Why stand ye here all the day idle?

"They say unto him, Because no man hath hired us. He saith unto them, Go ye also into the vineyard; and whatsoever is right, that shall ye receive."

THIS is recognized at once as a fragment of those strange illustrations used by our Lord, which we denominate parables. In this instance the kingdom of heaven is like unto a man that is a householder, hiring laborers into his vineyard.

I take it for granted that our beloved Saviour always employed his illustrations with adaptation to the occasion that called for them. He had an intention to meet the difficulty which was then pressing. And the main drift, or if we may so say, the moral, of His parable is always to be found in the same region where the difficulty lay that demanded His solution.

The parable of the householder and his hired

laborers originated in St. Peter's question, "We have forsaken all, and followed Thee; what shall we have therefore?" Our Lord's first object is to answer this inquiry as to compensation. He announces that the sacrifice involved in following Christ never is unrewarded. It is not only repaid, but comes back with a Divine plenitude, the best seed best nurtured on the best soil, and is in the harvest a hundred-fold what it was in the planting. So much is God's way of caring for those who expend themselves and their treasure out of love to God. But on man's part there is great diversity in the disposition with which such sacrifices are rendered. There is a calculating kind of close accountant who demands precise stipulation of his spiritual advantages before he invests upon Divine pledges. And there is generous, whole-souled, ardent, trustful alacrity, that only hears the call, and without beating about for terms, or suspiciously scrutinizing the chance of recompense, flings itself unreservedly upon the righteousness of God, ban ters not for a price, but welcomes the chance of escaping from its useless, fruitless, hopeless inactivity. That which grace specially honors is the disposition which accepts it for grace, and not for debt. God's economy is not injustice, but it is stupendous gratuity. The work and labor which He will not in the slightest item forget, is that which cometh of love. There is a quality of readiness, heartiness, in our acts which heaven measures as above all amounts. The genuine quality fascinates the eye of God more than the great bulk fills it. And, therefore, our Lord's fulness of wisdom in replying to Peter expressed itself in a startling conclusion, "Many that are first shall be last; and the last shall be first."

But the Apostle could not have understood, nor could we have interpreted this dark saying without some illustrative pictures. Jesus paints them with words. And among the scenes is that of the proprietor seeking in the market-place for those that should, in the pressing emergency, labor in his vineyard. At the eleventh or last hour of the laboring portion of the day, he would reinforce his band of hirelings. The men he accosts had not been exacting exorbitant wages, and conspiring to interrupt labor. They were not idlers of their own choice, nor restless, scheming plotters against the public welfare. They had their excuse for standing all the day idle in the very place where, of all others, employment was to be found. If any man had *sought* their services, no mischievous disposition on their part would have held them lounging around this centre of resort. And when the proffer of employment came, they dictated no terms, paltered not on the score of their claims, but closed with the simple bargain that whatsoever was right they should receive.

Now, if this was the original idea which our Lord's words would paint, we are not justified in so applying His parable as to militate against this Divine intention.

We do not propose to ramble through all the inquiries that have been ingeniously pursued respecting the meaning of those various hours of the day, when laborers were called into the vineyard, whether commencing with Abel or with Abraham, with the Apostles first proclaiming the gospel, or with the youth of the individual who has heard of the vineyard of grace. It is the system of mercy here disclosed, that addresses itself to our spiritual nature. It is the fact of men first finding themselves summoned to the duties of husbandry for the soul, at the eleventh hour, which surprises us into some solution of this event which may exhibit the mercy of God.

It seems to me that the point of this application to eleventh hour souls lies in the simple statement of their apology. They had not labored, because employment did not find them. They were unoccupied, because where they were likely to be sought no man had asked them to work.

There are two classes of souls in the spiritual order, then, to whom this eleventh hour encouragement does not belong.

These men that stood waiting for a petitioner cannot symbolize those unwilling, resisting, inflexible, and unimpressible natures which reject the calls of grace, and refuse the terms of salvation. If there was any intended resemblance between the searchings of the householder for laborers, and the invitations of the kingdom of heaven to souls that might be and should be genuinely Christian, then those that remained unsolicited until the last hour of the day are no representatives of a class who deliberately spurn the call of the gospel from first to last. If there can be such a spiritual condition as that of deliberate mockery at God's call, it is not indicated by any class which our Lord here portrays. But there is too much in human character that runs close upon the margin of this desperation. How far off from a deliberate refusal of God's call was that trembling Felix, when Paul reasoned of righteousness, temperance, and judgment to come? How far off from refusing the gospel is the startled conscience that wakes to hear itself called to repentance and the confession of Christ, and then relapses into its slumber of unconcern? How much less than a rejecter of the gospel was that placid Herod Agrippa, not daring to disbelieve the prophets, nor daring to believe them and be a Christian? Is our condition more pleasing to God than his negative indecision, when we admit the heavenly birth of the gospel, but refuse to seek in it a heavenly birth for ourselves? If there is a difference in degree, is there not a resemblance in aversion from God, whether we boldly proclaim that we will not heed the call of God, or whether we tacitly indicate that it is deferred to a more convenient season? The whole question of surrender to grace resolves itself into the cardinal inquiry, whether we shall develop ourselves in God's creation after His method or our own method. The pivot of salvation revolves on this point. Jesus saved us, so far as God's share goes, by submitting to the ordeal, "Thy will, not mine, be done;" and they that follow Him rest upon the same decision. The unsubmissive will, the unregulated heart, the unresolved purpose, the undevout attitude of body and mind—all of these, visited by the voice of God's commands and summoned by the appeal of God's promises, are registered for eternal remembrance among those that hear the word and do it not. They may cherish some project of ultimate amendment, they may promise their consciences that the dregs of life at least shall be holy, though the whole substance has been without God; they may dream that the last stroke of doom shall startle them to a contempt of earth and a love of heaven, but their repeated rejection of God's counsel, their continued indifference to mercy's reproof, argue that they are not intended by those who came at the last hour into the vineyard, but came as soon as they were called.

But we are adopting our Saviour's classification of spiritual conditions. His reaching forth the sceptre of salvation at the eleventh hour is not to be grasped by the persistent rejecter of the gospel as a warrant of hope for some eleventh hour favor to him. With the same impartiality does that living truth in the person of Christ crush the delusive hope of the sluggish and languid and unambitious recipient of grace. The angel that ushered in eternity placed his right foot upon the sea, and his left foot upon the earth. And so, the parable tramples alike upon the stiff and rocky hardness that will not answer to God's call, and upon the treacherous and unstable elements that yield to the impressions of grace, but drown it in the mere waves of emotion. There is a view of the gospel in which it is to be regarded as a call to labor. The householder was not abroad, from hour to hour through the day, inviting guests. He did not hurry into the market-place, where men's cares and amusements were clustering them, in the morning, and towards the close of the day, for the sake of finding men that would refresh themselves with his fruit or his shade rather than with the jests or the chafferings of the public concourse. He was in search of men that felt the need and sought the blessing of industry, of aiming at useful results, and turning their strength into products. The pleasures and the refreshments of the greatest of kingdoms are very prominent features in its attractions. They are genuine and eternal, and stand thus in contrast with the transient and the deceptive. But that pleasurable side of the gospel is only a part of its demand upon us. That belongs to its upper and unearthly aspect. It is sure to be a cross on this lower sinful side of its contact with the world, and is rather secretly and hopefully a feast. But one thing it must be to every one of us that blends grace with temptation, and that is "a labor." We have not solved the problem of working immeasurable happiness out of these wretched materials of mortality and sin by simply accepting the gospel, taking its lovely message to our embrace, and entrancing ourselves in the delicious consciousness that we love Jesus and are glad to be saved in his arms. That is the sentimental gospel which too often takes the place of warfare with the crucified, and work with the man that went about doing good. The echo of grace is not a melodious song, that sweetly tells the praise of Jesus, but the voice of a trumpet with the breath of an angel stirring us up to the rescue, "Work out your own salvation." The entertainment of a well directed soul is not idleness, but delight in work, and repose after work. What man needs for his immortality corresponds with what he finds imposed upon him for his enjoyment of this lower garden of God; not release from occupation, but an object worthy of his abilities, and a healthful pleasure in their exertion. God's parable is around us, and speaks through the whole system of nature. And it pronounces God's salvation to be dependent not only upon our feeling what He has done, but upon our laboring at that which we must do. The sentiment is morbid that expends itself in sentiment. Such a religion belongs to aerial unembodied creatures, and not to these complex beings which Christ redeemed. Labor for that meat which endureth unto eternal life, and you shall find your religious sentiments the more healthful, the more vivid, and the more disposing you to love your God, and to love that better image into which He, by your own labor, would shape you.

Let none of us deceive himself, or permit any shallow pretender to spiritual science to mislead us by any phrase or any theory that cuts the sinews of exertion, and leaves us languid and helpless recipients of grace, panting in weariness of life and counting upon the raptures of a saintly reward, because we have once thrilled with the luxuries of a devotional spasm. Serenity, that defied the cross and the devil, summed up its confidence in this language: "I have finished the work which Thou gavest me to do."

And if any conceit has lodged itself in our minds to the effect that our eleventh hour will come, and nothing shall then deaden us to the call of God—ah! who hath revealed to us that any messenger will then be heard? Who hath encouraged us to believe that those who refuse to accept the terms of the gospel, will be importuned when shadows are lengthened, and the opportunity of grace drifts beyond even the reach of our vision.

I offer you no mutilated gospel. I proclaim no scheme of my own devising. I speak for conscience—for the sanctities of truth—for the wants of our own truth-seeking souls. And I say to you, in the name of your own immortality, that whatsoever is right that shall ye receive—that there is no work done according to the light we have which shall be left uncompensated. Go into the vineyard. Enter the gates where Jesus claims the right and the power to employ and to reward you; be ye doers of the word, and not hearers only, deceiving your own selves. "Why stand ye here," in the market-place, in this thoroughfare where cares and jollities and devils will ever jostle and never reward you? "Why stand ye here all the day idle?" Jesus tells me to say that He will give you "whatsoever is right."

II.

THE VISION AND DEATH OF MOSES.

DEUT. xxxiv. 4.

"I have caused thee to see it with thine eyes, but thou shalt not go over thither."

WERE it not for the plain record of Holy Writ, we should have presumed that Moses would be transported from earth in some such excellent manner as Enoch was lured away to his God, or Elijah was wafted in the raptures of prophecy. We should have expected an equal sublimity in the close of the lawgiver's career, had *human* wisdom dictated the progress of events, or had *human invention* framed a fabulous narrative. Such was the human hand, uninspired and unhallowed, with which the Jewish historian attempts to condense the materials of the sacred history. He ignores entirely the offence, aggravated, public, and against Deity, which was remembered and visited upon Moses in his death. Waiving thus the mention of his signal crime, a gloss of imperfection is laid by Josephus upon all the subsequent history, and when he comes to describe the departure of this man from the scenes of life, it is with an unauthorized effort either to imitate the Christian statement of Jesus caught up from the view of his disciples in the clouds, or to eclipse the brilliant exaltation of Elijah in his burning chariot, or to bestow a heathen apotheosis upon the national hero. In this spurious narrative, he is represented as ascending Abarim in company with the whole senate of the Hebrews, as sharing with them in the view of the land of promise, as dismissing the senate to rejoin the body of the people, while his successor in the command, and the high-priest wearing the robes of Aaron, remained with him upon the summit of Pisgah; and (the narrative of Josephus concludes), "as he was going to embrace Eleazar and Joshua, and was still discoursing with them, a cloud stood over him on the sudden, and he disappeared in a certain valley, although he wrote in the holy books that he died, which was done out of fear lest they should venture to say, that because of his extraordinary virtue he went to God." Now here, we say, is a transcript of the plan which human art would have followed in delineating the death of this illustrious man. It would have buried from view the crime whose shadow lies upon the sacred page. It would have enveloped with the halos of glory the disappearing body.

We have already discovered the true narrative, although divested of expected splendors, yet luminous to the eye that looks for moral truths. It flashes upon us the persuasion, that God is a chastening Father—that He cannot suspend His moral government—that for our wanderings from righteousness we must be chastised. It displays, also, the provision of pity in his government by which He *prepares* the righteous to endure the severities of chastisement, and opens the prospect of Canaan before he buries in the valley of Moab. In the presentation of these truths, the event, as it occurred, is a thousand-fold more instructive, and far more in unison with the purport of Scripture and the methods of Divine discipline around us, than when embellished by human ingenuity.

We have, then, a chastisement upon the lawgiver, excluding him from the honor of completing the march into Canaan. We have, also, a special recompense for his former fidelity in the cheering view of that territory, towards whose fertile fields he had panted. The blow and its alleviation—the wound and the soothing—the chastening of a Father and the pity of a God, are before us. Is there no other moral truth involved in this event? Does it display God in no other character? What other view does it give of man as a moral being?

We see that a righteous man suffers. This is not strange. It is a sample of life—of life everywhere, in spite of increased refinement. But we see that he suffers particularly as a chastening for sin. What does this evince? That there are to be no penalties in an after life? Not at all. It evinces just the reverse. The penalty was not consequent, but subsequent. It was not an effect of his transgression, as remorse is an effect of guilt, or pain an effect of a wound, or loss an effect of imprudence. We can see no necessary connection between the trespass of Moses and his exclusion from Canaan. His working a miracle with ostentation and pride did not disqualify him for a leader of the people—did not destroy their allegiance or their courage. No doubt there was a connection between the sin and the penalty, but the connection rested upon some other principle than than that of disability for his office, or that of inward self-punishment. And the principle, which is thus required to connect two things so far separate as the unadvised speech of Moses, and the solitary, and premature death of Moses—that principle, we say, is the fact of a moral discipline over mankind.

We see, also, that a righteous man is prepared to meet his sufferings—that this preparation was not a hardening of his heart against fear, nor a flattering song of commendation, as if angels had come rehearsing his virtues and entertaining him with a description of his merits. No, there was nothing like this mechanical system of recompense—no such paying of equivalents for his good deeds. The recompense, when it came, was discerned by faith, and enjoyed by faith. It was received and relished by the same affection which had brought him towards it—in the exercise of the same faith that exiled him from the palace of Egypt, that braved the wrath of the king, that parted the waters of the sea, and grappled with his giant cares in the wilderness. By faith he looked upon the prospect before him, as the certain home of his people. By faith he connected the land of beauty with the promise of guardianship. By faith he discerned not only a luxuriance waiting for the chosen people, but a hand leading them to the possession. By faith he discovered that his word had not been in vain, but that Divine power and Divine truth should complete the remnant of his task. His blessing in beholding the land from his mountain post was dependent upon the exercise of this faith. It was not a negative satisfaction with hit past life, as being on the whole conscientious. Is was not the hardening of his sinews by reflecting that he had come safely out of dangers. It was a positive comfort derived from a positive faith. What, then, was the principle which made this vision a recompense and a preparation for the future? It was *this* obviously—that he was under a moral discipline. This made the view of Canaan a strength to his faith. This increased his endurance, while it rewarded his fidelity.

We are, by these observations, prepared to regard the event of his death as, in all respects, a fragment of moral discipline—a specimen of crystal from the revealed throne of Providence, in whose hues and pellucid form we may perceive the qualities of the mass.

To the lawgiver the vision was disciplinary. It was a test of his submission. Could he behold, and not desire to enter? It was a test of his obedience; for he went up by command, and went up for the purpose of completing thus his mortal career. It was a test of his delight in God; for.

he could not go over thither. And what was thus tested was by the testing improved. Apart from the necessity of bearing the penalties of his sin, the preparation for his death was, in all its appendages, disciplinary.

For his discipline in meekness, he was summoned to solitary communion with God, and a death around which man could array no flatteries.

For his discipline in courage, he was bidden to ascend the mount and deliberately confront the penalty of his sin.

For his discipline in faith, he was told to view the land as a promised possession.

For his discipline in earthly affection, he was called upon to die with his task undone, and in the full glow of bodily vigor.

And while his own virtues were thus trained and illustrated by the course of Providence, it was so ordered that his death became a discipline to others. In his removal from the view of the people, their revolts against his beneficent authority were punished. In his excision from the earthly heritage of Israel, they were taught to fear the penalties of transgression. In the favor of God, which presided over his fortunes to the last, they were called upon to view the blessings of his piety. In the submissiveness of his spirit, they beheld the triumphs of a nurtured virtue. In the secret burial of his body, they were saved from the peril of idolatry.

This, then, is the moral truth to be deduced from the wearying life and the lone death of the lawgiver—that the righteous man is under a blessed discipline. Though he recognize and feel a chastening hand upon him, he is neither hardened against it, nor lifted in rebellion to complain against his God, nor broken with fear and sorrow. And when he counts his sunny days of privilege and comfort, he reckons them as trusts, and pays his debt to a bountiful God with gratitude and devotion and trustful joy.

How elevating the thought! How sublime the victory of a righteous soul! It is not here merely to accomplish the toils and bear the rigors of life. It is here under tuition—tried with sorrows, tried with cares, tried with want, tried with possessions, tried with ease, tried with success. In all things and at all times it is under discipline. Animating, consoling thought! It gives nerve to my race after an imperishable life; it extracts the poison from these earthly wounds. Blessed discipline! How it makes of our afflictions a Jacob's ladder; and every woe that separates us from the love of this world is but a round that carries us up higher! Blessed discipline! How it consecrates our pleasures, and by converting them into thanksgiving and the love of God, clothes us with the robes of angels, which are the garments of praise!

But what mean we by asserting this blessedness of the righteous? Not that they alone are under moral discipline, for this embraces all mankind. Not that the righteous are exempt from the calamities of life, for these are essential to the carrying on of discipline. We mean rather that all the experience of life, all its accumulation of cares, all its seductions of vanity, tend to discipline the virtues and amend the defects, and enhance the blessings of the righteous.

This is the record which God has given. He has let us so far into the secret of His Providence. He has opened to us this page in the learning of heaven. "Great are the troubles of the righteous; but the Lord delivereth him out of them all." He goes, as a trusting child, that has occasion to fear, but leans against the Protector and is secure. And this is his attitude through life. But when life is over, what shall be the end of his discipline? He is fitted for the fellowship of God; he is ready for the study of all wisdom; he is come out of discipline, and his garments are washed in the blood of the Mediator, and he passes from the life of discipline to the rest that remaineth for the people of God, where temptation has no power, and chastening does not bruise his soul.

But I hear the murmurs of the human heart, and it asks why this should be so. Why should this discipline of sorrow and trouble be necessary to fill heaven with tear-washed sinners? Why? Go, ask the aged man. Did he know why his limbs were exercised in the sports and activity of youth? Did he foresee the effect upon his muscles, when he leaped and tasted freedom, while others smiled and sighed at his merriment? And when the gentle hand of restraint sets limits to their sportiveness, do children know what good for them is meant? And when it comes to discipline and tasks, and making ready for a life above merry childhood, it is a hardship that lays its fetters on them. But what know they of its advantages; what knows any one so well as that aged man bending down to pick up shedding memories?

Why should a discipline of temptation be needed for a world of holiness and rest? Why! Ask the tenants there. Is it a world of feeble, sickly, timid virtue? Is it a place at all congenial with a hesitating virtue? No, it is the home of exercised and vigorous goodness. For aught we know, there may be some necessity in moral nature that it should attain certain degrees of resistance and force, before it can stand secure even in a holy world. We may need to acquire an angel's resolution, a seraphic love, a muscular and winged virtue, before the soul can get a place in that world. And when we take the view, which God has, of our own nature, depraved, prone to sin, impatient, mistaking most grossly the advantages and disadvantages of good and evil; that it is a fallen nature which is to be reared, and not an upright nature to be carried through one life into another; we may confess that what discipline we need, it is entirely beyond our scope to decide. The soul is that bird of Paradise whose plumage has been ruffled, and the wings clipped, and the joints broken. Ambitious of ethereal flight, it flutters and wounds itself. Pained with the healing, it is injured by its own impatience. Let it bear the discipline of its cure, let it wait till its strength is confirmed by little acts of daily renewal, and at the last, unimprisoned, it shall go up above the clouds, and bring its plaintive moans into harmony with the melodies of a peaceful world.

Such is the discipline that suspends its obscurities over the righteous. It is a discipline not destroyed but solaced and blessed by the gospel. It is a great shadow, but to the Christian soul it is a shadow under the wings of the Comforter. It came to the lawgiver as an instrument that would repair his shattered meekness; and when he prayed earnestly that God would remove it, the dark dispensation was not taken away. But it came with a view of Canaan; it came with repairs to his faith; it came with unutterable joys in the contemplation of God; it came with the restoration of his forfeited character as the meek man. Such was the discipline that stung the flesh of Paul. And he prayed thrice for relief. But it was discipline, it was his school before the manly life, it was the mending of a broken spirit, and the answer to his prayer was a voice, "My grace is sufficient for thee." And all along through this childhood of the spirit, we go catching visions of a blessed life beyond, but the fruition may not come till the discipline is finished; and at every chastening stroke of trouble, the voice is heard speaking to faith on its enraptured mount of vision, "I have caused thee to see it with thine eyes; but thou shalt not go over thither."

III.

INGRATITUDE.

St. Luke xvii. 17.

"Were there not ten cleansed, but where are the nine?"

ORDINARILY there is no more reliable test of character than the measure of gratitude. It depends so much upon the constant predominance of better impulses, it carries itself so far beyond any single act of return, it is so essentially cordial and continuous, and consists so much more in permanence of feeling than in any one expressive action, that no one can be persuaded into confidence where he discovers ingratitude. I ask if any other trait so moves our indignant disgust as ingratitude? What so soon stifles the sympathies of nature? What so often withers the active hand of benevolence? What so excites the grudgings, wherewith we behold another successful? No; there is a kind of complacency which we all feel, in beholding the assurances of merit and virtue, the buds of gratitude, bursting tokens of fruitful goodness. We witness it in the repayment of a child's gratitude, and we set a value upon it not from the caresses or the ardent expressions or the flatteries of childish affection, but from the picture of the heart that is spread before us. Gratitude is honesty in paying a debt, but not the cold, rigid, and proud honesty that renders purchase-money; it is a generous, unselfish, cheerful integrity that both confesses the obligation and delights to be paying. Gratitude is the accomptant that writes the debt upon the heart, and the sign of gratitude is not in seeing benefits returned, but in finding them recorded on that inner ledger.

Ingratitude is the reverse, described as a "marble-hearted fiend," upon which cruelty can chisel a record, but gentleness and the breath of kindness leave no impression on the cold surface. You never see ingratitude in one of human kind without inferring a stock of ill-nature out of which the vice has grown. You look at it as the leper-spot, which shows disease within. You take it for an evidence not of corruption merely, but of corruption growing. Great vices, like any other human greatness, must have attendants to wait upon them, and minister to their sway. Ingratitude is by this rule discovered to be a monster-vice, served by mammoth and hideous traits; lifted up by pride so as to overlook kindnesses; a granite mountain-top above the lowly acts of common gratitude, elevated but proudly barren, and always attended with hard-heartedness and want of compassion, as insensible to other's miseries as to their kindness. See it in that first rebel against Infinite Love, the Arch-fiend, whose ingratitude was caressed and crowned by his ambition, by *pride*, that prime minister and great chancellor of hell; and not only by pride, for he put on at once, when he put off an angel's virtue, a devil's cruelty and malignity, dragging down his enticed army, and stealing, a glistening but venomous thing, into Paradise. See the human career of this vice in Absalom, the rebellious son of an indulgent father, with his fingers not only itching for the sceptre but reaching after the very head of his exiled and houseless parent.

But as corruptions of the heart are always worst in those who should by their nature be best, so human ingratitude has been most horrid in ambition and in cruelty when raging in a woman's breast. See it in those "unnatural hags," Goneril and Regan, with their crazed father, a beggar-king, "a poor old man, as full of grief as age, wretched in both!" See it most savage of all, in Tullia, daughter of a king, married with great dowry to Tarquinius Superbus, then inciting her husband to kill her royal father, then usurping his throne, then in bedizened pride, instead of funeral weeds, driving for a spectacle of jewelled splendor through the streets of Rome, and with no more compassion than a putrid carcass ordering her shuddering coachman to crush with the horse-hoofs and the wheels the yet palpitating and bloody body of her newly murdered father.

Such are the tragedies of filial ingratitude! Such are the horrors which ungrateful human nature can enact toward those of nearest human tie.

Let us learn to transfer these suggestions to our own individual characters as recipients personally of the Divine blessings.

It is evident, in the first place, that the measure of our religious gratitude will be the index of our character. We would like to resolve our religion into a round of devout actions. We are prone to content ourselves with certain specified acknowledgments, and to regard any extra zeal as rather putting Providence in debt to us. Partly because we do not meditate on the Divine goodness, and partly because we are unwilling to be counted debtors, our religious gratitude does not mount above absolute requirements. We see no need of advancing beyond the terms of salvation. And while the motives of a generous gratitude would prompt us to self-denials for the sake of promoting religion, or for the sake of expressing emotion, we restrain ourselves within the round of necessary duties.

And this sort of religion pleases the world. It calls itself Christian now, and whatever be its perversions or wrestings of Christian scripture, it claims the name of all that is good. But this world is not so utterly thankless as to refuse an offering. On the contrary, it has festivals and seasons when it expects to show gratitude. Care is taken, however, that this gratitude does not lessen the means of enjoyment. Its offering is not even borrowed from the fund for pleasures. It is put down on the list of necessities, and a tax of this overruling necessity alone can extract the tribute. Now we say that these returns to God are no suitable index of character. They may be urged by various motives not strictly religious. The test that we can apply with safety is that which will evince the amount of gratitude. This is goodness ; this is hope this is a tie between the Great Giver and the mortal restorer. This indicates the degree of filial feeling. Religious objects are set up in the world for the purpose of calling out and cultivating this feeling. God's language is by every day's sunrise, and by every cloud's shedding—by His benefits to the just and the unjust, "Son, give me thine heart." We give Him our heart in obedience ; that is well. We give Him our heart in worship ; it is well. We give Him our heart in *gratitude ;* and it is all. Earth can do no more. Here then is the touchstone. Apply it to your character. What does it reveal? Are you moved by a sweet gratitude? Are you delighted with the privilege of testifying a religious emotion? Do you come into the atmosphere of praise, as the happy child rushes to the caresses of affection, to the offices of respect and gratitude? Do you listen to the voice of God, speaking in His prophets, as an obliged friend waits upon the counsel of his best benefactor? Do we seek for occasions and modes of showing what we feel? And when the spirits flag, and the flesh chills the ardor of nature, do we still persevere as knowing that we ought, with all our powers and against all obstacles, to glorify our God? Let such questioning be the magnet among the affections of the soul. Watch the attraction which may exist between your gratitude and your soul's affections. It will show, as no other test can show, our real character.

It is evident, in the second place, that as our ingratitude towards men is never a solitary vice, but, like a guilty man afraid of remorse, seeks shelter in society, so our religious ingratitude will carry along its concomitants. It grows out of spiritual pride, as the other out of worldly pride. What is it that disposes one to be ungrateful but a false estimate of his rights, as if he had claim to a greater share in this world than another, and as if he could demand more than by justice he can earn. And this conceit of a proud spirit makes it insensible to the kindness and courtesies and the incessant favors of others. So is it towards the Great Goodness. Our proud spirit scorns subjection. It *claims* from the Maker all that by which we *live*. It accepts His gifts, as a sort of testimony to our deserving. It challenges the Almighty to withhold from us what we have fairly earned. It is not thankful for its faculties; industry and exercise have made them. It is not thankful for its gains; they came in spite of hazards. It is not thankful for the gifts of grace; for God gives us no more than He finds pleasant and delightful to Himself to give. They are poured, the bounties and the grace of God, upon proud spirits, like sunlight and showers upon the topmost crags, which court the earliest and the latest rays, and draw towards them the passing clouds, but they produce nothing, they render nothing, and the very drops that water them are exhaled to heaven from the valleys below.

I am not saying that the ungrateful soul gives utterance to all this pride. Far from it! It is, like that of the nine lepers, discovered by its silence. They were afraid to return and expose their malady.

It is a similar spirit that cuts off the feet of gratitude. It comes halting to the sanctuary of praise. It refuses to surrender itself to the fealty of a redeemed sinner. It must be lured by the voice of attractive eloquence to the house where God's mercies are acknowledged. It comes as a civility to man, where it should press through storms and through threats to own and to publish the ceaseless benefits of grace. It is indifferent and unhumbled, as if God had not made us debtors, or as if we were under some exception to the law of gratitude. With what loathing do we look upon the pride that receives the little acts of courtesy without an equal politeness. Can we make these trivial acts articles of faith, and count it of no consequence whether the Almighty be adored? If the appearance of humility draws us to so strict observance of ceremonies that shall make society happy, oh! what constraints are there to humble us on our knees before the everlasting God, and to waken the tones of praise in echo of the seraphic hymns and the eloquence of gratitude above.

Religious ingratitude is not only base through pride, but hard of heart. It indurates the soul. It grows upon us, like cruelty upon the heart of passion or avarice. You see it stalking like premature guilt upon the fields of earth, where the unworthy offering of the ungrateful Cain was rejected of heaven. He lost the very chance of acceptance by the effect of his ingratitude. Because he slighted the benefits of God, his heart was deserted of God. He was hardened in the very process of neglecting to praise. The fear of God was taken away, as the love of God was stifled. And the same hardening came upon the heart of Judas. He was ungratefully bartering the life of his Master, and all the time he was selling himself to a desperate deed. In this way, the terrible proposition is justified, "Whom He will He hardeneth." He pours more benefits upon their rocky insensibility. He makes their vice to grow by giving it occasion. He wills to show the inveteracy of corruption, by exhibiting its resistance to arguments of love. God hardens by His Providence, but it is kindness and the outpouring of gifts that should soften and melt; and the ungrateful heart is hardened. It goes on like the nine cleansed lepers, conscious of benefits, but conscious of wilfully deserting the Benefactor. So we harden the offender who escapes through our clemency and wallows again in the mire. So the parental indulgence hardens the stubborn tempers of depraved childhood. So the image of gold hardens the hand that digs for the metal and graves it with art and cunning device.

But why, we ask, why should human nature be debased into ingratitude towards God? What temptation can we have towards this vice? That it is possible, daily observation evinces. That there is a proneness to it, every penitent heart confesses, every tongue reluctant to join in His praise proclaims. Incredible as it might seem, the reality stares upon us, when the mere system of worldly pleasure, empty pleasure, makes drafts much larger than religion, and finds them honoured; when the cost of a year's struggle in politics exceeds the expense of religion, and is met without a murmur; when the decencies of attire are more onerous than the honours of God's worship, and no one suggests retrenchment there; when the elegance and the comfort of our homes far surpass the offerings we make to God, and no one feels the inconsistency and the inverted order of things. Is there not some disease upon the muscles of the hands that get, when they open to receive, and cannot be lifted up to bless? Is there not some unhinging of the doors to the heart, when they let in such a throng of earthly delights, and send forth so few messengers to heaven? Is not the heart smitten with a curse, that admits all tax gatherers except the princely form of gratitude to our Saviour?

But what are the errors or the persuasions that have converted the heart into a dead sea?

Why, they are simply these: false ideas of God, with Whom we have to do, and false ideas of His control in earthly affairs.

By the former error, we conceive of God as an Almighty and Infinite Spirit, of all perfection, but we do not realize in Him emotions suited to His divine nature. He is to us a Lawgiver, but not a lover of justice. He is to us a wise God, planning salvation, but not a Redeemer, yearning over us. We think of Him as removed from us, and wrapt in His own sublimity, when He is near us and affected by our every moral act. Ye that rely upon such a high and distant and abstracted intellect for your God, tell me; ye many that live in Christian lands, and call yourselves believers of the

Word, tell me, what your Bibles have to do with such a being as you imagine? What part has that isolated God in revelations and prophecies and the gradual uncovering of His glory? What part in your cold system has that crowning fact of the incarnation? What need in your philosophy of a Saviour, Who went about doing good, flesh of our flesh, touched with a feeling of our infirmities, bidding the leprous scales to drop, banishing the diseases of men, and remanding the dead to cheer the homes of desolation? What has that far-off majesty to do with our services, our homage, the little act, the suppressed feeling, the struggling prayer, the vocal praise? Oh, no! you have put God away from you when He would draw nigh; you have denied Him the emotions which He has come near to ask, come near to encourage. When He bids us cry "Our Father," you have no thought of the affections He would express. When He sends the Spirit of adoption into our hearts, we choose to live as strangers. When He tells us that our thanks and praise gladden His untroubled Spirit, we will not receive the truth. When He tells us that our actions jar upon the harmony of the universe, and while our repentance wakes a melody in other worlds, we doubt the grandeur of our being. When he descends and hears our cry and sweeps the curse from us, we question whether the Incarnate Redeemer is to be praised. We receive the benefit and depart from the Christ that heals us; we catch at the gospel sound that God is gracious, but we lose the gospel sound that tells us of the Father rejoicing because we obey; and for our persistency in this erroneous view of God, the Saviour of man is compelled to inquire, "Were there not ten cleansed, but where are the nine?"

The second source of our ingratitude is the failure to recognize the personal intention of God's benefits. This applies to two classes.

The first class are those who count their privileges as so many indications of their safety. They are not attuned to thanks, because they dread no danger. They find their houses stand, and their harvests come, although they live on the sides of a volcano. They are not quickened into religious praise, because they have no need of religious comfort. In the lot of life, they have enough to do to manage affairs of earth, and carry their burdens. It is their expectation that God will warn, that He will awaken, that He will give them spiritual gifts when their time comes to receive them; not considering that now is the accepted time, and that every joy, as well as every trial, is a personal messenger, sent to ask for their tribute of gratitude.

The second class are those who have received eminent mercies, and permit them to pass without a special acknowledgment. See how many are spared by the blessing of God from "threatening graves," and their vows are never rendered! How many have cried unto God in the hours of alarming sickness, and resolved to consecrate their living days; but with the glow of health came the chill of ingratitude! How many have looked unto God in affliction, imploring His grace, and in the tumult of the surrounding world have forgotten their promises and their duties! What person, educated amid holy influences, has not at some period recognized the yielding of his heart to the persuasions of the Holy Ghost? Alas! the many receive the grace of God in vain. Raised from their distress, snatched as brands from the burning, they are lured away to their old and stronger habits, the flames of corruption are kindled anew, and Christ stands at His altar and asks, "Were there not ten cleansed, but where are the nine?" How many washed at the font, and cleansed from their sins by the promised gift of the Spirit, have trampled upon the crown which God gave, and counted the blood of the covenant wherewith they were sanctified a common thing!

The voice of Christ is addressed directly to these entangled victims of sin. They, above all others, must be speechless in the judgment. They have been gathered to the household of the Father, and ungratefully desert again its shelter. They have been possessors of the inheritance, and sold their birthright for a trifle.

Oh! shall the ungrateful heir of God reply that the treasures were not given, that the title was contested by temptation, that the inheritance was a struggle and a sorrow, and all its bliss lay far off among the palaces of the upper world. Child of God, this is thy privilege. Thy glory in that other sphere will be fixed by thy patience and thy fidelity here. What! shall God buy us with His Son; shall He visit us with His Spirit; shall He make a covenant with us; shall He give us the arms that win the victory; shall He call us His sons and His heirs; shall He bring the atmosphere of heaven around us; shall He give us all that resolute goodness could need? and, because the man's estate is not ours at once; because the trusts of the tried are not ours without trial, shall we desert Him, and spurn His gifts, and throw our contemptuous neglect back against His grace?

Think how the breath of ingratitude freezes our compassions. Think of the odious character which attaches to an ungrateful child. Think of the pierced breast of parental love, wounded by a child's ingratitude—

> "How much sharper than a serpent's tooth
> It is to have a thankless child."

Ah! no tenderly caressing father, no melting pities of a mother, can compare with the love of that Father, can equal the compassions of our Redeemer. His wounded heart is ever pouring out intercessions for us.

Bleeding Lamb of God! wound by Thy Spirit, wound in Thy love, our hardened hearts.

Almighty Saviour! draw us to Thy feet. O, our Father! open Thy arms of compassion for ingratitude washing itself in tears of shame. If there be but one that loves and lives as a child of God, teach me to be ambitious for this honor.

IV.

FORGIVENESS NOT IMPUNITY.

2 SAMUEL xii. 10, 13.

"Now, therefore, the sword shall not depart from thine house.

"And David said unto Nathan, I have sinned against the Lord. And Nathan said unto David, The Lord also hath put away thy sin; thou shalt not die."

IT may often seem a strange thing to us that in the Holy Bible, designed to portray examples of the most exquisite purity, and to inculcate precepts of the highest virtue—it may seem strange to us that in such a volume, representing in word and symbol the Divine perfections, so much space should be allotted to the history of David, and to the effusions of his inspired soul. He stands forth upon the sacred page as a sort of model approved by God, as a man (to use the Scripture language), after God's own heart. He stands forth as quite a solitary example of perpetual devotion, and the very words which God accommodated to his experience are transmitted to us all, for our instruction and for moulding not only our language but our hearts. Yet we behold him, according to the testimony of the same record, implicated in the grossest crimes, confessing himself a wilful sinner, and published to the world as the instigator and plotter of a treacherous murder. There was a season in his career when he *seemed* to be, and *was* the worst of men—a tyrant, brutal, lewd, guiltier than any of us, abhorrent even to himself when Nathan drew his likeness. But the record that is faithful in these particulars warns us with the sequel. Before the monarch had displayed any compunction, the prophet approaches him with his ingenious parable. The rich inheritance of the king on the one hand, and the little treasure of his servant in the bliss of a happy household, are plainly pictured by the king's reprover. To use the words of David, the Lord takes the wicked in his own net, and makes the king his own accuser. And then, without waiting for him either to extenuate or to confess his guilt, the Almighty brings forth, from the armory of His justice, a weapon that may vindicate His own holiness, while it leaves to the sinner the opportunity of repentance. "I anointed thee king over Israel, and I delivered thee out of the hand of Saul. Wherefore hast thou despised the commandment of the Lord? Now therefore the sword shall not depart from thine house." Fearful weapon to be wielded by the Eternal God! Fearful threatening to follow him through all his days, to hang over him in the appalling remembrances of death, to descend upon generation after generation, and to stain the stone of his sepulchre from age to age with the vengeance and the shame of his forgiven transgression! Fearful threatening fearfully fulfilled! How that one short season of wickedness changed the whole current of David's life, and opened a flood of misery upon his descendants. "The sword shall not depart from thine house." You wielded it in defiance of God, He will wield it in vindication of His insulted Majesty; you made it the instrument of sin, He will make it the instrument of vengeance. I know well enough that David was forgiven, I grant that he was a most thoroughly penitent man, I remember that he was patient and that he was ever afterwards a most earnest servant of God; but his sin never forgot him, and because he was a penitent, he never forgot it. The sword was pursuing him, and not only him, but, so far as the sacred record extends, it was yet piercing his lineage, and marking its way with blood, and I know not but its blows are yet hewing in pieces the house of David, unless its work was done in the slaughter of the Son of David, as He bore the sins of the world in His own body on the tree. I see one of his sons conspired against by another, and slaughtered with the sword of his own and his father's punishment. I see this slaughtering son rioting in the temporary success of his wickedness, until the darts of Joab pierced his heart, and "the young men that bare the armor of Joab compassed about and smote Absalom and slew him." And I see a third son, spared till the burial of his father, and then slain with the sword of his brother. I see the Edomite and the Syrian raised up as adversaries to Solomon, and unsheathing the sword against him all his days, though his whole aim was to live in peace, and though he had an excellent wisdom for his help. I see the tribes then rent asunder, and war between their princes all their days. And afterwards I trace only a history of confusion and carnage, until I behold the Son of David pierced on the cross, and His mother, who was of the house and lineage of David, beholding the fulfilled prophecies of her royal ancestor with a sword piercing her own heart also. Fearful wages for a few days' sin! Ages did not wipe it out. God forgave it, but its punishment lingered. David rested in the arms of God's mercy, but the world was reading in his children's woes the sentence of unrelieved judgment—"The sword shall not depart from thine house." Observe, here, that this threatening was a consequence of the sin, neither founded on the king's repentance nor mitigated by it. It was a part of the penalty laid upon the transgressor, and only a part. According to his own judgment, the rich violator of the poor man's peace must surely die. In the sight of men he had broken the bonds of society, and by the voice of the king he must die. Not so with the royal offender. By the voice of the law, he was banished from God, he was shut out from the hope of mercy. But repentance brings back his soul from this future doom, while it leaves the earthly retribution to bow his soul in sorrow all his days, and to carry the tide of punishment as far as the sin might reach. For whatever it might imply, there was a putting away of David's sin, when he confessed it as sin, whatsoever men might esteem it, and did this with a passionate sorrow. "And David said unto Nathan, I have sinned against the Lord. And Nathan said unto David, The Lord also hath put away thy sin; thou shalt not die."

Observe, also, as a part of this history, that the punishment, which hung upon David, notwithstanding his repentance and God's forgiveness, were not only outward troubles, but inward afflictions for the rest of his days, and sorrows of soul, uttering their mournful strains upon that harp which had cheered away the griefs of Saul, and been ever tuned to praise. His life was spared, but it was, at the best, a burdensome life, heavy with the chastenings of God.

From this history we have now some instruction to elicit.

In the first place, we see in this history that sin has a double consequence, partly in this life and partly in another: the former in vindication of God's honor, the latter in the necessity of the soul's unfitness for heaven. It was so in the very beginning of transgression. "In the day thou eatest thou shalt surely die," was the sanction of the law; and, in its fulfillment, death has passed upon all, although all are not irrecoverably out of the favor of God. We are daily witnesses of the temporal penalty of the first transgression, while we are ever in hope that its full condemnation may not pass upon all.

In the second place, we observe that forgiveness of a sin does not include the remission of this temporal penalty. The truth of God's word demands this, while the loss of His favor as a consequence of sin is required by His nature. This favor may be regained by a change of our character and relations, a change from the love of sin, or indifference about it, to an abhorrence of it as sin; a change from an open or careless despiser of God to an open and earnest searcher for His mercy. This change, wrought in us by that grace which Christ died to purchase, may restore us to a condition of acceptance, and then only the temporal penalty remains to be exacted. I know not whether the drift of this remark is yet understood. My meaning is that God's nature makes a sinful nature by necessity abhorrent, incapable while sinful of His joys or His favor. His grace or gracious gift, on the other hand, relieves such a nature of its absolute sinfulness, and if it go so far as to make that will like His own, truly abhorrent of sin, then the nature is, though imperfect, yet for Christ's sake accepted.

It is impossible to illustrate this, because there can be no such relations between creatures as between God and His creatures. But when we come to speak of the temporal punishments for sin, we see that the honor of God's law is concerned, and the truth of His word; and for the sake of these He will visit every sin of every soul, however good, however bad,—will visit every sin with a temporal penalty, whether the sin be forgiven or not. I do not say that it is of no avail to seek forgiveness or to find it in this life. Every moment of delay is aggravating this world's penalties, while it may cast us with unforgiven sin into the world where grace never enters, and repentance never comes. I suppose this temporal penalty might be divided into two kinds, one in the way of chastening, the other in the more severe way of loss of opportunities. And this will be a sufficient answer to those who inquire after the punishments of one repenting at his last hour. He loses opportunity of retrieving his name among men, and doing good in his generation, and gathering rewards. David's sin was taken away; he lived a long life in God's favor, but it was a life of repentance, chastened and corrected, loaded with the temporal penalties of sin. If you would know how a Christian Apostle looked upon this, hear his appeal to the Christians at Corinth, when they came with unprepared and unworthy hearts to the feast of the Blessed Sacrament, "For this cause many are weak and sickly among you;" whether it were the body chastened or the soul distressed, it was for this offence. "But when we are judged, we are chastened of the Lord, that we should not be condemned with the world." Hence the prayer of that ancient Christian, "Burn here, wound here, that Thou mayest spare in eternity." His own perfect nature does not foreclose a sinner from hope, while it does exact the chastening which one man's offences have deserved, and another's righteousness shall escape. Thus are mercy and truth met together in the gospel, the one sealing the sinner for heaven, the other bowing down the accepted soul with the Lord's chastenings. I know that it is common to speak with piety of our distresses and tribulations as hidden mercies and disguised blessings, and I believe it to be true. But they are blessings and mercies only because of overflowing grace, which brings them home to our consciences, and uses them to arrest the dominion of some mastering sin. What, I ask, are all the woes of this life but so many temporal penalties pursuing men's transgressions, penalties of that opening sin, which Christ has blotted out while the temporal woes remain? How else can we reconcile the sufferings of innocent infancy with the mercies of God, sufferings loading the soul with everything but remorse, and the body even with death? They have committed no sin, and are exposed to no eternal vengeance; yet they are racked with tortures, and sometimes taken away from a life which has been to them worse than death. We believe that the price which the Redeemer paid secures to their departing souls the saving grace of God, but here the temporal penalties of the old transgression are heaped upon them. For them at least the sin which was theirs by the heritage of Adam, is forgiven by the heritage of Christ, but the temporal penalty is not taken away.

Lastly, we see plainly in all this, that punishment is not reformatory, but retributive and in vindication of God's glory. David was thoroughly reformed, was penitent even without punishment, was laid in his grave ages before the punishment had ceased from his house. It was not designed, then, for his reformation. And if men will still insist that his example was for the reformation of others,

I surely have no desire to dispute it, since this concedes the whole question, and makes the consequences of his sin punitive towards himself. I have no desire to doubt that God's chastenings make the good better, but I cannot refuse to say that his punishments are nevertheless the retributions of justice and the vindication of His glory to the sufferer, to alarmed men, to a universe. But do we not thank God for His inflictions? Do we not glory in tribulation? Do we not trace the birthday of everlasting hope to some occasion of Providental chastisement? Has not God reformed us by our very sufferings? Truly may we say, on the cross we found our Jesus. But what erected our cross? What brought us beneath it? What but the punishments of a Father, Who remembers our iniquities, and scourges us back to our salvation.

"The Lord hath put away thy sin, but the sword shall not depart from thine house." It speaks to us all. It bids us to recall the past, and wipe away every little sin by repentance. Our tears of sorrow shall be our penalty, and mitigate the judgments of time. Woe to the man, whose whole life has been a heaping up of punishments! At one day they will descend in arrayed vengeance, and write the past in fiery characters along his path or on the walls of his everlasting prison. Woe to him who is greedy of gain, woe to the drunkard, and the reveller, and the adulterer, and blasphemer, and scoffer! Even repentance will not screen him from the earthly vindications of wrath. Already are beginnings of punishment falling upon us. In them we hear the accusation of God, "Thou art the man." In the tortured victim of his passions we are discovering the fruits of his sowing in sin, but who hears in his own calamities the voice of God, "Thou art the man?" In the recompenses of human law, God's viceregent, we rejoice, but in the tribulations of our lot, who hears the message which the past is sending, "Thou art the man?" In every woe as it fastens upon you, God's messenger is dwelling, and uttering his faithful accusation, "Thou art the man?" It is not an accident that perplexes you; it is not the mere devising of man; it is an old sin coming back to accuse you, and to leave its record of warning, "Thou art the man?" Oh, fling away, I pray you, that proud and self-righteous habit of boasting that the Lord has chastened you. He did it for your sin, He did it in remembrance of the forgiven past, He did it for your old murmurings, for your secret sins, for your worn-out and discarded pleasures; He did it in the faithfulness of a Father's love, but in the truthfulness of a holy God hearkening to the accusations of His law, "Thou art the man." We hear Thee, O God, in every joy that crowns our days; we hear Thee in our daily ills. Grant us grace to repent of all the past, that in the struggles of death we may have no sins to track us then, but go out in peace as the day sinks into night.

V.

THE WARNING OF LOT'S WIFE.

ST. LUKE xvii. 32.

"Remember Lot's wife."

THERE are two peculiarities in the allusion here made. The first is the omission of the woman's name. No name is given to Lot's wife in the sacred record. None of the genealogies, with all their precision, mention it. The narrative in Genesis describes her fate, but omits her name. No sacred writer records it. Our Lord copies this silence of canon, and cites her history with no other title to distinguish her but that of Lot's wife. The Jewish gloss upon the narrative assigned to her the name of Adith; but that sounds like an after-thought, for although many names were prophetic, there is no intimation that God's foreknowledge had described her as being a testimony of His displeasure.

Another peculiarity in our Lord's mention of this woman is her sudden emerging from obscurity by His allusion to her fate. Her righteous husband is borne upon the memory of the inspired penman, but the woman so signalized in the history, fleeing with her guiltless husband from the doom of Sodom, becomes for a moment the object of chief historic interest, shares with him in the rescuing love of God, and in the obedience of hasty departure from the polluted city; reaches with him the suburbs in the plain amid whose luxuriant fields they would fain have found some equivalent for the home that had grown too corrupt for human occupants; hearkens with him to the mandate that hurried them beyond the coveted fields; trembles with him as the blackened heavens roar with tempests of fire, and the quivering earth echoes its groans, and the clouds that burst from the yawning plain send up the sulphurous spouts to kindle with the lightnings that crackle through the sky. As suddenly as the flash that heralded the vengeance of that judgment-day, she is paralyzed—a pillar of salt. She stood, and motionless and silent and unmentioned she remained from that recital of her fixedness until the lips of Jesus recalled the warning of her fate, and pointed a moral with the admonition—"Remember Lot's wife."

The very use of this occurence by our Lord rescues both the woman and the whole history of the vengeance falling on the cities of the plain, from the imputation of fable or exaggeration. What wisdom, or what seriousness, what fidelity to truth, or what authority among men can attach to a teacher of heavenly morals and a pulpit of divine rebukes, when the illustration of his weighty truths melts away into fiction, and his quotations of divine judgment are falsified as either extravagant or fabulous? To reject the narrative in Genesis is to impugn the authority of Jesus. To cavil at the conflagration of Sodom and Gomorrah is to deride the Saviour of mankind. The sulphurous desolation that swept the valley of Sodom, and, first suffocating, then covered and incrusted the disobedient woman who loitered behind the fugitive patriarch, startling and puzzling as the narrative may be, is involved in our reverence for Jesus. The mysterious elements of His character are so many attestations of the transaction recorded by Moses. Every miracle of Jesus argues that Sodom was punished and that Lot's wife was an example of Providence vindicating itself. The Divinity that was in His messages, the faultless perfection of His ethics, the sublime tenor of His revelations, the sanctity of His person, and the intensity of love that prompted His admonitions, all these conspire to hush our whispers of distrust and to command our wayward hearts.

Our Lord's use of this incident throws some light upon its obscure particulars. He is charging His disciples not to expect any such indications of His coming and His day of triumph, as will force themselves upon men's observation, or divert the ordinary tides of human care. He tells them that the Son of man will come under the dynasty of grace, as the angel of Jehovah came under the rule of the Patriarchs,—"As it was in the days of Noe; as it was in the days of Lot." He affirms that the world will be no more concerned as to impending judgment than the corrupt mass of mankind while the preacher of righteousness launched his church to float upon the deluge, and that the dominant vices of men will be just as defiant, and fattened hearts of irreligion just as heedless, as the populace that vexed the righteous soul of Lot and wassailed in the pride of their martial conquests and the luxury of their teeming acres. He fairly pictures to His disciples the cool, brave indifference with which men buried their souls in earthly pursuits, as if there were no God, no heaven, no laws but those of commerce, no pleasures but those that perish, and no higher tribunal than the figment of a fashionable etiquette. He was to come for the purpose of dissolving these falsehoods. But no gospel sent before Him would revolutionize the traits of human nature, no kingdom that He erected would annul the tempers of depravity. Whether they considered that judicial approach of Jesus as exemplified in the destruction of Jerusalem, or as fulfilled in the crushing of the Roman conqueror by one more barbarous and brutal than himself, or as verified to each soul in the solemn appeal of the gospel to the conscience, or as completed to the man that dwells in a Christian atmosphere when death palsies the body and eternity demands his soul; whenever they regarded the coming of the Son of man to be realized, let them heed the admonition which was sounded in the ears of those imperilled, which echoed in the ears of those rescued and spared. The fires of Sodom were a signal to those who would not amend and could not escape. The incorrigible and the scorner, the votary of pleasure and the debauched victim of unbridled lust, saw pictured before them in the days of the Son of man the same irreversible judgment that hung over the splendid opulence and the infatuated vice of Sodom. But along the borders of the plain, where the saline waters refused life to vegetation, and where the belched gases and alkalies of the earth's bowels showed that nature had turned from motherliness to tyranny, from a bosom of fertility to the ashes of death, from the loveliest valley of Jordan to a sea of mockery and to a tomb of sterility,—there, upon the margin of this vast burial-ground stood the monumental pillar that marked the fate of one captured by mercy, drawn with the cords of affliction, extricated from the pollution and the curse of sin, but overtaken by the floods of returning desire, and transfixed with the penalty of disobedience because she would not hasten where mercy led. Pointing to this monument of relapse, Jesus publishes it as the law of responsibility in the days of grace—"He that is in the field, let him not return back. Remember Lot's wife."

My brethren, we accept this warning as it was intended. It images to us the dangers that attend even a condition of grace. It is Christ's parable of salvation defeated. It seems to say there are three robberies of your immortality to be shunned. We may have in our hands that stupendous gift of God, eternal life, and may lose it. Catechismally, we say, the world, the flesh, or the devil may defraud us of what is our own—*life eternal.* By parable, we say, fires may overtake us, stifling, burning, hardening our souls, like Lot's wife in the valley.

The figure that warns us is no emblem of a soul refusing gospels, banishing angels, unwilling to escape. It is that other side of alarm, that shrieks to a soul once saved and then lost—once guided by angels and then loitering for devils—once tasting the powers of heaven and then smothered in the ashes of vanity.

Is this thy own peril, O my soul? Jesus reveals it. Study it reverently, trace it minutely, O heart so treacherous! Immortality so jeopardized! Note every shadow of danger which heaven has painted to your eye, "lest any of you be hardened through the deceitfulness of sin."

Three sources of peril attend a condition of grace.

The first is represented by the abundance of Sodom, the luxurious comfort of those valley-homes, and the enchanting beauty of nature which emulated a Paradise lost, in the romantic scenery and sumptuous clothing of that fertile plain. It was this that tempted the choice of Lot. And regaling herself with these enjoyments, the wife of the patriarch little felt the stifling oppression of sin that rioted around her ungrateful for the wealth and the health, the harvests and the homes which were nestled in that magic valley. Perhaps her enchantment with this beautiful region had induced Lot to venture the hazard of his piety amid such ungodliness. Perhaps her delight in the dissipations or the display of the people had chained the righteous family to a home hedged with temptation. And when God's violence tore away the charm to save her soul, lingering appetites dragged her back to the scenery of beauty and indulgence. She could not deny herself, at least, the privilege of tarrying along the borders of this delight. The field of pleasure from which loving angels led her, and her faithful husband fled, still decoyed her worldly heart. Read the parable, O my soul, of worldliness re-asserting its dominion—of the trampled lust rising again to conquer thee—of the serpent's eye gleaming beside thy path—of the ease and carelessness that once betrayed thee, again inviting thee to tarry and to die.

A second peril lurks in those innocent affections which throb by nature within us, and often symbolize to us the most that earthly vision can behold of the purest rapture in heaven. Lot's wife shared in these joys, and found those emotions exercised amid the Sodomites. Closely allied with her own family were those who were imbued with the scorn and the profligacy that dared the justice of God. Her own sons-in-law mocked when the gathering storm was foreboded. No appeal of the venerable Lot touched their fears; no disclosure of angelic warning smote their consciences. The patriarch, his vacillating wife, and the two daughters that cheered his home, were the only denizens of the four cities that were worthy to escape. Ten righteous persons would have averted the vengeance. But the kindred of Lot, with all his steadfastness, could not supply that quota of mercy.

Painful, no doubt, it was to every kind sentiment thus to be thrust out from associations which nothing but the universal impiety had alloyed. The test was more than the fond heart of the woman could undergo. She could cling to her husband—she could console herself with the daughters that escaped to the mountains; but when obedience demanded that she should hear the voice of God rather than the outcry of affection, the sentiment of the woman was stronger than the faith of the saint—the love of kindred was greater than the reverence for God—the promise of heaven to make duty blessed was treated as a mockery. She sent her heart back among the contaminations of unrighteousness, and suffocated amid the fumes of an over-anxious heart. She felt the bitterness of that sentence which the Saviour of humanity writes against humanity, "He that loveth son or daughter more than me is not worthy of me."

The fiery ordeal of Lot, and the monumental fate of the woman, suggest to us the third, the insidious, the deadly danger that besets our salvation. There was a secret whisper in her heart, "God will not devastate all this beautiful plain." "The men of Sodom are sinners before the Lord exceedingly," but the pleasant fields are not rebels—the meadows invite not His curse—some vestiges of this innocent nature will escape. She loitered because she doubted. She would not charge God with such indiscriminate justice. It was no harm to tarry and see the bounds of His scourge. It would be an honor to His mercy to cast herself upon it amid the quiet tokens of His bounty that fringed the plain. Thus crept into Eden the wily author of unbelief. Thus whispers to the trembling heart the seducing spirit of affected humanity. It speaks of mercy, when it means self-indulgence. It quotes the attributes of God, when it means disobedience. It argues from the harmless aspects of nature, when nature itself waits for a redemption. It pleads for salvation amid the valleys of Sodom, when God urges us with the decree—"Stay not thou in all the plain; escape to the mountain lest thou be consumed."

"Then let thine angel seize thee by the hand,
And lead thee onward to a happier land,
While thou art able yet to hear his call,
Ere bound within by Passion's secret thrall."

VI.

THE FEAR OF THE LORD.

PROVERBS i. 7.

"The fear of the Lord is the beginning of knowledge."

IN mapping out before the mind of his supposed pupil the ways of safety and the ambushes of peril, the wise man deduces all the elements of character from a just sense of our relations to God.

He indicates at the outset of his instruction the primary sources of counsel and admonition which if duly heeded will anticipate for us the harder lessons of our own experience. Subsequently he proceeds to expose the insinuations and enticements that beset, and inveigle, and mislead men. The charms of evil company, the plausible promises of crime, the alluring prizes of recklessness, the glittering purse of the gamester, the disguised snare of the knave, the guarded confederacy of the profligate, the easy prodigality of the spendthrift, the cunning smoothness of all that lead the way to death,—these are the dangers that are sure to lurk along his path.

As a fortification against these blandishments of

woe, God has appointed natural preceptors and guardians. "My son, hear the instruction of thy father, and forsake not the law of thy mother." Remember that God has implanted within their breasts a natural affection, that they have a conscience over your conduct and a natural longing for your good, which they can scarcely stifle, and which prompts them to advise you more wisely than they admonish themselves. Their dear-bought experience they willingly give to you. Regard them as, under God, the nearest keepers of your counsel, and the best expositors of your safety. Extend a like confidence to all who stand in similar relations of guardianship and affection. These are the instruments of God's goodness and care. These are the Providential securities against those wiles and deceptions of evil that are ambushed for your ruin.

But before even these, and in order that you may be disposed to heed your Providential safeguards, place a principle that opens into the avenues of wisdom and safety: "The fear of the Lord is the beginning of knowledge."

When we consider what accumulations of experience are condensed in that Book of Proverbs,—what depths of the human heart are there fathomed, what suggestions of practical wisdom are comprised in it, what results of experience are here presented, what precepts of sound morality are embodied in it, what multitudes have derived from it the warnings that saved them from temptation,—we may appreciate the importance of that foundation which is here laid for all the instruction it conveys, "The fear of the Lord is the beginning of knowledge."

There is perhaps no surer way both to vindicate and to explain this wise proposition than to expand into its full sense the principal term which is here employed.

The terseness of expression is characteristic of the proverbial language. The expression comprehends, as a proverb is meant to do, a variety of topics under some one term. And in like conformity with proverbial use, the proposition is to commend itself to the experience of those who are qualified to judge, and to the faith of those who would learn in a wiser and a safer way.

It is an every-day proverb that he who will not be wise by counsel must be left to learn in a harder way; and so he who expects to attain the knowledge of divine and eternal truths, of things that his senses cannot grasp, and his conjectures cannot certify; he who expects to know the satisfactions of a good conscience and the value of a religious life, without the fear of the Lord to guide and to teach him, must learn by a slow and severe experience that he has disdained the beginning of knowledge.

Most treatises are written with the idea of leading the reader by degrees to a conclusion. The Book of Ecclesiastes is constructed upon this model. It seals the result of a life's vicissitudes with the conclusion, "Fear God and keep His commandments; for this is the whole duty of man."

But the wisdom of the Proverbs is based upon a disposition to accept the teachings of experience. It accordingly opens its treasures, as the wise men opened their treasures before Christ, not waiting for the sceptre of manhood and the robes of royalty, but proposing as the suggestion of all experience that we must be disposed to wisdom by the fear of the Lord. It assumes that there is a wisdom which can be learned through no other means. It virtually denies the claim of worldly sagacity, and sets religion at the threshold, not at the remote and secret corner of wisdom. It scouts the whole system of learning moral truths by tasting the penalties of disobedience. It unlocks the imposture with which cunning is apparelled, as if its ways of caution and evasion were the lessons of wise forethought. It puts us upon the art of defending ourselves by being armed for the assaults of temptation, instead of compromising with sin and practicing on its principles with the reserved right to denounce them. It disputes the pernicious maxim of the devil, that none better knows the worth of heaven than he who feels the bitterness of hell. It pronounces the evil of sin to be best known, where the love and the passion for it are unknown, and like the voice of God in Paradise teaches that the fear of the Lord and not the flavor of disobedience is the beginning of knowledge.

In looking at this leading maxim of wisdom, our attention is first arrested with the term by which a disposition to learn is expressed.

"The fear of the Lord" is an expression either

for the predominant character of a person, or for the occasional sense of guilt and danger. In the former sense, as denoting the characteristic qualities, it is used in the text. Its converse is represented as the life of wickedness and folly, practically despising wisdom and instruction, or rushing upon the course of sin without regard to the sense of guilt and danger. The term with which this practical folly is contrasted, must therefore denote the bent of the disposition and the life towards a practical fear of the Lord.

In the sense of character this fear stands directly opposed to the paroxysm and passion of fear. It excludes the latter by precluding the occasion for it. In a similar way, the fear of dishonoring ourselves by a base action, protects us against the fear that pursues the conscience of baseness. Fear is an affection of the soul, and its character depends entirely upon the relations of the person to the object. The fear of a good man's censure supposes our exposure to blame, but the fear of a wicked man's enmity supposes only our collision with his passions. The fear of the Lord is therefore an affection of the soul corresponding with our relations to Him. If we are only the sullen expectants of His rebuke, it is a tormenting sense of impending danger. The soul that drowns the reproofs of conscience in the louder demands of sin, is described as the wicked with no fear of God before his eyes. But the trembling fugitive before the awakened wrath of God is represented as hiding in the clefts of the rocks for fear of the Lord.

When the same expression denotes the accepted and tranquil soul, it is not God himself that is transformed, but the relations of the man to Him on which the affection of the soul is founded. He stands before the inner eye in both cases, the same majestic Being, the same infinite wisdom, the same omniscient God, the same spotless holiness. In the one case His majesty convicts us of our affront, His wisdom condemns our resistance, His omniscience penetrates our guilt, His holiness accuses us with deserving His punishment. The soul is not in a condition to regard Him as an object of complacency. It is full of the prevailing thought that there is a penalty upon it. The greater fear of suffering, suffering inevitably, possesses it. Its relation to Him is that of aversion and estrangement. Its inclinations have unfitted it to behold Him with sympathy. He is revealed before its perceptions in all perfection,—but the affection that guilt brings uppermost is the fear of guilt returning to lacerate the memory.

Take it as a passion startled by the panics of bodily harm. What is our fear, then, but the overpowering of all other affections by the sense of danger. We are driven out of our self-command, surprised out of our better judgment, and pressed from every side with the thought of danger. It is the soul all thrown into one feeling, the twisting of every faculty into the one posture of alarm. So with the fear that remorse wakens. The soul is disturbed from its slumber, and rousing only in the sense of alarm gives itself wholly to the affection of alarm. Memory, fancy, speech, and muscle, all tremble in the overpowering sense of danger. And that fear shrinks into utter despair, as the onmipresence of God leaves it no escape, the omniscient eye leaves no disguise, the omnipotent arm leaves no shelter.

In the other case, where the fear of the Lord has already formed and colored the character, it is not a paroxysm of guilt and danger; it is not a soul thrown into tumult, and absorbed in the feeling of alarm. It is the sense of God's majesty and wisdom and omniscience and holiness wrought into the habit of our thinking and feeling and acting.

The fear of the Lord thus expresses the components of a reverent, a devout, a conscientious and an upright character.

It is reverent, for it recollects that God has a sacred name to be honored, sacred places of His special presence, sacred offices to testify our homage, a sacred word to be received with meekness and attention. It is affected with the thought that the Almighty is not only to be spoken of and spoken to, as the Most August of Beings, far, inconceivably far removed from our puny faculties, but as the Revealed God who has solemnities of place and act to cultivate our sense and express our awe of His infinite greatness.

The fear of the Lord is devout, for it knows that the great power of God is His ability to condescend. He can hear us, and accept our tributes, and enter into our feelings, and yet be supreme and wise. It is devout, for the treasures of wisdom are with Him, and they are imparted to them that love Him, and in this love are likened to Him.

The fear of the Lord is conscientious, for it lives in the sense of His searching eye. It opens every chamber of imagination to His scrutiny. It finds His eye reflected from every thought and intent of the heart. He is with it at the door of every act. He is with it in the memory of every hour. It has no rest, till it abandons every concealment, and lives with a conscience void of offence. Its first suggestion is "the eye of God." It aims to look upon all things as He beholds them. And such is the abiding sense of His fear, that every footstep of the downcast soul, and every vision of the lifted thought is surrounded with the legend that Hagar found even in the wilderness, "Thou God seest me."

The fear of the Lord is upright. It recognizes no fear as equal to that waiting upon the paths of iniquity. It is upright, for this is the character which God will protect, which no evil shall utterly discomfit, and which His infinite truth is pledged to reward.

The fear of the Lord is but a synonyme for that character of devout and conscientious religion, which draws its wisdom, its hopes, its desires, its *fears* from the source of every noble endowment, and the object of every salutary dread. Fear is the passion most deeply planted in our nature. It commands and controls the soul more than the milder sentiments, which are pleased with the excellence of virtue, and lured by the splendors of recompense. It is used accordingly to express the deep and thorough hold of God's majesty and truth upon the soul, and it again and again signifies in saints the surrender of the affections to the fear of those things which offend God, and the pursuit of those things that please Him. Can we wonder that this disposition should be made the first element of practical wisdom?

If true knowledge is the learning of those things which we have the greatest use and the greatest necessity to know; if true knowledge is the employment of our thoughts about things in their own nature the most excellent, and in their relation to us of the utmost importance; if true knowledge be the improvement of our minds with practical truth, and not our amusement with empty speculations; if the knowledge of a happy and satisfied conscience be more desirable than endless anxiety, horror, and despair; if the study of God's favour be more desirable than the art of making the friendship of the world; if the experience of a blessing from an almighty Benefactor be preferable to the knowledge of companionship with the profane and the vicious; if it be better to know how the happiness of the world may be promoted, than to know the secret of making each other miserable without cause and without end; if true knowledge consists in perceiving and adhering to whatsoever things are true, honest, just, pure, lovely, of good report, things that promote the health of our bodies, and secure the peace and quiet of our minds, things that establish the order of the world and make other men happy as well as ourselves, things that make our present enjoyments easy, and the remembrance of what is past comfortable, and the hopes and expectations of what is to come secure; if the knowledge that thus leads us to God and elevates man, be true and worthy knowledge, then is the fear of the Lord the beginning of knowledge, for without it we cannot know these things as our experience, our assurance, and with it, we increase and abound in knowledge and all judgment.

VII.

THE SMITTEN ROCK.

NUMBERS XX. 11.

"And Moses lifted up his hand, and with his rod he smote the rock twice: and the water came out abundantly."

MEEKNESS tempted, and Christ the fountain for the thirst of the soul—these are the first suggestion and the ultimate lesson of the history whose pith is given in the text.

Moses, betrayed out of his transcendent meekness, hurried into rashness and irreverence towards God by the justness of his indignation towards men; the servant of God who had deserted the palace and the royalty of Egypt for the sake of his conscience, now when more than a hundred years had bleached his honorable head, warmed and transported into hasty speech by the impatience of his people—piety selling itself for a moment to the follies of human infirmity—practiced and habitual meekness roused into a sally of passion—our expectation of saintly strength and unconquerable prudence disappointed in the exhibition of weakness and precipitancy; man in his best estate, with Jehovah for his companion and miracle for his daily scene, yet revealed as the victim of temptation and the defeated wrestler with sin — this is, at first, the picture of discouragement thrust upon our view.

What confidence shall we indulge, when Holy Scripture thus confesses the betrayal of the meekest man? Where is the boasted vigor of human virtue, when the master-spirit of a dispensation is vanquished on his own field? Where is the security of human perfection, when the aged lawgiver, neither sustained by his own years of discipline nor awed by the sullen discontents of his people, forgets the majesty of his God, the weakness of his own heart, the gravity of his age and his station?

My brethren, man is the boastful trumpeter of the greatness which his nature achieves. God is the teacher of the frailty and the imperfection and the instability which no strength of man can banish from himself.

He describes man as the grand argument of discouragement. He pictures humanity, as, in itself, a life-long weakness. He puts a blemish upon every human boast. He writes the truth of our moral infirmity. He records the unceasing dangers of temptation, and displays the human heart in one continuous panorama of discouragement in man, that God may be disclosed as the secret strength of all His servants.

What an absolute contradiction is the pride of our heart to this express verdict of heaven against us! Tempted, unstable, erring man, where is wisdom but in the self-abasement and self-distrust that kneel and hope in prayer?

> "The gray-haired saint may fail at last,
> The surest guide a wanderer prove;
> Death only binds us fast
> To the bright shore of love."

We say that such a picture of discouragement attaches to the history with which our text belongs.

The transaction here narrated is, no doubt, a similar instance of popular murmuring and of Divine interposition to that which occurred at the rock Horeb when the smitten rock poured out a supply for the two millions of thirsty pilgrims.

In either case, it was the outcry of the people against God's chosen instrument of mercy to them that gave occasion to the miracle of bounty. In either case, it was the disposition of man to charge all the difficulties of a good work upon his leaders and benefactors and guides in its accomplishment—the disposition to fault those who conduct us toward great results by great efforts, which woke the ready tones of censure and complaint, and challenged the Providence of God.

The miracle of the first supply from the rock had its subduing effect. The forty years of wandering were nearly terminated when this second outbreak of murmuring assailed their lawgiver.

He meets the difficulty by presenting it before his God.

Heaven assumes the remedy as its own. It regards the voice of rebellion as a denial of Providence, and moves to vindicate itself. Moses, as its instrument, shall yet be honored, but God much more. The lawgiver and the priest are to stand before this desert rock. They are to speak to it, and the waters shall gush. In haste and heat of spirit, Moses wields the rod—God's long-entrusted token of his authority—and, more strenuous for his authority than for God's means, exceeds his commission to speak to the rock, and smites it twice, and "gave them drink as out of the great depths."

But, alas! he had copied that distrust of God which his own excited heart would rebuke. And in the same excess of human passion, "he spake unadvisedly with his lips." The lawgiver, the type of human sinfulness in its highest moral achievement—the type of the utmost conscience could do—the ear that could listen to God and the voice that could speak for Him—the meekest of men was but a guilty, mortal sinner, and to Jesus alone of human kind was left the praise, "He doeth *all* things well."

When we recollect that the conduct of the lawgiver at this crisis was the subject of special reprehension from God, and that for his offence herein Justice was compelled to write its sentence of exclusion from the land of promise against him, we may be prepared for that typical revelation of Christ which attended this failure of Moses.

It is no fancy of the rabbies, or of Christian mystics, that has found herein the revelation of Jesus. The Holy Ghost, by the testimony of Paul, assures us that the Rock was Christ.

With us it is of little regard whether he intended to say that the power and the goodness which lay under that mass of rock, and came out abundantly to refresh the church in the wilderness, was the hidden presence of Christ, long before His incarnation, giving the refreshments of mercy to men, or whether the rock was only, at that juncture of Providence, a sign of what Christ should be at the great juncture of man's fate in the universe.

It seems to me manifest that the tenor of the Apostle's argument in the 1st Epistle to the Corinthians, where he makes this allusion, requires us to regard the waters issuing from this smitten rock to stay the thirst of Israel, as, at least, representing those powers and virtues and gifts which emanate from Christ for the refreshment and invigoration and salvation of the soul.

And, to my mind, it is beyond dispute that the Apostle intends its application first to His gifts in His Sacrament; but, consequently, all His gifts by any means of grace.

With the whole scope of significance in this type, I would not meddle. The briefest experience in God's word ought to teach us that we cannot exhaust its resources at a glance. And none but the disciple of a theory, rather than of Christ, will essay to limit that testimony of Christ which lay under the whole system of types as the spirit of prophecy.

I am constrained by the very stress of this Scripture to concentrate all reflection upon the nucleus of wisdom here revealed. It sets before us, in the supplemental fullness of Scripture, what nature could see but blindly, and tell but obscurely. It is such a concourse of objects—Moses and Jehovah, and the people and the gushing rock,—of Providence, and the law, and the Church and Christ, as brings into contact and into contrast elements the weakest, and elements the mightiest. The Psalmist says that he never understood Providence till he went into the Sanctuary and saw the end to which it was coming. And St. Austin was a scholar and a libertine and a disputatious "know everything," until a voice put the Scriptures into his hand, and told him, "Take and read," "take and read." So we come into this shadowy region of types with the discernment of God's purpose to inculcate something that nature alone could not have taught. He is adding here a higher lesson, and showing us that there was a mystery beyond the great work of daily Providence. God was the miraculous Redeemer of His people, but that they easily learned to disregard. They put it all to the account of His Providence, and when that resource seemed exhausted, they had no idea of anything beyond. This was repeatedly their character. And now at this time it breaks out again, and in its re-appearance He puts into typical signs this truth, that man must have a Saviour over and above Providence. Here is the thought, my brethren. Let it not escape from us. Man is in absolute need of a Saviour, that shall make up for him what Providence does not supply. Man is not only a creature to be kept alive; he is a sinner to be saved. Providence does not keep him from sin, Providence does not remedy the evil of his sin. Providence places him in difficulties, in temptations; and he sins the more. He needs a Saviour, a recovering power, a cleansing ocean of love to purify his nature. He must have—Oh, that mercy would meet his need!—he must have a Saviour. The drought of the wilderness is parching his soul. He perishes in the thirst for life, and Moses can bring him no succor but the dry sands of a natural Providence.

Was not the sign a lucid representation of the sinner's need, the Saviour's gift?

Moses is deficient, but Christ is sufficient. The law can only apply to the Power that acts in Providence, but grace opens in the desert its fountains. The type of conscience smites the rock, but the type of the Saviour yields its streams of refreshment. What were the word of Moses, what were the power of his staff, what were the virtue of his smiting, unless that Spiritual Rock had been the symbol of a Saviour?

As it was typified in the desert, so is it realized in life. The open hand of Providence may satisfy the soul for a season. God is wonderful in nature, and bountiful and kind; and man may live contented with his conscience and contented with his lot. But ever and anon the drought comes. Ever and anon the soul feels its destitution in a barren and dry land. It drinks of the dews, but it thirsts again. It drinks of the pools of excitement, but it thirsts the more. It drinks of earthly satisfaction, but it fevers with the draught. Something to refresh, something to purify and cheer and to quench the thirst for immortality,—something to be a happiness lasting, pure, and safe,—this is the want. Who knows it not? Who feels not the burning of this desire? Who is not ready to murmur that Providence withholds the draught?

Oh, it is not in nature to give,—it is not in the power of the law.

It must come from the smitten Rock. Jesus, the wounded and the crucified of Moses; Jesus the Rock of our salvation, He is the source of that happiness which swells into abundance.

We may hear that such an apostate has abandoned the Saviour as a delusive source of rest; that such a disciple has shrunk back with the disappointed cry that his religion was more of a hardship than a comfort; that such a practiced follower of Christ once rejoiced in the pleasures of his Christian calling, and now pronounces the whole a delusion. I doubt none of these things. Thousands are misled; thousands are deluded by their own emotions; thousands substitute their own schemes for the gospel of Christ; thousands are saved from some besetting vice, without living in Christ; and the evidences are poured in floods, in floods of delusion, that the life of apparent religion and the life of Christian integrity are easily interchanged. But I do deny that ever one soul from the days of Judas' remorseful confession, from the days of Peter's penitent tears, that ever one human soul has truly and fairly tested the reality, the peace, the blessedness of the pure-minded Christian, and then as truly and fairly pronounced it to be anything less than a Divine gift and an unearthly sweetness and rest to the soul. Millions from their dreariest tribulations in this life, millions from their repose beneath the smile of Jesus, millions from every tongue unite to beseech us, "Taste, and see that the Lord is gracious."

And the smitten Rock, Whose head pierces beyond the clouds into the splendors of heaven, echoes with the assurance, "Whosoever drinketh of the water that I shall give him shall never thirst; but the water that I shall give him shall be in him a well of water springing into everlasting life."

VIII.

COBWEBS.

JOB viii. 13, 14; xxvii. 8.

"The hypocrite's hope shall perish; whose hope shall be cut off, and whose trust shall be a spider's web.

"For what is the hope of the hypocrite, though he hath gained, when God taketh away his soul?"

THE language evidently implies that some satisfactory enjoyment or expectation is already in the possession of the hypocrite. Probably the constitution of the human mind is such that no one could live short of despair unless buoyed up by some present contentment or some hope for the future. It matters little in what path or in what complicated paths of pleasure we move to our destiny, the same law holds throughout this state of mingled happiness and misery, a decoy of hope must be our incitement.

It is easy to be sentimental on this topic, but we choose to be plain and direct, as looking to the helps of salvation and eternal joy, rather than the food of transient entertainment. If I were standing among the persecuted band of the early disciples, tempted to swerve towards the compliances of philosophy, I should draw my topic from the heavens and the graves of the righteous, and set forth the sparkling recompenses of patience and perseverance unto death. If I were standing among the professed disciples of heathenism, with nature for their teacher and the sibylline whispers of tradition for their religion, I should draw an argument from the works of God, and bring in the gospel as the light issuing from the home of Deity, and the solemn utterances of the Divine carpenter in Galilee. But among Christians, and such Christians, I dare not copy the boldness of my Master—"Woe unto you, hypocrites;" but I must venture upon the wisdom of the Shuhite, "The hypocrite's hope shall perish; whose hope shall be cut off, and whose trust shall be a spider's web."

I will ask you to consider, first, What is understood by the appellation of hypocrite; secondly, To whom the text may be applied; thirdly, The certainty of a miserable fate, the fate here represented; and lastly, The measure of the evil that awaits the hypocrite.

The appellation of hypocrite literally applies to any one who acts an assumed part. It was first used to designate those who played a fictitious part upon the stage. As carried into morals or into the transactions of real life, the same idea is retained. A hypocrite is one who wears the mask of a feigned character. The history of the stage is the best explanation of the forms which this vice of hypocrisy may assume. There, as we all know, the most profligate corruption may walk in the majesty and attire of. unsullied integrity. The cringing coward of the streets struts in the bearing of some ancient hero—lisping ignorance wears the robe of a Solon—a villain that has cheated the gallows will play the part of the upright judge—lips that never sent a prayer above the ceiling of the play-house will mouth the supplications of saints—the profane swearer will wear the vestments of the minister of God, and the painted face of pollution will mock the blush of maiden modesty. In religion, he is a hypocrite who counterfeits a character which is not his own. It may be defined as an affectation of the name joined with a disaffection to the thing, "a form of godliness, while denying the power thereof." There are plainly two classes of men to whom this appellation may be given. He is, in the first place, a hypocrite who is an intentional and corrupt dissembler, who knowingly and with effort wears an appearance directly contrary to his inward character, and absolutely disguising his real condition. Such are they that, under pretences of friendship, worm their way into others' confidence only to betray and to ruin them. Such are they that make great professions of simplicity and honesty that they may overreach and ensnare. Such are they that put on a religious profession only to further their worldly interests, and to gain credit among men. Such are they that make great noise and ostentation in their public religion, and are Neros catching flies in the hours of secret meditation.

The stage, when spoiled of its primitive purity, and pandering to the most degraded tastes, is the image of this masked dissimulation. A hypocrite of this description is the very hyena of the moral world, prowling among the graves, ranging by night, with every noble trait extinguished. Meekness itself broke into denunciations against the outward varnish of such noissome sepulchres.

Another class of hypocrites is far above these instances of designed dissimulation. The more refined hypocrite is not bent upon deceiving others, but is carried along with the deceiving of himself. He has a reverence for conscience which the other possesses not, and so sincerely aims at some degrees of virtue. He has less idolatry of men's opinion, and so rises above the pretences by which the other hopes to win. There is a vast distance between these two forms of hypocrisy. But both deserve the name; both await the consequences. Deceit is the element of corruption in both cases; but the one is managing to deceive others—the other has managed to deceive himself, The one will resist every appeal, and needs, for the good of others, to be upbraided and unmasked. The other needs only to pause and seriously to consider the truth of his condition, when the mask will be detected, and the illusion that betrays him be broken.

I think it to be evident that the language of the text is to be applied to hypocrites of this less corrupted class. Only of such a one could any hope be asserted. He that persists in a bad course, knowing it to be such, can entertain no hope for the future. His hypocrisy must assume some of the character of self-deception, or the element of hope could not quicken it. It is not the destruction of the hypocrite himself, the designing dissembler, which is here declared; but it is the hope, the stay of his soul, the web of his weaving, that is to perish. The particulars of this class need not therefore be explained. The general description is enough to distinguish the subjects of this moral disorder. Would you see the array of hypocrisy, thus fashioned into self-deceiving, which Christian lands present, the name of its victims is Legion. They swarm over desolate Christendom like the plagues of Egypt. Their fabrics of cunning delusion hang around the structures of the gospel, as the webs of the spider around the ruins of a deserted home. You see the symptoms of the disease fastening upon minds that err concerning the essential duties of the gospel. What one has said of eloquence, might be asserted of repentance or conversion or any other root of Christian hope, "Many would have been able to have reached it, had they not deemed themselves already to have arrived at it." A season of alarm and trouble concerning the soul has passed for the foundation-duty of repentance, and the work of daily anguish over the record, and of momentary struggle against besetting sin and tendencies to sin, has been left undone. A temporary change of habits, or a successful amendment of some glaring faults has passed for the duty of conversion, and left the hypocrite to a hope strong enough to buoy him into death, but frail as the web of the morning, which snaps in the mid-day wind, and fruitless as the almost persuaded conversion of Agrippa. You detect the same element of hypocrisy in the perverted promises of Scripture. It would weary to follow the whole detail of men's subtle evasions. Take, for instance, the gloss which thousands put upon the passages which record God's scrutiny of the heart, and His acceptance of a willing mind, and His dispensation of positive precepts. Know they not, can we otherwise believe than that God demands the deed where the performance is possible—that He requires a law to be observed unless it contravene some other law of equal obligation? He puts it into our power to do, as well as to will, and then expects both the one and the other. Where the hindrances of His providence forbid the act, there and there only is His majesty sufficiently honored with the intention and desire. It is one's bounden duty, as he would live in the favor of God, to read His Word, to hearken to its instructions, to frequent the place of public worship, and to bend the knee in private homage. But blindness may seal the book of wisdom to our vision, and sickness may chain us to postures of irreverence and to places where we cannot share in the public tribute of adoration and praise. God will accept the heart that yearns for the withholden privilege. It is our duty to remember the love of God who gave His well-beloved for us in the memorials of the crucified Jesus; but if the Almighty cast our lot remote from the scenes of the sacrament, the pantings of the soul for the inward communion of Christ will be supplied from the fountain of compassion. It is our duty, each of us individually, to see that the offerings in God's house are sufficient for God's poor, and His daily praise and His purposes of mission to famishing or benighted men. But some are too poor to bear the whole burden, and the rich may revel and leave the gospel to languish, and yet *he* loses not his reward who longs and labors in lonely sacrifice for the end; for "if there be first a willing mind, it is accepted according to that a man hath, and not according to that he hath not." But the refined hypocrite neglects all these duties, and omits that he has the means to perform under the vain persuasion that God asks no more than the offering of the heart. The hypocrisy strikes still deeper. It belies the attributes of God. It shapes Him to its own desires, and converts Him, the Almighty Ruler, into a changing patron of our passions and caprice. If it be only fashionably worldly, and decently averse to self-denial, and morally negligent of the worship of God, it is content to acknowledge God's justice, yet as an attribute that is only aroused against some gross and flagrant sinner, some offence that is visibly exposed to the present retributions of misery.

Are not my words the language of soberness? Is not the mercy, the exceeding mercy of God, made a daily offset, not only to His spotless holiness and His abhorrence of iniquity, but to our open and habitual and presumptuous transgressions? Is not grace converted into a bounty upon sin? Are not children taught to be hypocrites, to grow up as if religion and obedience were meant for manhood, and mercy would make a blank of youth and iron-linked habits? Are not Christian duties neglected, Christ's commands despised, with hearts as cheerful as hope can make them, and with no breach in the delusion of peace, till the winding-sheet is worn? To whom, then, does our text apply? It renders its own answer. To the Christian legions of baptized apostates—to the merry hearts of civilized and polite ungodliness—to the many that listen without obedience, and the more that forsake the house of prayer. "The hypocrite's hope shall perish; whose hope shall be cut off, and whose trust shall be a spider's web." "What is the hope of the hypocrite, though he hath gained, when God taketh away his soul?"

The sequel of this hypocritical career now opens upon us. As surely as that hope is built upon false foundations, so surely shall it be removed. What is the experience of the world in hypocrisy which regards only the affairs of the world? Disappointment to the schemes of dissimulation, and contempt without the pity of mankind. How much more certainly, if greater certainty be possible, must the dissembler in religion, and the builder upon the foundations of sand, find his refuge swept away by the storms of calamity. The truth of God's word is pledged to this result. It originates the appalling question, "What is the hope of the hypocrite, when God taketh away his soul?" It determines the narrow bound of impunity: "The triumphing of the wicked is short, and the joy of the hypocrite but for a moment." Which, then, shall stand, the truth of God, or the waywardness of men? Which shall prove victorious? Which is sealed for an everlasting security? The 'covenant of the hypocrite with his own soul shall moulder upon his grave — the judgment of God shall live to confront the offender.

Observe on what the persuasion of the hypocrite rests, and the certainty of the fate awaiting him will be the more evident. Errors and unbelief are the only pillars of his expectation. Can these survive the unmasking of the grave? When God's nature cannot be misunderstood, when the heinousness of sin cannot be blinked from our thoughts, when the happiness of the soul must be a love of obedience instead of a hope of impunity, when the righteous are scarcely saved, where shall the ungodly and the sinner appear? How is it here, I ask you? Do designs founded upon errors succeed? Is ignorance successful, because it refused the guidances of wisdom? Does this state of God's forbearance manifest any such arrangements of lenity? What ground, then, in reason, what ground in experience is there for the hypocrite's hope? Merely the reason that sin and delusion will ever travel on, that they love to have it so. The wisest and the purest hypocrite that breathes can find no better reason for his hope of heaven, than his fear to lose it, and his desire, in spite of forfeiture, to win his rest at last.

Finally, where shall we look for the measure of the evil that is rolling upon hyprocrisy? The day is coming when the besom of wrath shall sweep from their hold upon the pillars of the temple of God the cobwebs of human art. It is the last of the hypocrite's confidence. His trust shall be a spider's web. Systems of religion spun from his own brain, like the threads of network from the insect's body, shall not mask him from the eye of God. Hope is the last relief that misery can use. What unmigitated woe must swallow souls whose hopes have parted company with them forever? Amid the sorrows and discouragements of this world, whereof the hypocrite shall inherit his full share, he is accustomed to console himself with the thought of rest and comfort in another world. The world is filled with such hope. It is the buoy of immortality on these tumultuous waters. Imagine the surprise of the hypocrite, as he comes to his journey's end, and as the wayworn traveler, where he expects refreshment, finding want and hatred and slaughter. The language of prophecy glares, at last, in a terrific fulfilment—"Fearfulness hath surprised the hypocrites. Who among us shall dwell with the devouring fire? Who among us shall dwell with everlasting burnings?"

Search, then, your inmost heart, lest your hopes of heaven be more delusive than your fears of hell. Keep back thy servant, also, O Lord, from presumptuous sins, lest they get the dominion over me.

IX.

THE BROKEN HEART.

PSALMS lxix. 20.

"Reproach hath broken my heart."

THE desolate complaint of this Psalm, and the imprecation of avenging penalties it contains, would unquestionably have been applied by us solely to the person of its persecuted author, had not the inspired teacher made known its reference to the suffering Saviour. It is His oppressed and desponding soul that utters the cry of unconsoled and utter grief—"Reproach hath broken my heart."

We take it to be a literal description of the spiritual suffering He endured. We assume that no other language can so exactly indicate the actual cause of His distress, and the actual effect of His sufferings. In the face of all the incredulity which may sneer at the proposition, we scruple not to affirm that our Blessed Redeemer was an instance of one who died of a broken heart.

The phrase itself is heard with skepticism. Men of a certain turn of mind cannot imagine such a thing possible as a broken heart. They put it aside among the fancies of poets, and the tragical dreams of romance. Or they class it among the cases of madness or of imbecility, and note it among the pitiable signs of disease and defect in heart, rather than the product of sound feelings rightly controlled and acting. It seems to them to be the result of faulty affections, and the needless consequence of mistaken grief and undue sorrow. They regard it as a decided case of mismanagement. They blame the brooding over disappointment, and the laying of troubles to heart. And to them there is no reality in the imagined breaking of the heart; but the sufferer and the victim has, in truth, given up all heart, and ceased to feel as becomes our nature.

Now, in answer to all this skepticism, it may suffice to recall the manifold forms in which this broken heart is recognized by the Word of God. It is regarded as that state of feeling which is above the scorn of heaven—"A broken and a contrite heart Thou wilt not despise." And as if to picture the contrast between the pitiless cruelty of earth, and the tender compassions of heaven, the wicked man is described by his disposition to be unmerciful and oppressive, carrying his high hand so far into the excesses of hatefulness as even to "slay the broken in heart." And lest any countenance should be given to the notion of the worldly votary that the broken heart is a fault, and a triumph of the worst elements, and an unmanly condition that puts one out of the pale of respect for his heart, it is mentioned as a sort of especial claim to

God's consideration—as a separating ourselves from what God abhors—as a title to His peculiar indulgence, a preparation for more intimate privileges, that "the Lord is nigh unto them that are of a broken heart." And so eminent does this broken heart rank among the objects of God's regard, that He sent His Son, as it were the sign of His own broken heart; and He anointed that Son in the flesh with all the gifts of His Spirit, in order that He might "heal the broken-hearted;" and as if to illustrate the reality, and to make it the more certainly incident to human nature, even though innocent, He makes even the spotless man to confess that this was the calamity which God had ordered and God's own act produced: "Thy rebuke hath broken my heart."

It is impossible, then, to escape from the conclusion that God's Word, at least, is not ambiguous. It looks upon the "broken heart" as a reality, a pitiable reality, a laudable, and, in some degree, sacred reality. It speaks in contradiction of the world's surmises. It pities this state, as a noble and a generous, and, in the highest degree, *manly* suffering. It makes the "broken heart" such a misery and such an excellency, at the same time, that God's compassions were excited by it, and He was moved to do it honor. And it is so compatible, not only with innocence, but with true greatness of soul, that Christ was never so superior to common men as when He died of a broken heart.

The term, however, is so variously employed,

that we must give different shades of meaning to it as it is differently applied.

We are led, therefore, to inquire, first, in what sense it is understood in the world; and secondly, how it applies to Christ.

In common phrase, the broken heart is expressive of utter grief occasioned by disappointment in that which engages our most intense affections. It is not possible to one who does not live in his affections. It is not possible, unless one is so eagerly and cordially enlisted in a cause as to merge all other objects of desire in it. It is not possible, except also where one has found some object which, in a measure, has entertained him either with the possession or with the hope. Who wonders that the cold, selfish, scheming soul should be skeptical? Who wonders that the man who puts his heart into nothing save himself and his own self-sufficiency, who counts nothing beyond himself really a part of his happiness, that he doubts whether there is such a thing as a broken heart? Who wonders that the withered affections of the heartless voluptuary, or the mechanical earnestness of a calculating charmer, or the schooled insincerity of the man of the world, or the woman of fashion, that these should turn into pleasantry the silliness of broken hearts?

It is the serious tragedy of life; the life-engrossing and the death-coveting earnestness of Romeo and Juliet; it belongs to the region of unartificial emotions; and they that only act a part and wear the dress and speech of sincerity for the making up of a scene, can have no faith in others' sincerity. Of course, every little obstacle is not sufficient to crush a strong affection. And the heart is not bruised by the mere shadow that lies across it. To complete this work of violence, the heart must meet a calamity that offers no alleviation—that neither soothes it with a better hope, nor leaves it a happy recollection to caress the wound of disappointment. It must be an affliction that lays its stroke upon the affections. It is not loss that makes it, it is not loneliness, it is not privation; for all these are easy to bear when there is a solace within. It is not the thought that effort has been a failure; for, while the heart remains, it will scorn to be subdued. It is not the sense of shame, or the exposure to derision; for all this our natural pride resents as much as it feels. It is not abject servility of spirit, cowering before a difficulty or a dread; for this is the weakness of one who begins without heart, and has nothing to hazard, nothing to be injured. It is not the want of resolve and affection and will, which even, in the worldly sense, forms or contributes to the broken heart. No; the very foundation of the idea is the intensity of the affection coupled with the entireness of purpose. There must be emotion—there must be an object that calls for our faculties and our feelings, and there must be activity and animation pervading the whole soul, and centering upon some chief desire, or there is neither a wound nor the heart to wound.

There are two reasons, therefore, why this misfortune scarcely receives the respect of the world. With some it is the most egregious of follies to be so much overruled by the heart. And they seem to deduce this principle from the best of authorities; for wisdom itself avouches that he who "trusteth in his own heart is a fool." It is presumption to dispute a sentence so loftily derived. Yet we very much question whether this is, after all, such a slur cast upon the living and acting with a heart. The same charge is laid upon him who trusteth in his own wisdom, or in uncertain riches; and yet not even the sagacious world has taken this to be an argument against the having or the using either wealth or wisdom. Perhaps the danger is about parallel in all the cases; and the folly is not in the possessing, but in being afraid to spend and to use and to turn to right account, and to convert into active talents. And, in this sense, who is the wise man's fool but he that shuts up his heart in cold imprisonments of selfishness, or buries it in napkins of civility, and has no show of its use to exhibit.

There is a part of the world with whom it is the original sin to be carried away by zeal, and by having more heart than is really conducive to our comfort and our profit. They represent the Arctic and Antarctic extremes, and, like the greasy Esquimaux, count it a distinction to have the power of laughing at the ardent natures that loathe the smooth blubber. They are diverted with the calamities which men bring on themselves, by indulging and strengthening their affections, and they imagine that an affection is worth nothing except as we can so moderate it as never to suffer any deep affliction from it. They say that if it must be wounded, it might better not live—if we must suffer in heart, we might better put our pleasure in such heartless living as to save the suffering. Need we say that this disposition, flattered, as it may be, by philosophy, is the remotest from Christian wisdom. *That* puts the substance, not only of character but of devoutness towards God *in the heart,* and that sets before us, on the pedestal of super-angelic elevation, the man of purest affections and of most generous sympathies, who wept at the grave of his friend, owned a beloved disciple, baptized himself in blood out of love to man, and consigned himself to the fate of a broken heart. O mightiest of friends, most tender of brothers! "not as the world giveth, gavest Thou unto us." It was not for a return, that the life of Christ was given for us. It was not that we should repay this incalculable debt with our miserable constraints of affection. It was out of the abundance of his own heart, because it was excellent to have affections, though they wrenched us with anxiety and took our blood for their cost.

2. By far the greater part of the world shuns these frozen regions of glittering heartlessness. With the most of men, the crime is not that original sin of having a heart and cherishing it, but the allowing such a great and noble and angelic part of man to be overpowered and broken. They

put the very virtue of the heart in its intentness, and resistance, and superiority to disappointment. With them it is only excellent by its strength against difficulties—its endurance in spite of disaster. They would have a heart within a heart, and the inmost of all to be the determination never to feel or confess ourselves baffled. We may be wounded in the outer circumference of affection, but this is only to drive us into the entrenchment that never yields. This unbroken purpose, to be above the control of our affections, is what most men call *heart*. The broken heart is, in their estimate, a heart demolished, annulled, and they count it a moral impossibility to make a manly heart out of one that has been thus despoiled of its integrity; nay, converted into no heart. It is, to their mind, an extinction of life, and nothing but a miracle can give to the shattered material a resurrection. We reach the very idea with which we first described the world's skepticism. The broken heart is the sign of *defect*. It matters little to the carnal eye how this misery is incurred. It is not an inquiry whether the affection has been misplaced, whether the heart has leaned upon a treacherous staff until both broke together. It is enough that there was a shivering into hopeless abandonment of effort. The radical defect, the world says, is betrayed, and the secret is that there was not a genuine heart—that there was not the manly will which defies the hammer of tribulation. And however the world may commiserate the sorrow (for we know ourselves to be all of kin in that), yet, for the broken heart, the world has no respect—over it chants no elegies to greatness, rears no monuments of commendation. It carves an Alas! for the epitaph, and it symbolizes the broken heart not by a cross on which heaven and earth meet, but by the broken column, or the shattered vase of ashes, emblems of an unfinished work.

In what sense, then, we inquire, can the broken heart be predicated of Christ? With deference to the suggestions of Scripture, and with the conviction that we are representing the spirit of its testimony, would we enter the mysteries of this sacred subject.

It is lawful for us to infer that the human soul of Christ was not unconscious of those hopes and fears which innocently agitate our own souls. We have reason to regard Him as ignorant of the amount of sacrifice to be required of Him in bearing the iniquity of us all. And we have reason, therefore, to regard some of the most consoling hopes of a righteous soul as made to Him the sources of disappointment and sorrow. The fact does not at all prejudice the submission of His will, but rather explains this, and shows how His suffering, as it proceeded, was a progressive and continuous sacrifice of the will to that of the Father. We say that these were sufficient reasons for His entertaining some expectations of consolation and success to mitigate the severity of His sufferings, and vindicate, while He was living His wronged and execrated name. Holy Scripture gives us, at least, two distinct intimations of the sorrow that came in this way of disappointment to break His heart.

Our text tells us, that it was reproach which broke His heart; and it has an explanation immediately ensuing, as if the weight of what so surprised His strength was too much for his heart, and left no room for any consoling thought—occupying and possessing the heart—till it was "*full* of heaviness." And to identify the cause of this unexpected grief, the Redeemer is represented as declaring His hope and His disappointment: "I looked for some to take pity on me, but there was none; and for comforters, but I found none." There seems to have been a cherished hope that some tribute of affection, or some act of gratitude, would mitigate for Him the agonies of His painful cross. He seems to have counted upon some exhibition of human affection which might, at least, suggest that His love as a man and a brother had not been entirely wasted and frustrated. By the miracles of healing, by the miracles of supply, by the raising of the dead, by the drying of the mourners' tears, by the gladdening of parents' hearts, by the light he had diffused over the disconsolate, by His own warm affections, by His tears for others, and His ever-ready offices to the sick and the dying and the dead, He might have supposed that the cross and cruelty he awaited from Scribes and Gentiles, would yet be pitied and comforted with some recognition of the love and the debt. What God designed for Him to suffer, He does not seem to have entirely known.

And the hand of God, by His prayer, He would not stay or limit. But of *man* what should He receive? Would *man* so utterly forsake Him? Could *man* be so heartless as to leave Him without a sign of gratitude? Was there any barrier so high and so strong that *man* would not reach to Him at this hour of need even one poor word of *pity*, one sigh to relieve His own?

It is easy to believe that in the expectations of His human soul there was all along a comfort in the thought that mankind, who would not be recovered by anything else, might, at least, be drawn by affection. So far as human feelings were alive in Him, He must have been full of confidence that man could not universally resist love. But when this last hope of drawing men to Himself and so to life was dashed—when his desolation uttered that hopeless language, "Thou hast put away mine acquaintance far from me and made me to be abhorred of them. Lover and friend hast thou put far from me. All my inward friends abhorred me, and they whom I loved are turned against me"—was it strange that the work of recovering men by love seemed to His human soul a failure? With a love for mankind so intense that life was consumed in the flame, and yet with mankind so intractable that neither his innocence nor his sacredness nor his love could be a protection—that he must be not only neglected, but spit upon and scorned, and reviled, and hated—oh! was it not a reproach—a reproach upon his life's whole work, his heart's last hope—which dashed every prospect to human view into atoms, and literally broke his heart.

There is, however, a farther intimation of the cause that desolated His heart. The mention of *reproach* carries the eye back to a previous passage in the same Psalm—"The reproaches of them that reproached Thee, are fallen upon me." That this refers to Christ, and how, St. John hath taught—"The zeal of thine house hath eaten me up," and the reproaches follow as the consequence of this zeal. And what this zeal imports, the act of Christ has made manifest. It seems, therefore, to be the record of Scripture that the Redeemer's heart was broken by the reproach which His zeal for the house of God incurred. It was His demeanor of authority in driving profanation from the Temple that awoke the fatal wrath of the priests and elders. It was His language concerning His authority and power over the Temple that was produced for His conviction. In fulfilling the office that was laid upon Him, He must exercise authority, He must command obedience. Man resisted. Man would put religion in the heart only, and not in the Temple. Man would use the very sacredness of God's house to shelter his own avarice and minister to his own aggrandizement. Was it not singular that a man so despised and so weak should have put to flight the whole crowd of buyers and sellers, of great men and holy men? And might not the hope be framed out of this fact that His zeal for God's house commended itself to men's conscience, and was a source of power, and must give him undisputed claim to their reverence? But alas! it was this very zeal that consumed Him. It was the source that seemed to be full of power, that betrayed Him into the enemy's power. It was the very authority that God gave Him, and on two occasions made conspicuous, which was turned into accusation of blasphemy. Listen to the tenor of all that taunt and ridicule and invective which was flung at Him upon the cross. Hear how vindictively they threw in His face His claim to authority over the Temple. Mark the sting that lay in their words, when they thus laughed at His claims, and boasted that His great success in the Temple was the cause of His failure. And He could see that the work was all in vain—that the Temple He had cleansed was doomed to ruin. His office as a man—that which had warmed His soul with its most glowing zeal—that which had taken up every fear and every affection into its own surpassing force—this was a baffled, disappointed work; nay, by the very death He bore, the very triumph He gained, this delight of His human heart was crushed. Was it strange that, in the bitterness of an utter, a certain disappointment, "the reproach had broken His heart?"

My brethren, there is no need that we should dilate upon the fact of Christ's thus offering, with His death, the very sacrifice which heaven exacts of man. He had no heart of sin to break with shame and sorrow for what was in it, and so His innocent heart was broken with defeat and reproach.

God took that as the noblest offering which human nature could present. Wait not, then, for gold or for success—wait not to bring money or price. The broken heart, that yields the hope of saving itself except in God—the broken heart is the frankincense whose perfume is welcomed at the altar, is welcomed at the throne.

God took the broken heart of Jesus and made it the heart of the King of Kings. And He will make the broken heart anew. He will turn its sense of degradation into the majestic consciousness that the new heart makes us invincible. It will come to a joy which the world cannot give and hell cannot take away.

God of all pity, break—though it be by tribulation, though it be by saddening earth to us—break these hearts of clay, and make us to live as chosen to be, through the broken heart (of Jesus and our own), kings and priests unto God.

X.

YOUTHFUL CONCEIT.

LAM. iii. 27,

"It is good for a man that he bear the yoke in his youth."

THE best days of life are soon gone; and time, that stayeth never for man, seems then to fly with greater speed. Death lingers to the old, the night is long to the sick man, the freshness of the morning will not bring him his strength, and he crieth out in vain for the peace of the grave. To all these the sun is slow in its course, and they bear the burthen of their days; but youth is a dream of gladness which comes but to vanish; it is sweet as a smile that perishes; it is bright and rapid as the arrows of God when He shooteth His lightnings in the heavens.

If youth, thus, is the season when the foundation of wisdom is to be laid, and if that season passeth away thus rapidly, we must not suffer occasions to escape us which admit of no substitute; nor neglect improvements which no other period of life will ever enable us to attain. Whether we can see it or not, it is true beyond all disputation, and God has not yet in nature or in revelation found it necessary to make you or me, or any uprising scion of mankind an exception, nor has He expunged a syllable of the record of His truth, "It is good for a man that he bear the yoke in his youth."

By *the yoke*, I understand the sacred writer to mean, in general, a state of discipline; everything which education teaches; the restraint of passions, the formation of habits, and the cultivation of faculties. It is not my intention, at present, to launch into so wide a range as that to which this explanation would seem to lead; but, in pointing out a few of the characteristic faults of youth, to show in what manner the young are most likely to prove intractable to that yoke which the pulpit advises them to bear, and to make it clear what those sins and infirmities are which present the most serious obstacle to their progress in Christian improvement.

The first error I shall notice, and to which I consider *youth* to be more exposed than any other period of life, is *conceit*; that which our Saviour characterizes under the name of self-exaltation, and St. Paul reproves as being "high-minded," not in our modern sense of elevation above any mean or degrading motive, but in the sense of being "wise in our own conceits,"—an overweening opinion of our own good and great qualities. The thorns of life prick these bubbles. Youthful inflation seldom lasts, except ludicrously. Time brings a pressure, and conceit collapses. But the wisdom that gives us insight into the reality of human nature, both the boldly masculine and the modestly feminine, assures us that conceit is not an imaginary peril or error of youth.

The reason of this is very obvious. The comparisons the young have made between themselves and their fellow-creatures are few in proportion to what they must make hereafter. Absolute standard of excellence there is not. We think ourselves great because we think others little, and the more human beings we mingle with, and the more frequently we institute the comparison, the more probable it is that we shall find our equals and our superiors in every accomplishment and in every virtue.

The Jerome Bonaparte, whom the success and the favoritism of the first and great Napoleon made king of Westphalia, because he was a brother, was a man of less experience and of narrower observation than the emperor, and was amazingly elated with his importance. He paraded his conceit foppishly and airishly before the Napoleon whose wit was often as pungent as his penetration. Jerome imagined that the majesty of his office must irradiate the very features of his person. "Travel, my good brother," said the emperor, "travel and learn something that a king ought to know. If the majesty of kings is supposed to be stamped on their countenances, don't be alarmed. You may travel through Europe incognito. You will not be discovered."

We often observe men, whose sphere of life has been extremely confined, to be conceited through *every period* of their existence, for the same reason that the young are conceited in the *earliest* period, because they have measured themselves with very few of their species, and mistaking all that they have seen for all that there is, have so confirmed themselves in habitual conceit, that the delusion is totally impregnable to all future conviction.

Growing experience forces upon the young a perception of their unjust pretensions; they begin to discover that the world had made some progress in knowledge before their existence, and that their birth will not be hailed as the great era of wisdom and of truth.

It is necessary to live for a considerable time, and in various scenes, to perceive fully the wisdom of those practices which the world has established, not at the suggestion of any one individual, but from the gradual conviction of all that they were best adapted to promote the general happiness. Our fathers, in their youthful days, questioned with as much acuteness, and decided with as much temerity as we can in ours. If the progress of life has taught them to *respect* what in its origin they despised; if they have traced to the dictates of *experience* many things which they at first attributed to prejudice and ignorance; if they have learned to mistrust themselves, and to confide more in the general feelings and judgments of the world; we ought not to suppose ourselves protected from the same revolution of opinions, or imagine that those early conceptions of human life shall be permanent *now* which have *never* been *permanent before.*

But I must protect myself against misconstruction. I must beware that I mislead not you. My remonstrance is against conceit. I proclaim it a failing as injurious to the acquisition of Christian as of human improvement.

My remonstrances are by no means directed against the spirit of *free inquiry.* From this a strong mind cannot and ought not to be debarred, any more than a strong body ought to be from perfect activity and motion. But this let the young consider. It is not a necessary consequence that no reason can be found because they can find none, or because they can even obtain none from a few persons to whom they have proposed their difficulty, and who, perhaps, can see and practice right without the power of explaining and defending it.

To incline to the one side or the other is natural and not blamable in the young; but when you are so liable to error, do not decide so that you cannot directly retract; avoid the fatal mistake, the weak but common mistake of youth, of being so violent and positive, where good men have not been unanimous, and eternity is not in the scales, that you are either tied up for life to the crude system or the novel vagary or the untested cause you have adopted, or are forced to abandon it hereafter with the imputation of folly or of guilt.

Courage and firmness in maintaining important opinions are worthy attributes; but in proportion as any opinion is marked by moderation and formed upon reflection, it is most likely to be retained with spirit. Inflexibility is then a virtuous steadfastness and not a vicious obstinacy. The granite has a right to be hard and durable, though it protrudes amid the soft shale of the surface, because the granite is primitive, and has in itself all the elements of a world's foundation.

Extravagance in opinion is the parent of change, and frequent change produces at last a profligate indifference to all opinion. The person who is *firm* and *consistent* in his *manhood* has most probably been *modest* in his youth ; so true it is that all the humility so strongly enjoined by the gospel is not calculated to repress and extinguish human powers, but to adjust the degree of confidence with which they are exercised to the degree of excellence with which they are endowed, and to take care that whatsoever is fallible should not be presumptuous. All those who judge of the world by *ideal* rather than *actual* models of excellence are in some little danger of becoming too contemptuous ; the imagination can easily represent somewhat superior to what ever existed or ever will exist. By assembling all the excellencies which nature has scattered among many real beings into one fictitious one, and by omitting all defects, we have at once a monster of perfection, to which our sad medley of good and evil cannot be compared without disgrace. Such is the case with the young, who despise imperfection because extended observation has not yet shown them that the realities of life always fall far short of the pictures of the mind, and that they can easily conceive what they never will be able to find. The increase of years, with many *evils*, brings *this good*, that our expectations of life are more accommodated to its true state; we are no longer surprised at flagrant inconsistencies in character, nor disgusted that prejudice and weakness should twine around the loftiest virtues; we are contented with mixtures of good and evil, as it has been mingled for us, and do not despise our species because God has made them lower than the angels.

Prudence is, perhaps, another cause that checks the indulgence of contempt as we advance in life. The world, we find, has inevitable difficulties enough without the wanton exasperation of our fellow-creatures.

Contempt is commonly mistaken by the young for an evidence of understanding. But no habit of mind can afford this evidence, which is neither difficult to acquire, nor meritorious when it is acquired, and as it is certainly very easy to be contemptuous, so it is very useless, if not pernicious. To *discover* the imperfections of others is penetration; to hate them for those faults is contempt. We may be clear-sighted without being malevolent, and make use of the errors we discover to learn caution, not to gratify satire. That part of contempt which consists of acuteness we may preserve; its dangerous ingredient is censure.

Contempt, so far from being favorable to the improvement of the mind, is perhaps directly the reverse. It increases so rapidly that it soon degenerates into a passion for condemnation. The sense of what is good withers away, and the perception of evil becomes so keen and insatiable that every decision we make is *satire*, not *judgment*. All things have a double aspect; the contemptuous man sees than only on one side, and does not believe they have any other. He has sacrificed an excellent faculty to a malevolent indulgence.

Wisdom consists in doing difficult things which the mass of mankind cannot do; there is a much more compendious road to reputation in *doing nothing* and in *blaming everything*, in pointing out where others are deficient without proving where we excel. In this way a contemptuous person gives himself virtues by implication, as if the opposite perfection were immediately infused into his own mind the moment he had discovered a defect in the mind of another. *Real wisdom* rather delights in positive exertions, and seeks for reputation by showing what itself *is*, not by boasting what others are not. Contempt and conceit are twins of the same parentage. Pride begets them; humility strangles them. Youth in its waywardness fondles them; age, if it outgrows the errors of youth, flings them aside, as the experienced and athletic swimmer discards the bloated bladders that have given him false appearances of buoyancy and skill.

The contemptuous habit and the conceited mind are the outer bark and the inner pith of the same shrub.

The young in their short-sighted fallacies presume with this withe to whip the rock. It staggers not, but the frail instrument cracks and splinters, and betrays itself to be contemptible. Thou, man of virtue, man of sense; thou patient, unresenting object of contempt and conceit, art the wise teacher to the young; whilst in thy fortitude thou art silent, in thy humility thou pitiest and forgivest.

> " They that overween,
> And at thy growing virtues fret their spleen,
> No anger find in thee."

It is this sweet morsel of conceit which intoxicates our youth to render our age insipid and morose. It is these dainties of conceit and contempt poisoning the youthful tongue, which turn to bitterness and sourness as life and God's justice grow ripe. These are the passions which Christianity so often condemns, as the likeness of hatred, and the resemblance of the fallen enemy of man, proud but miserable, ambitious but cursed, full of accusations against them that seek a good conscience, but as futile in his complaints as the stone we fling against a fellow-sinner is futile to stop the flowing mercy of God.

Surely, if any one has a right to look down upon the world with contempt, it is not he who has just entered into it; if great actions, admirable qualities, and profound knowledge are sources of superiority, they most probably will not be traced in that person to whom so short a period of existence has afforded little leisure for thought, word and deed.

When *pride* cometh, then cometh *shame;* but with the *lowly* is wisdom. Before *destruction* the heart of man is *haughty*, and before *honour* is *humility*.

XI.

THE MIRACLE AT THE RED SEA.

1 Cor. x. 1, 2.

"Moreover, brethren, I would not that ye should be ignorant how that all our fathers were under the cloud, and all passed through the sea; and were all baptized unto Moses in the cloud and in the sea."

THE Hebrews are here claimed as the ancestors of Christians, not on the presumption of lineal descent, but on the ground of religious precedence. They were the partakers and possessors of that covenant which God made with men. Natural religion, if there be such a thing, belonged to all men, holds now the sway over unevangelized lands, and determines the destiny of those who inherit not the gospel. But the Church, the visible body with a revealed covenant and special privileges from God, has been always exclusive. And the descendants of Abraham by the flesh were "our fathers" as the sole possessors of that covenant religion, once Jewish, but now Catholic; once limited to a nation, but now as expansive as its institutions; once confined to genealogies, now distributed by universal laws.

There is, accordingly, a practical wisdom to be

deduced from the main elements of God's moral government over "our fathers."

In selecting them as the depositaries of His truth, miracles attested the fact of His intervention. And there was something like a compend of all miracles, in those two symbols, the cloud and the sea—the sea, that natural power most widely diffused, first reversing its properties and then rushing back to its pristine condition to rescue our fathers, and the cloud, that emblem of perpetual beneficence, hanging its daily curtain of protection and refreshment and instruction over the tents of Israel. So nature has recoiled by miracle, and again resuming its order has been the means of rescuing the church of God, and overthrowing its enemies. So also natural forms, as changeful as the clouds, yet always returning, have sheltered and refreshed and conducted the wearied church in the wilderness. It does not comport with my purpose, to expatiate on the uses and significations of that miraculous cloud. The Divine will, as manifested in the control of the sea, is the special subject before us. Its withdrawal as a solid heap, like rage frozen by fright, to make a way of escape for Israel; its return, pouring a retaliatory death upon Pharaoh and his army; these are the materials of our theme.

What were the effects upon the parties interested?

What moral instruction does this event convey?

What typical wisdom was designed by this miracle?

The effects of this miracle upon Egypt are too manifest to be overlooked. We need to recall the fact that the ten plagues inflicted upon that land had been not only judicial visitations, but blows of correction obviously aimed at their idolatry, in derision of the objects they worshipped, in contempt of their sacred rites, in defiance of Osiris, the god of light, and, as they thought, of life, and in contradiction to their prevailing superstitions. Their punishments were calculated to disabuse the mind, while they stung the conscience. It was the glory of the Invisible, making the creature to proclaim His praise, after man had converted this instrument into a Deity. The Egyptians may have argued like the Syrians in the reign of Abab: "Their gods are gods of the hills; therefore they were stronger than we; but let us fight against them in the plain, and surely we shall be stronger than they." They might have questioned whether this conqueror of their magicians could exercise his art beyond the clime of Egypt. They may have doubted His ability to command wonders among the mountains-deities, or near his shepherd-home in Midian. And at least, while they had feared His power over the irrational creation, there was no evidence that He could command hosts of men, and convert fugitives, encumbered, unarmed, unskilled in war, into a resisting army. It was necessary to convince Egypt, that the sea was as subservient as the river to the God of the Hebrews, and that the very waters which protected their territory on the east were made and moved by the breath of the Lord. It was necessary to intimidate this rapacious nation and subdue their recklessness by terror.

And the effect was in correspondence with this design. "I will be honoured upon Pharaoh and upon all his host; that the Egyptians may know that I am the Lord."

What more appalling lesson, than to read the helplessness of the army, on which Egypt leaned? What higher indications of the Supreme, than to behold nature changing its uniform laws on behalf of His people? What more direct reproof of their grossness, than to find their nation's last resource turned to very scorn? What clearer evidence that neither mountains limited, nor station escaped this Omnipotence?

The pride of Egypt was effectually shattered by this overthrow. During the forty years, that Israel wandered in the wilderness, their oppressors never lifted hand against them. The miracle was a merciful restraint, if it proved no more. It prevented the combination of this empire with the Canaanites in resistance to Israel. And it was a check upon the Pharaohs, for which the world may be thankful,—the Waterloo of an Egyptian Bonaparte,—the disgrace and disaster that saved the Eastern World from subjugation by that swarming nation. Upon the fugitives, the effect was no less remarkable. They had hesitated to own the commission of their leader, but now "they believed the Lord and His servant Moses." They had been contaminated by the idolatries of Egypt, but now they "feared the Lord." It was the open victory of the Supreme Being, and sealed upon their memories forever the certainty of His existence, His power, His justice, and His truth. It was a plain declaration, that the Lord was on the side of the defenceless, and that He valued the lives of infants, which heathenism had devoted to the offices of cruelty, or to the service of superstition. "They were baptized unto Moses in the sea." The law, of which he was the mediator, became by every obligation of reason and of affection, their only guide. And the astonished gladness of their hearts was turned at once to praise. The oldest hymn upon record was chanted upon the coasts of that sea. It was repeated by the choirs of Israel from that day onward. Music and the exhilarating accompaniments of skill were on that brink of miracles consecrated forever to the worship of God. And that oldest hymn, which man now reads, was the monument in the mouths and hearts of sire and son to show that the first and typical redemption was by miracle, and in the distant prospects of the Revelation, is the chanting of this hymn by those who have gotten the victory over the beast, who "stand on the sea of glass, having the harps of God. And they sing the song of Moses the servant of God, and the song of the Lamb."

This consummation of Pharaoh's career is replete with warning. The conduct of this monarch is a continued display of the infatuation of wickedness. His fate is a signal display of the judgment that descends on our obstinate infatuation.

How presumptuous the scheme of his hardened heart! Soliciting mercy from the Lord, he gains the desired relief, but no sooner does the answer of mercy come, than his heart again swells with folly. Had he not every reason to expect that the next blow would be aimed at himself and his army? Had not the judgments that softened his heart, come so near that himself must be the next victim? Was there any indication that the Power, which had compelled him to submit, was exhausted or withdrawn? Such is the blind impetuosity of sin. It swells the veins of guilt by the very breathing-spells of mercy. It is hardened—no man can tell the process—it is hardened by the forbearance which gives it respite. It escapes a present punishment only to invite a redoubled indignation. The very rock will yield to continual droppings, but the hardened heart is like the avalanche that hangs on the side of Jura, which feels the melting ray only to precipitate itself into ruin.

The sad infirmity of sin is its weakness of vision. It is wise for a brief compass, but the looming dangers beyond are hidden from its view. When it is recalled to the light by some afflictive stroke, it comes up like a prisoner from a dungeon, or the miner from his shaft. It sees the light, but it is blinded still. It is in the blaze of a new world, but the objects of this creation are obscured and distorted. There is a pain in the very novelty. The soul is restless under this new condition. There is an obligation fastened upon it, which it would shun. It hates the light, and retreats from the very irksomeness of blessings to its own caverns of toil, and gain, and danger. And the sentence of Jesus is verified, "Men love darkness rather than light, because their deeds are evil." They may not repent, because they will not stop to reason with themselves. They may not choose the reproach of Christ, because they have not paused to gaze upon the lustres of the recompense. They may not see the folly of sin, because they have not exercised the eye of the soul to see its proportions in the open light.

If this braving of the Divine judgments, and this infatuation, were the ruin of Pharaoh, why may they not have the same tendency for all? Was he not raised up, and made eminent and capable of yielding power, for the very purpose of showing in him the methods of the Divine government? The same moral system under which his heart was hardened till he dragged the walls of ruin down upon him, the same moral system now exists, and will to the end exist. Where there is not the will to seek unto God, the disposition to love the soul's health, then will infatuation come, and reason itself will be confounded, and worldly wisdom will appear like foolishness, and the punishments of that soul will illustrate the excellency of God's government. But some one will say, the ways of the Lord are not equal, for whom He will He hardeneth. Yes, but He willeth to harden only those that have resisted His government.

God took away the equilibrium of Pharaoh's faculties, just so often as Pharaoh refused to sanctify those faculties. God was increasing his stupidity, but it was because the monarch chose this, rather than to forsake his crimes and passions.

Pharaoh does not stand out in history as a fiend or a brute. His traits were human, his infatuation such as man must expect. But he was eminent, he had the power of great good, or great evil. The magnitude of the consequences was not in the atrocity of his offences, but in the elevation of his position. He towered in obstinacy like one of the pyramids of his land, and the wrestle with his heart was a battle with the embodied idolatries of Egypt. Suppose some fiend had been incarnate to illustrate the pertinacity of sin. Would it have touched our case? Scarcely at all. His crimes would be monstrous, his spirit would have wanted human compassions. We could not analyze the motives of such a creature. We would have disclaimed the identity of our temptations. The only points of contact would have been in the hearing of the same law, and the same certainty of its vindication. But we have in distinct characters upon the throne of Egypt a man, human in his wilfulness, human in his relentings, human in his covetousness and oppression, in his fears and his promises. His example is the handwriting on the wall of the human heart, and God has inscribed there, as if we were reading it on the lintels of the soul, "Beware lest any of you be hardened through the deceitfulness of sin."

If this be the admonition that issues from those drowning waters, equally distinct is the encouragement resounding in the hymn upon the shore. It sends its thrill to the heart of obedience, as it celebrates the rescuing and protecting hand. Be not ignorant that "our fathers passed through the sea, and were baptized unto Moses in the cloud and in the sea." They came out of Egypt by temptations. They were encompassed with fightings and fears. Could pen have written it more legibly, than they now read in the waters of the miracles, "He will also with the temptation make a way to escape, that ye may be able to bear it." Temptation is the touch-stone of religion. God has no place of safety for it in His universe, if it is too weak for temptation. The hazards of virtue, the trials of holiness, these are the tests that lay the foundation of our joys. It is in these that God manifests Himself, though not by daily miracle, yet by daily grace. Ye servants of this world, tell me if the good actions of which you are not ashamed, were founded upon any other principle, than the way of escape from temptation. Ye that have persevered in the obedience of Christ proclaim it, as your rejoicing heart must testify, that "with the temptation there is always a way to escape." When there is no other remedy, we may "stand still, and see the salvation of the Lord." Though the threatening world, like pursuing Egypt, may exalt in the hope that you are entangled and the wilderness hath shut you in, God will make "a way to escape." Though the faintness of discouragement may come upon you, and your cries may be the ejaculations of terror, rather than the petitions of hope, He will make "a way to escape."

Though you go down to the brink of death, and walk as it were sentenced to the grave, He will make " a way to escape." Though you are amid the waters of tribulation, baptized by the clouds of earthly woe, and walking through the deeps of new experience, there shall be " a way to escape." Though you follow your Saviour, as the Israelites ventured after Moses, into the yawning avenue of death, you shall find between its congealed walls of terror "a way to escape," and on the shore of safety and viewing the scene of triumph, shall sing the song of Moses and of the Lamb.

I cannot doubt that this miracle was typical of lofty spiritual truths. St. Paul in our text makes it the figure of baptism, and our Liturgy has so pronounced it in the prayer before baptism. It was the act by which God of His own mere grace received them as His church. It was the sprinkling of the covenant, which bound them by every good motive to serve the Lord, and which pledged to their faith His very omnipotence. And, as that baptism was effected by the ministry of Moses, and was the sign of their duty to cling to this ministry, they were baptized unto Moses, so we in the name of the Trinity, and unto the ministry of Christ. And as they were by figure buried in the waters, so we are buried by baptism into death. And as they passed through the Red Sea on their way of escape to Canaan, so we through the grave and gate of death and a joyful resurrection enter into the inheritance of the saints in light.

We stand then by nature on the Egyptian shore.

Death must be passed. And it is at our option, to go trembling but triumphing through its waters with the people of God, or to enter it with our worldly schemes upon us, and our delusions fixed, and in the service of the prince of this world, and find there the doom of everlasting destruction.

The use made of this type by St. Paul is to demonstrate that no covenant relation will save us, except as we keep our covenant. The covenant was immensely blessed to the Hebrew, it was his life, it was the fountain of his after joys, it was the mainspring of his persevering courage. But the covenant did not save the sinning Hebrew from the plague and the pestilence of the wilderness.

And our baptism is more blessed than the sprinkling of those dews from the cloud and those drops from the sea. For it was not the water then that gave the blessing, but the power of God, and the covenant. And it is not the water that blesses now, but the resurrection of Christ, and the gift of the Spirit, and our adoption into God's family.

But when they sinned, it was a double contempt, nay, it was manifold contempt, a contempt of God and of their covenant, of their own souls and of their mercies, of the angel that led them, and of the land that waited their coming.

Whether we behold the fate of the proud Pharaoh, or witness the vengeance-stricken corpses of Israel in the wilderness, the warning is read, "If they escaped not who refused Him that spake on earth, much more shall not we escape, if we turn away from Him that speaketh from heaven. For the God of our fathers, *our God*, is a consuming fire."

Brethren, I would not have you ignorant of this. But I would have you to remember, that their deliverance was from the groanings of Egypt, ours is from the miseries of eternity. They were saved from them that kill the body, our rescue is from them that strangle the life of the soul. Their escape left a fiery wilderness between them and rest, our salvation plants us among the odors of Eden, and makes the very wilderness of arid suffering to rejoice and blossom as the rose. Oh, what rapturous praise, what zealous vows, what consecrations of every faculty, are due to Him who hath redeemed us from the hand of the enemy, and leads us through pleasant places till we pass over Jordan!

XII.

THE CALUMNIATOR AND POLITICIAN.

1 SAM. xxii. 22.

"And David said unto Abiathar, I knew it that day, when Doeg the Edomite was there, that he would surely tell Saul."

DAVID and his cotemporaries; the anointed shepherd exchanging his staff for the sceptre; the Psalmist flinging melodies upon the breeze of every clime; the monarch unawed by the colossal grandeur that overshadowed the East during his reign; the father of Absalom, most impious of rebels, and of Solomon, most illustrious of sons; David, the stripling, that defied the lion and the bear; the ruddy young man that challenged the Philistine giant; the applauded champion of his nation taken to the family of the king, beloved of Jonathan, jealously pursued by Saul; a good man, so far beyond his times, and yet a passionate, cruel criminal, falling so far beneath his standard; a man so amazingly prospered, the very Achilles of numberless adventures not fabulous, and yet a man so severely and so sadly injured and afflicted; David, the epitome of all kings and of all vicissitudes;—how vast, how instructive a theme in himself! yet himself but a single source of light in the constellation of human greatness which glimmered around him. David and his cotemporaries. I have often regarded it as a subject on which the pen of political wisdom might guide itself by the just monitions of sacred oracle, and write lessons of experience for king and courtier, for statesman and priest, for reformer and patriot, for the ambitious aspirant and the corrupted possessor of power, for scheming and shrewd and laborious but wilful men like Saul, for conscientious but unfortunate and injured men like Abiathar; for the wearers of the temple linen, clothed with prerogative, yet not always inviolate; for the winners of battles; for the managers of peace; for the arbiters of justice and the counsellors of authority; for them that accept trusts of power, and for an impatient people in their bestowal of trusts. Grouped around the royal history of David, how bold and magnanimous an examplar of the faithful prophet is Samuel, faithful ever to God, to the people and the king; beside him towers the athletic Saul, model of impetuosity; then the affectionate and valiant Jonathan; and among the pictures of domestic character, Nabal, rich but penurious, prospered but churlish, and Abigail the wise-hearted and generous but thwarted wife, and Jesse, that royal father of royal sons, and Michal, that short-sighted and unhappy woman, proud of her family but despising her own husband; while in the front of public affairs we see such strong outlines of character as marked Nathan righteous in reproof, Shimei the cowardly reveler, Joab and Abner jealous rivals and both unscrupulous, Ahithophel, the cunning man, capable of great mischief, but dying when the remedy begins, and others a number, each a representative of a class. Of greatness how many models, of virtue how various examples, of crimes how abundant specimens; men of profligacy, and men of integrity, lofty in purpose as Solomon, and impious in ambition as Absalom ; while in the background from the shadows of obscurity crawls forth that image of sycophancy, of servility and of disgusting meanness, Doeg the Edomite.

David appears to have discerned at once the insidious character of this man. When as a fugitive from the wrath of Saul, David was sheltered at the house of Abimelech the priest, Doeg was present, completing his period either of vow or of discipline under the sacerdotal charge. David was suspicious at the time that his traits would render this sanctuary no asylum, and that his mischievous propensities would involve the house of Ahitub in danger. Passing by the other cotemporaries of David, we would inspect the character of this Doeg.

His name indicates his extraction from the degenerate race of Edom. By some insinuating qualities he had ingratiated himself with the king, patron ever of men whose best quality was their readiness to serve him. He was one of that class who measure their importance by the amount of art which they abet. It was his pride to win a prize from Saul at the expense of David and of Abimelech. The radical defect in the man was the want of true independence. He was a mere attachment upon the success of those from whom he sought to gain. Without worth, or without principle, he scrupled not to employ others as instruments of his own aggrandizement by lending himself for an instrument of their schemes. His preferment had been earned by such services to the king, and David knowing the only point of value in the man, supposed that he would gain as an informer what he never would have acquired by higher services. He is a specimen of those creeping, unprincipled, self-seeking men whose promotion is the reward of pandering to the caprice and jealousy of their patrons. Elevated by such means to his position in the kingdom, there was no reason to suppose that the habit would forsake him, and no reason to confide in his sense of honor. "I knew it that day when Doeg the Edomite was there, that he would surely tell Saul."

Let us observe more closely the history of this man, and perceive to what such a dishonorable character tends.

When David had escaped the fury of the monarch, and had gathered around him the disaffected subjects, Saul was incensed at beholding the alienation of his people, and the want of affection that displayed itself even among his own bodyguard. Upbraiding his attendants, and eager to find some object for his revenge, he attempts to draw an accusation from the servants that waited upon him. Doeg rejoices at this chance of reaping the harvest of an informer. Abimelech, odious to this sycophant by his very virtues, is represented as having assisted David and conspired with him against the king, to have given the fugitive the benefit of his sacred offices, to have provided for his bodily wants, and to have equipped him with the sword of Goliath taken for that purpose from the treasury of the Lord. Saul seizes upon this opportunity for sating his vengeance. The priest is summoned not to a trial, but to sentence and execution. In vain does he disentangle the falsehoods of Doeg. In vain does he insist that loyalty and affection to his rightful sovereign had prompted every act. In vain does he attempt to appease the anger of Saul, by protesting innocence. The enraged king dooms Abimelech and his father's house to extermination. The curse upon negligent Eli receives its fulfillment. His house falls before the entail of punishment. Yet note by what instruments this result is attained. Saul commands his own body-guard to fall upon the priests. The sacred rites and officers of religion, ever venerated by the true soldier, will not be violated by these servants of Saul. Grotius tells us that no civilized nation ever allowed injuries to the priests of their enemies. The same reverence for religion, as the real foundation of their allegiance to Saul, withheld the hand of the soldiery from Abimelech and his father's house. But the king's wrath, kindled by the breath of Doeg, must now be fed with fuel from the bloody and impious hand of Doeg. He became the executioner, and without reverence for either the innocence or the sanctity which he himself had falsely accused and convicted, he murders four score and five of the priests, and the city of their habitation he devastated, sparing neither the brute nor the child nor the mother.

Of the life and the character of this Edomite we read no more, except the comment of David upon his barbarous acts, "I knew that he would surely tell." It appears also from the caption of the 52d Psalm, that this man was noted among the Jews, and is to be regarded by all generations, as a sample of mischievous and false and deceitful wickedness. This Psalm may be read by us profitably as a comment upon the species of guiltiness which distinguished Doeg. And the close of his career, though not recorded upon the historic page, is so distinctly indicated by the prophetic pen, that it stands out upon the sacred canvas as a picture of warning. "The righteous also shall see, and fear, and shall laugh at him."

"Lo, this is the man that made not God his strength, but trusted in the abundance of his riches and strengthened himself in his wickedness."

With such insight into his character as these few circumstances furnish, let us first define what was the real position of the man, and then deduce the instruction conveyed by his history.

It must strike us in the first place as singular that David after hearing of the barbarities which Doeg had practiced, of his profane assault upon the priests, of his calumnious accusations against Abimelech, and his false testimony, should yet as it were forget these crimes, and inveigh against none of these vices, but wander away from the subject of atrocities to the trifling accusation, "I knew on that day when Doeg the Edomite was there, that he would surely *tell.*" My brethren there was philosophy in that mind of David. He read men by their true faults and not by their appearances. Doeg was a man who relied for everything upon his tongue. He was a butcher because he had been a tattler. The source of the whole mischief was his disposition to make his fortune by his tongue. He had no principles to proclaim, no generous emotions to utter and to impart, but he had ends to serve, and he knew of no smoother and surer way to reach them than by his tongue. That was the secret of his favor with Saul. He flattered and he profited the prince. There is no indication of his being a meddlesome or officious man, farther than his own advancement required. It was not a pragmatical or trifling temper that characterized him. It was the deeper and more ruinous vice of a smooth and plausible, but deceitful and malicious tongue. With this he rose upon the swelling tide of princely favor, but rose by trampling every envied object beneath his calumny. The voluble or the intrusive man mistakes perpetually his own interest or safety, but the Doegs in all their prolixity have a first and ceaseless regard to their own aims and meanings. Habit has made it easy for them to feign the tone and to frame the language suited to the occasion, He was of that class who emphatically live by their wits, for his conscience or his usefulness was no measure of his success. By a strict scale of phrenology his character could only be measured from his brain, not at all from his heart. David's philosophy rested on the two facts that Doeg was present and that Doeg had an end to gain. His being controlled by consequences of injury to others, or by self-respect and an unwritten law of honor, this was no element of the calculation. He would surely tell, for his tongue was his capital. Hence it is that in the Psalm, he is described as if the tongue had taken the place of a soul and was itself the seat and source of thought and device, and with accumulation of invective the tongue is described as cutting when it seems only to shine, "Thy tongue deviseth mischief; like a sharp razor, working deceitfully."

Doeg was by trade a politician. His business was to keep on the winning side. Office and emolument did not at that time come from the popular majority, and it was easier to decide where the strong party should be found. So long as the priests were in the favor of the king he was submissive to their sacred authority, but the moment they became obnoxious to the king, Doeg was thirsting for their blood. No doubt he was regarded as a man of the greatest luck, and sometimes as a very oracle of political sagacity. But the truth was that he was unincumbered with the unfortunate burden of principles, and could move like a wandering Bedouin wherever the largest caravan was marching. Let me not in stigmatizing that Edomite as a politician, be suspected of a fanatical antipathy to the business of politics. Not to follow politics as a science, but to be a politician by trade, is the suspicious, the odious character. It is to have no theories, no laws, no conscience, except the platform of policy; to stand as it were upon our own planks, but these unmoored, unanchored, a drifting raft steered only by the breeze. Party alliance is almost a necessity, almost a sacred duty of citizenship under our system. To eschew it entirely might be only sensitive selfishness. To stigmatize it would be to arm factionism, and leave us at the mercy of them who make merchandize of their country. Political attachment and trading in politics are as far asunder as good and evil. It was the unprincipled course of Doeg that made him so pestilent a politician. He resolved it all into a strife of tongues. The falsest and the boldest was the best. His representations were coloured for his cause. The truth was manufactured into a weapon for his party. Fabrication and insinuation, enough of the facts to inculpate Abimelech, but not enough to do him justice, these were the staple of his trade. Was it wonderful that Saul's throne decayed, when he built it with such materials. Is there any political security when falsehood is at the base? Surely as Providence, the forgotten element in the calculations of iniquity—surely as Providence rectifies at last the reckoning of dishonesty, so surely will Providence baffle at last the cunning of politicians. Doeg with his falsehood shall sink into oblivion, as he passes his zenith of success. Before the kingdom leaves the hands of Saul, the heartless politician is buried among the ruins of his schemes. The priestly influence which he envied is not dead, and its reviving power shelters the righteous cause of David, while it triumphs over the unrighteous instruments of Saul. The prophetic language of the Psalms becomes an accurate history, "God shall pluck thee out of thy dwelling-place, and root thee out of the land of the living."

Such examples of wickedness may be profitable to us, if we deduce from them the instruction which wisdom has inscribed thereon.

Thus it is no part of the Divine wisdom to picture the fiendish disposition which could at last without compunction massacre the whole family of priests. The Scriptures rather direct us to those sins which lie at the root of brutal crimes. A human trait, a disposition formed of human motives, the sin which may by habit become familiar and pleasant to the thoughts of a man, this is the radical depravity. At these roots of evil we must strike, if we would reform a soul. It is all in vain to trim the branches, and to lop off the leaves of sin. And among those radical sins, which must be extirpated, are the plausible iniquities of the mischievous and deceitful tongue. This little member "setteth on fire the course of nature, and it is set on fire of hell." It has such resources of evil at its command as to be termed itself "a world of iniquity." It multiplies vices by its own power, and from its hiding-place surveys the malice and the mischief it has called into being. It planned and it effected the fall of man from his primeval uprightness, and opened through its mouth of deceit and flattery the whole flood of human woes. Banish this root of evil, and how quickly would the harvests of misery dwindle upon the earth. Oh, that the enthusiasts of reform could look upon sin and woe, as they are seen from the realm of light! How soon would their zeal be withdrawn from the futile effort of damming the rivers of guilt, to the wiser and more blessed work of purifying the fountains. Give men an awful reverence for truth, give them a conscience to abhor deceit, give them a desire for the noble satisfactions of integrity, and you have broken the spell which binds the soul of Doeg. And so it is with laws, and constitutions, and social order. Not the terror of a bloody penalty, but the majesty of God presiding in religion, residing in law, abiding in the faith of men, is the true conservative power.

A warning is also contained in the history of Doeg's progress from habitual and natural vices to acts of unnatural barbarity. His implication in the persecution of David could not terminate with the mere part of an informer. He must exaggerate to give his complaint importance. He must falsify to sustain his accusation. He must assail the character of the priest, he must violate the claims of hospitality, abuse the weakness of the king, gain a dastardly advantage over his fellow-servants, malign the purest motives of Abimelech, invade the sanctity of the altar, and bathe in the innocent blood shed by his own perjury. Each successive act was but the consequence of the first crime with his tongue. "Thou lovest all devouring words, O thou deceitful tongue!" The series was wrapt in the iniquity of the beginning. If the nature of that initial sin shows it to be radical corruption, and indicates turpitude at heart, the consequence shows it to be the root of flagrant crime and indicates a preparation for the most cowardly and the most cruel excesses. Sin, that has got command of the tongue, asks for no other mastery. If it can make us willingly profane, we shall unreluctantly carry curses. If it can break the girdle of purity, the drapery of our thoughts shall hang in shameless looseness. The Egyptians, when sacrificing to Harpocrates, the god of silence, used to cry out in the midst of their rites—*γλωσσα δαιμων*—"The tongue is a demon," "the tongue is an angel"—mighty for good, or mighty for evil, as it may read. And Solomon has expressed the same idea with a view to its final consequences. "Death and life are in the power of the tongue." "Winged words" we praise. "Winged words" flew from the lips of the god of eloquence. With them heroism is nerved, and holiness is wafted to hear the welcome of its God. But when the same power of language is wielded by a calculating and ruthless Doeg, it is the lying subtlety of a fallen angel.

The history of this man serves also to illustrate the manner in which the unscrupulous politician makes a convenience of religion, lifting himself upon the prostrate honour of God, and of the uniform fact that detraction and falsehood find their first victims and the chief objects of their envy and their cruelty in the ministry of holiness. David's times were in this but the prelude of history in every generation of scheming politicians and faithful priests.

Speech and thought and influence, talents of immortality! How great their winnings! How miserable their loss! Consecrate them, take them from the service of selfishness, and use them to elevate our own nature, and in the regions of a higher existence we shall have the tongue of the wise, the lips that speak in accents of harmony the praises of God.

XIII.

NO IMPOSSIBILITY OF A RESURRECTION.

Acts xxvi. 8.

"Why should it be thought a thing incredible with you, that God should raise the dead?"

THE reason that the Christian Scriptures insist so strongly upon the doctrine of a final resurrection, I take to be this, that the universality of the resurrection is involved in the office of Christ. "If Christ be not raised," says one, "your faith is vain; ye are yet in your sins." The fact that Christ was really a Saviour on the cross, implies that He was really a Redeemer in His resurrection. If He has not risen for mankind, He did not die for mankind. If He was not bearing the sin of the world upon His crucified frame, He is not raising the flesh of men by His own resurrection. We cannot remove the one without impairing the other. Either our bodies are to follow the risen Saviour, or our sins were not expiated in His body. The question of salvation by Christ is therefore involved in the doctrine of the resurrection. It is not to be thrust back into retirement, but made a prominent evidence of our redemption by the Mediator. It is only as we withdraw from Jesus, and begin to carve out our own way to life, an independent salvation, that this doctrine fades from view, and becomes first an unessential item of belief, and finally a mere conceit of the philosophers. Look at the representative office of the Saviour,—look at the fact that He has broken from the grave, and "Why should it be thought a thing incredible with you, that God should raise the dead?"

One man, subject to death as we are, yielding up his life as we do to the mastery of pain and weakness,—one such is already lifted by the hand of God from His grave, and "death hath no more dominion over him." Is not the resurrection possible, then? And if it be possible, why is it incredible that He should accomplish it who has infinite knowledge to understand the manner, and infinite power to command the means of executing it.

The question that rises at this day is not respecting the fact of Christ's resurrection, but respecting the possibility of a general resurrection which we predicate on this fact. To answer this question as to the possibility of the event, we will glance at some of the difficulties upon the face of this doctrine of universal resurrection. And may God render it profitable to our salvation!

All the difficulties in this doctrine, which are worthy of notice, must consist in the position that there are circumstances rendering a general resurrection impossible, which were not found in the case of Christ. To assert that God cannot re-unite body and soul, is to deny that He could create them. While this is absurd of itself, there is the fact that Christ is risen from the dead, directly in the face of the assertion. The difficulties of a general resurrection are not found in the impossibility of reuniting the elements of flesh and spirit, but in the supposed impossibility of commanding the identical elements of the body for the purpose of this resurrection.

There is a manifest difference between the reviving of a body that saw no corruption, and restoring elements that have undergone corruption and dispersion,—between the resurrection of Christ's body wrapt in its grave-clothes and undissolved, and the resurrection of our dust scattered, perhaps, by the winds or waves, and distributed over every continent. I say there is a manifest difference in these resurrections. But it is a difference of operations only. Whatever operations are possible, are equally easy to Omnipotence. There is no such distinction as difficult or easy, the moment the act is possible. Those terms belong to creatures whose powers are limited, and who may be approaching the extent of their ability. Possibility is one thing with us, and another with God. With us it is the measure of strength; with God it is the whole scope of Omnipotence, compassing every thing except a repugnancy or contradiction. The care of this globe in its broad orbit, and the care of the rolling dust in the whirlwind, are equally easy to the Almighty. It was no more difficult for Him to build the symmetrical form of Adam out of clay, than to create Eve out of the sleeper's rib. It was no more difficult for Him to breathe a living soul into the shape of Adam, than to gather the materials of that frame from the ground, and accommodate them to the organism of life. Why speak we then of difficulties, when Omnipotence is the workman? Omnipotence knows no such thing as difficulty, save in impossibilities. We should have pronounced it difficult for God to create a Universe out of nothing. But does not the very name of Deity imply that He is the only self-existent Being, and is not the whole material creation therefore an argument, that our Maker is impeded by no possibility. Show me then the impossibility of His collecting the dispersed particles of our body and replacing them in their order, or you show no difference, so far as God is concerned, between raising the undissolved body of Christ, and raising the disintegrated bodies of men. He said "Let there be light, and there was light;" to remotest worlds it darted. With one word, with the same power that created, could He recall the scattered rays from every sun and every star, darkening all the fields of space, and collecting every luminous atom into the dwelling of His glory. Shall He have less power over atoms that probably never leave this sphere,—this little dot in creation? He wields myriads of worlds, and knows the path of every grain in all these thousands of globes. And is He unable to keep watch over the particles that form our bodies,—unable to track the wanderings of atoms on one of His myriad globes, when every atom here moves by the impulse of His power and the guidance of His law. Nay, O worm of the dust, do not stultify thyself in striving to nullify the power of God!

What if the components of this body were dispersed everywhere! If the Almighty were only a skillful machinist, He surely could reconstruct a piece of mechanism like this body out of the parts. And how can the parts be wanting, unless atoms are annihilated? Reduce your Deity to a mechanic, and one of two things must be proved, or a resurrection is within His power. If matter is constantly annihilated, and so annihilated that the same matter cannot again subsist,—or if, the bulk of creation remaining as it is, there is no possibility of atoms returning to the same form they once composed,—then there is a contradiction in the doctrine of a resurrection. But so far are these propositions from being proved, that the exact reverse is quite demonstrable. All things indicate that no annihilation of matter occurs; and our living bodies are examples of identity undisturbed by the changes of atoms. I know that this mortal frame is a very intricate piece of clock-work, but the readjustment of its parts is in the hands of one who knows every wheel and joint, every pivot and jewel of this ingenious fabric. What would you think of the artificer's skill, who could not arrange the pieces of a clock, because its steel was from Russia, and its wood from the Indies, and its brass had come from the crucibles of Tamul? How then shall we find a difficulty in the corruption and dispersion of the corporeal elements, when they never pass out of the hand of God?

We are reminded of other difficulties. Not only are the elements of our bodies dispersed, but they are, in the constant transmutation of matter, becoming components of other bodies. The moistures evaporated from the mummy are distilled in the heavens and swallowed by the thirsting Egyptian. The dust of Alexander mingles with the food of the beggar. And I, when I leave this flesh in my grave, part with portions of other bodies received into the blood and humors of my own.

Nay, we read of cannibals living almost entirely upon human flesh, and seventy bodies are digested by one, and that at last is burned. We propose the Sadducean question, In the resurrection, which of the seventy shall be entire?

We might repeat the reply of our Lord to similar carping: "Ye do err, not knowing the power of God."

We might originate a doubt whether cannibals are not to be reckoned with brutes, whose nature they have substituted for the human, and are thus debarred from resurrection as having scarce conscience, scarce soul enough to make men of them,—to make them either fit for heaven, or capable of remorse.

But with these anthropophagi disposed of, there is still a residuum of imaginary difficulty.

The elements of one body in the course of change and dispersion may enter into the composition of a thousand others. If all are raised entire, what is to become of the frame whose elements are distributed in all.

To estimate the real amount of this difficulty, consider that no more than a hundredth part of that which nourishes the human body enters into its substance, and that the whole substance of our flesh is lost and gained in every period of seven years. What then are the chances that any great proportion of another body shall enter into the substance of one now yielding to corruption? It is but one chance out of millions, and is this the kind of difficulty that men will call impossibilities? There is one chance out of millions that all of us shall wake up idiots on the morrow. Is it therefore incredible that any of us should have our senses on the morrow? There is one chance out of millions that the earth will refuse to produce either herb or plant during this season of annual resurrection. It is therefore incredible that the verdure of the spring will re-appear,—all other things continuing as they are?

Suppose even that the cannibal has been assimilating within his system the devoured flesh of two hundred human beings. Was this beastly prey his only repast? Has this alone entered into the fibre of his muscles? By no means. The flesh of his own kind has not been the tenth part of his food. The substance of his body, though he died in the very satiety of his horrid gormandizing is only partially composed of his victim's body.

Take away then from each body, all these admixtures,—withdraw from each resurrection-body all the possible contributions from others raised with it,—and where, even then, is the difficulty? It is not at the best so much as the loss of a limb. It is not equivalent to the wastings of many a sick-bed, that prepares its emaciated possessor for the grave. What, if God by a sudden exertion of power, should restore the wasted frame of the consumptive to full proportion and vigor. Is the identity destroyed? Would the soul be a stranger in its new-garnished tenement? Is it another tree, that now stands in the dwindled nakedness to which winter has brought it, from that which soon will spread its leaves to refresh the sight, and ripen on its boughs the fruit that shows its latent value? If we measure the power of God by our fears, the beast of the field is sometimes stronger than Deity. Behold what He does, and understand the gloriously enacted description of the resurrection to come. He raises the impaired frame of the invalid to a life of robust vigor, and he scarce knows the change except in new powers and new comforts. He changes the appearance of the earth from bleak and buried winter, to teeming and variegated summer, and nothing has been subtracted from or added to the number of atoms. He wakens the helpless and inactive slumberer with the dawn of each day, and the body which a very spider might have tied in his web, bids the water and the air, the energies of animated nature, and the hidden subtilty of electricity be harnessed to its service. So shall the undeveloped bodies of those dying in infancy, and the mutilated bodies of misfortune, and the emaciated bodies of slow decay, and the ghastly corpses of the battle-field, and the ashes of the consumed martyr, and the fragments of the assassinated or mangled victim,—all re-appear in the integrity of a complete human form, supplied for its defects, and endowed for its new destiny, yet to all intents numerically the same.

I see no difficulty in a resurrection, that is not answered by the greater difficulty of creation. Do you believe that this world has an Almighty Creator? I know that thou believest. Then, why should it be a thing incredible with you that God should raise the dead?

I tell you whence unbelief comes,—whence an artificial indifference to this subject comes. It comes from a fear to recognize the true dignity, the true immortality of these bodies, lest we should be compelled to cut off the indulgences of the body, lest we should be constrained to make these bodies share in our holiness, lest we should feel obliged to confess our sins in the body, lest we could not evade the duty of worshipping God with our tongues and our knees, with prayers as well as thoughts, with the clasped hands of a petitioner, as well as the busy hands of honest industry. There is no good reason why the wicked should love to think of a resurrection. Though their bodies are raised from the dead, it will be as that Eastern prince was lifted from his funeral-pyre. Apparently dead he was laid upon the customary heap of faggots. The kindling flame roused him from his stupor, and in terror he begged for a resurrection from his funeral-pile. He was succored, and raised, but it was only to protract his misery under the lingering agonies of disease. So will the unsanctified sinner recover his body, only to find it a home of torture, and might better content himself with the flames of his first death. "Many that sleep in the dust shall awake, some to everlasting life, and some to shame and everlasting contempt." Some to everlasting life! Yes, the arches of heaven shall ring with their welcome. The sting of death shall no more rankle in their purified souls,—the victory of the grave shall end its putrid riot over their glorified frames. Friends wasted by disease shall meet to shine in the splendors of immortality.

The little child that could not speak the name of its earthly parent, shall be strong to execute the will of its Heavenly Father. The brother whose noble heart was shut up in a feeble body, shall be among the mighty ones that cast their crowns at the feet of Jesus. The sister whose gentle spirit fled from the rude contacts of earth's miseries, shall be happy to share with us forever the felicities of a holy world.

The beams of intellect shall again dart from the eyes, and the lustre of joy shall kindle upon the features, and the charms of kindness shall again glow in the countenance,—but no tears shall come to deluge the gladness,—no cares shall furrow the cheeks of them that are at peace with God.

XIV.

THE DIFFUSIVENESS OF GRACE.

ISAIAH lx. 22.

"A little one shall become a thousand, and a small one a strong nation: I the Lord will hasten it in his time."

THE language is intended to describe in terms that shall arrest attention while exciting hope, the expansion and the pervading power of the religion brought by the world's Redeemer. This predicted culmination of God's purposes presented itself to the prophetic eye in various aspects. At times it emerges upon the horizon of the future as a stupendous *Power*, breaking the iron bars, bursting the gates of brass, convulsing the earth, rending the heavens, bringing deliverance to the captive, and prostrating the formidable and the grand in its easy victory of force. Anon it is welcomed among the strifes and carnage of contending nations as the tranquil dominion of *Peace*, appeasing the angered passions of mankind, calming the native savagery of our inflammable hearts, and unfolding the scenery of pacified peoples, smiling lands, affluent harvests, propitious seasons, mellow moons and cheerful suns; old men and children grouped in social happiness, arms and bellowing war forgotten, the sword not even rusting as a trophy of honor but hammered into plowshares, and every one, satisfied with plenty, reclining beneath his own vine. The kaleidoscope of prophecy revolves again, and every object seems touched with the liberating and disenthralling effects of the gospel. It is condensed, for a moment, into such characteristics as can only be denoted by one word—"Emancipation." The sinner is seen dropping his chains. The oppressed of the devil goes free. The prison-doors are open, and the miserable victim of his vices comes forth to resume the franchises of grace. Where despair brooded, is now the brilliant coloring of revived joy. Where habit, like a huge tyrant monster, had been binding men hand and foot, trampling down their hopes of rescue, and stealing from them every promise of restoration, *there* appears a new element in the scene, a mightier Redeemer, and He proclaims release.

Again the vision of prophecy changes. It assumes not so much a new phase in the exterior view, as a new power to penetrate into the secret motives and to descry the inward affections of a gospel era. Under this power of insight, human nature becomes transparent. The crust of disguises is peeled off, and beneath the outward form we behold a wide mass of better impulses, and sanctified emotions, and kindly dispositions, and inwardly living piety. The tongue of the prophet calls it "the reign of righteousness;" the penetrating wisdom of Jesus calls it "the kingdom of heaven." Can prophecy add more? Is not this sufficient to cheer the waiting patience of the prisoners of hope? Here is *Power*, emanating from God and bringing the promise of all His resources. Here is *Peace*, reconciling hostile nations and shaming the blood-red features of conquest. Here is *Emancipation*, rescuing the pitiable victim of his vices and the remorseful conscience of sin. And, at last, here is the internal splendor of a genuine righteousness, that bespeaks man renovated, and shows itself to be a vital power animating the soul and kindling heaven within. What more can be needed? One element alone. We need to know whether this gift of God is a complete and finished production as first bestowed, or whether it is endowed with the power to extend and strengthen itself, and prevail more and more, and acquire new arguments to prove that it came Divinely, lives Divinely, and will be Divinely preserved. That additional light beams upon us through the disclosures of prophecy. We are certified that God has not left us with a complete gift to incur the responsibility of preserving it perfect, and to depend upon ourselves for its benefit by our strenuous effort to keep it intact as it came. No; the greater grace is not the greater burden. But that which God confers upon us in the gospel is a growing, enlarging, diffusive power that attests its own Divine origin by its own increase, and exhibits itself, not as a blessing once for all given, but as a blessing continued, given more and more, and assured to us by these widening testimonies of a goodness that defies exhaustion. And this is the assurance involved in God's promise, "A little one shall become a thousand, and a small one a strong nation: I the Lord will hasten it in his time."

We may put it into a single phrase—it declares "the diffusive tendency of grace." This at once presents itself to our minds in two aspects—what we may call the *intensive* and the *extensive.* Grace spreads and strengthens and multiplies itself intensively by its inward grasping of our faculties and feelings. It is sometimes called, in this sense, an *influence*, a streaming of power into the thoughts and affections and motives of a man, the flow of God's fullness into the first springs of thought and will. And then it strengthens into more than an influence, and becomes a commanding element of our inward being, or, as an Apostle phrases it, "bringing into captivity every thought to the obedience of Christ." Nor even here does its exertion pause; but it proceeds to reconstruct our spiritual being, shaping us inwardly after the new, the perfect model of the man Christ Jesus, till we almost lose our old identity of earthliness and grossness and ungodliness, and (in Scripture phrase) are changed into His image from glory to glory. These things we do not always realize, because they are spiritual results, out of the range of sense. They come not with observation. But they are the intensive triumphs of that grace which must diffuse itself and grow and put on beauties, or must vanish from our hearts.

This intensive diffusion of grace is not the aspect in which our Prophet is regarding the gospel. He is more intent upon producing before us figures that indicate the extensive diffusion of grace. Diminutive promise, extending into the force of thousands, and feeble individuality extending into the compactness and numbers and majesty of a nation—and all this accomplished with such disproportionate appliances and under such abrupt transitions, that man loses the chance of calling it his own work—it is the Lord's hastening after His own order of events—this is the imagery that occupies the prophetic eye. It was pictured of old to rouse the flagging hopes of a desponding people; it is rehearsed for our admonition upon whom the ends of the world are come.

Has this prediction been verified? Does it involve principles worth taking into our philosophy or theory of life? These are inquiries that every serious soul will make (and a soul not serious is a soul that has forgotten its immortality).

The prophet's words *are verified.* The kingdom of heaven was first epitomized in the Son of Man that came down from heaven. Into what is it extended? If you ascend into the realms of bliss, it is there. If you descend into the shadowy habitations of the dead, it is there. If you breathe the odors of Paradise among the disembodied righteous, you inhale a peace for the soul which attests your residence in the kingdom of heaven. If the wings of devotion transport you from continent to continent, you hear the chants of your forefathers in the hundred tongues of our dispersed race, but it is the same faith and the same Bible and the same salvation, all derived from that one Fountain, that Son of Man "despised and rejected of men," but "the pleasure of the Lord prospered in His hand." Do I recognize no extension of that kingdom beyond those objects which my own narrow-sighted eyes can behold? Here, then, is the obvious fact, challenging the contradiction of my senses: the crucified Man of Nazareth animating with His own impulses and uniting by His own doctrine thousands of thousands, and penetrating all barriers of empire and exclusion and jealousy with a system that binds together in Him people that know not each other's language, people made by their attachment to this system and by their undying determination to maintain it and spread it and transmit it—made virtually a great nation. So much the purblind eye of sense observes. But what is all this compared with the vision of faith? If the prophet is verified by the outward scene on earth, what shall we say of the less transient reality that looms in the wider scenery of faith?

Jesus treads the wine-press alone. Single-handed He wars with the iniquities of the ages and with the furious armies of spiritual malice. He might have summoned more than ten legions of angelic cohorts. But He battled alone. There was no intercessor. The blood of redemption sprinkled only His own garments. But the triumph, oh, how boundless! The Blessing! How it sweeps heaven and earth into one wide embrace! It kindles a new fire in the desolate heart of man, introduces a heavenly light into the chambers of the dead, calls down angels to discover to them the manifold wisdom of God, interprets to their understanding the obscure series of earthly events, and brings the sundered worlds of temptation and of rest into one communion. The lone victim diffuses a grace that reaches both worlds, reconciles men and angels, forms these tempted and those triumphant into one household, for of Him "the whole family in heaven and earth is named."

The *extensive* power of the gospel has thus been viewed by us with reference to the wide regions of existence it embraces. Regard it, again, with reference to its pervasive power, and see what a diffusive energy resides in this grace. It appears as a simple doctrine. Its propagation is committed to artless and unlettered men. No intricate or abstruse science is claimed to be embodied in it. Men disdain it for its simplicity. A brief history relates the career of its author. It is launched upon the world without patronage and without authority, save its claim of derivation from God. But it spreads into all the movements of society. It has a wonderful power to pervade the feelings and laws and customs of stereotyped society. It penetrates the mass of men. And while it is neither lawgiver nor ruler, neither revolutionary nor political—while it assails not the emperor and bribes not the judge—yet it moulds laws and influences governments, reforms society and actuates policies, compels emperors to profess Christianity, and induces tribunals of justice to mitigate the penalties that had ignored the brotherhood of man.

Some of us smiled more than two years ago* when our superannuated chieftain announced that we should conduct our civil war on Christian principles; and it was derisively asked if we intended to slaughter rebels according to grace, and to substitute the gospel for Hardee's tactics. Many a fiercely contested battle-field has been our answer. We have carried our doctrine of salvation in iron-clads and gunpowder, but we have humanized and ameliorated this dire, this demoralizing, this debauching necessity of war. Of all dreaded provocatives to the most hideous passions of our race, none threatens such barbarities and atrocities as a civil war. It is nothing but the power of the gospel pervading our hearts, and thrusting itself among the frantic excesses of battle, that has put such a curb of forbearance upon our hostilities, forced the maddened warrior to remember mercy, granted such humane indulgences to the prisoner of war, and rendered the hospital system, in all its stages of arrangement, from the ventilated cot of the sick recruit to the invalid corps of maimed veterans — rendered this whole sanitary provision just as important and valuable as the ordnance supply or the recruiting detail.

And herein is but the sample, in our day and our land, of what that simple doctrine has been effecting through all Christendom. It assumes not the power to eradicate the evils of so-

* This sermon was preached in 1864.—*Editor.*

ciety by *command*, and *instantly*, but it introduces and diffuses a humanizing principle that softens our asperities and relieves one another's miseries. And this is a doctrine expanded into a manifold system—a feeble institution in Galilee become an influential instrument throughout the world—a creed of twelve articles developed into a faith converting the hearts, and the laws, and the usages, and the very ferocities of nations.

We see, then, the verification of the prophet's words. Do they, then, involve any principle worth taking into our philosophy or theory of life?

This one idea seems to be involved in every aspect which this subject presents, that grace is necessarily diffusive. It is like the fragrant ointment upon Aaron's head, that bedewed his beard, and diffused itself to the skirts of his garment. No one receives it genuinely and uses it as a Christian, without becoming a participant in this work of diffusion. God imparts it to us not to be housed and secreted in our own hearts by some right of monopoly, but to be evinced in our lives and to magnetize society wherever we touch it with the attractive power of this grace. The property of diffusing itself is a condition of its abiding with us. It cannot survive any system of Christian living which treats the gift as only imparted for the luxury of self-enjoyment. As well might you attempt to shut up sunlight in a casket and preserve it there, as to take grace into a human heart and hold it there bright and warm and heaven-like while it has no outlet for diffusion.

The principle thus applicable to each one of us indicates the mode of the gospel's operation upon society at large. It is not intended to develop itself by commotion and ruinous upheavals of the social structure. It acts by patience and by moderation, by intrepid testimony and by winning example, by the silent power of consistency and by pacific methods. Thus it startles without confusing the minds of men. Providence sends alarms. Events arouse and excite men. The church sooths and calms and persuades and encourages. Its strength is quietness and confidence, and not agitation and clamor. God may send earthquakes and portents, may shake the jail-gates at Philippi and waken the inmates in terror, but the Church quietly sings praises unto the Lord. And by her very composure in the person of Paul and Silas, she is able to convert the agitated subject of alarm, and to answer the eager inquiry of affrighted conscience, "What must I do to be saved?" The religion of Jesus has by this quiet diffusion penetrated society. It is edified, as a visible system, by the diffusive power of love; and it operates to extend and disseminate its benefits with such orderly exhibition of truth and such tranquil confidence as disarms the antipathies of the world.

Were I speaking of the internal development of God's life in your soul, I should tell you that it is vital religion, not because it is enthusiastic and suddenly bnrsting upon your consciousness, but because it is patient and steadfast and growing from grace to grace, from prayer to perseverance, from the glow of the heart to the guard of the tongue, from the feeble buds of rapture and ecstacy to the riper fruits of courage and constancy—"first the blade, then the ear, then the full corn in the ear"—*vital* religion, not because it swells into volumes of excitement, but because it grows into the flavors and tints of a heavenly life. But I speak of the gospel in its outward action—of the life of God inhabiting and strengthening a church. And there I discover the same principle controlling its development.

It is the leaven imperceptibly leavening the mass. It is the life-blood purified at the vitals and secretly conveying health and vigor to the debilitated frame. It tingles through every member of society, and it imparts vital refreshment to every part of a nation, from the head to the foot, putting, as it were, that central heart which travels along in the blood—putting that heart into every muscle, every throb, every motion, every sensation of the whole body, and men know not whence it comes, that vitalizing power—and they atheistically ascribe it to the management of some *party*, or the operation of some *law*, or the effect of some popular *orator*, or the vehemence of some *selfishness;* but it is none of these. It is God hastening His own work. It is society moved by God through the heart, and that heart is His Church. If that heart ceases to beat, *we perish.* If that heart diffuses the blood of health, *we live.*

XV.

REDEMPTION.

EPHESIANS i. 7; COLOSSIANS i. 14.

"In whom we have redemption through His blood, even the forgiveness of our sins."

THE Apostle multiplies words because language is so inadequate to convey his ideas. It fails to express the sciences of earth, and new coinages must be uttered, phrases from one tongue must be borrowed by another, to put into words the inventions and devices that concern simply this narrow world. How much more is the earthly phrase impoverished and insufficient when it would declare heavenly things. But the language of men must be employed to convey Divine ideas, and the magnificence of heavenly grandeur must submit to the weakness of earthly words, or God must cease to speak to men. "The Redemption" is one of those vast Divine ideas, which comes limited to us in a word that in vain attempts to grasp the whole magnitude of the mercy. Paul feels its feebleness, and without discarding the word attaches an explanation, "Even the forgiveness of our sins." Redemption alone might involve no more than the "commercial" idea. It might suggest only the fact of a hard and unrelenting, though *just* demand on the part of the Almighty, exacting the full payment of the ransom, and buying the opportunity for man from the cruel and inexorable law of God. That was the original and natural force of the word. In this "commercial" sense it was applied to property. Usage, however, had elevated this idea of redemption. It had been for ages associated with the Hebrew's recollection of his nation's deliverance from bondage. It expressed in one word the lengthened story of a suffering and oppressed people conducted by God's hand and sheltered by His presence, until the fierce heathen could be dispossessed and the tribes of Israel peacefully instated in a land where they perpetually chanted, "He hath showed His people the power of His works—He sent redemption unto His people."

There was no difficulty, therefore, in bringing the religious mind to view the Eternal God as a Redeemer, as undertaking this office for man's necessity, as bringing rescue to a vast multitude, and as comprising in His act of redemption a promise of unwavering fidelity from generation to generation. But we needed to associate something still more heavenly with this thought of redemption. It was not enough to accept the "commercial" idea of a sufficient payment made by blood. It was not enough to accept the thought of its extent, that it embraced *all* men, and that it was "*eternal* redemption for us." This higher element must be recognized by us as the Christian meaning of the term, that it was a loving, a compassionate, a *pardoning* act of God. We are not permitted to dishonor heaven and ourselves by simply believing that some ingenious expedient has been found to satisfy justice, and so put it into God's power to open heaven for man. Neither are we permitted to pause with the comforting thought that the whole race has received this favor from God, and that it is an ample redemption for ever. All this may be true, and may exalt our admiration of the mercies of God; but all this is not enough. There is more involved in our redemption by the blood of Christ, more that represents to us the glorious excellencies of God, more that concerns the reality of our own nature.

It assails our hearts with its representation of the origin of the whole scheme of redemption, suggested in heaven, contrived in a counsel of perfection, the emanation of a love that would not desert us, a stream of forgiveness which is but the gush from the fountain we had been determined to seal up, God's tender mercy. Ah, how had we denied it, choked it, refused it! When it came to us with Paradise and promises, we scorned it. When it came with laws and ordinances, we disowned it and ascribed every command and every prohibition to the hard measures of a rigorous severity. And when, after all our obduracy, it came asking of us repentance, moving us to be pitiful and tender-hearted because God Himself was the Father of mercies, we flung our hard-hearted sins, like great masses of obstruction, into this fountain of mercy, as if we had desperately resolved to choke up the stream we had not been able to exhaust. And yet the Beloved came and brought the inestimable redemption. The whole of heaven was with Him, and the utmost of love was in Him. He had nothing to gain, for all things were made by Him, and He was the brightness of the Father's glory. He merely put into clearer syllables that original fact, "God is Love." There is one word in the language of Scripture which expresses all this history of God's manifestation, and that is "redemption." It sums up what the Apostle elsewhere expands into this form of theology, "Not by works of righteousness which we have done, but according to His mercy He saved us."

If the term thus condenses so much instruction concerning God, it is no less suggestive respecting our own nature. With rapid transition does the Apostle's mind hurry to the equivalent term that denotes the most deplorable reality which redemption discovers in us—the reality of inexcusable sin. Here was the necessity for all that tragedy of blood. Here was the occasion for God's attributes to be summoned for the most arduous task. Here was the evil that strained the heart of mercy to the last degree, and furnished the problem which none but God could solve. It was not some foreign power that threw the baleful hindrance between God and our own nature. We were the enemies by wicked works. We were our own wilful destroyers. Our iniquities separated us from our God. Our sins were the barriers between the trembling heart, and the happiness it lost. It was corruption that we had invited to inhabit the soul, and for which we had banished peace and purity. In ourselves, in the sensual thoughts and the ungodly devices of our own souls, was the misery that enveloped us, and through this thick shroud of ruin burst the redemption of God, "even the forgiveness of our sins."

Was it strange that the mention of God's redeeming act should instantly suggest this its principal triumph? No, this is the wonder, that such a picture of God forgiving, and of man despising forgiveness, should be viewed by us with as much unconcern and apathy as if it were some whimsical conjecture respecting the fashion of an angel's dress.

Perhaps there is some explanation of this indifference, though it be no apology, in the limited and unworthy sense which we apply to this redemption. Its scope is not appreciated. We narrow it to the few that seem to seize with holy eagerness upon its entire benefits. And we lose sight of the greatness of the mercy as embracing the whole world—as granted to the just and the unjust—for "God was in Christ, reconciling the world unto himself, not imputing their trespasses unto them." Or we depreciate redemption by not regarding the multitude of reliefs to our condition implied in this term. We use it as if no more than an expression to signify a change in God's purpose toward us, abandoning indignation and concluding to indulge. But it gathers up into one phrase far more than this—Father relenting. It means that God took upon Himself great humiliation, surrendering His majesty, sending out of heaven the dearest, noblest, highest being that heaven delighted in, permitting this puny, daring enemy of God, this corrupted creature, to shame and wound and trample on the loving Creator. It means that God took this cruel, sorrowful payment of tears and blood, which the sinful injustice of our nature wrung from the tender heart of Jesus, as if it were a great sacrifice offered by our nature to the inflexible righteousness of God. Redemption means that all the burdensome and blind ceremony by which men had been hemmed in to save them from the pollutions of their own race, was lifted off their consciences that they might be saved by the sweet and mild orderings of a Christian life. Redemption means that God substituted for the dark and hard thoughts of His Providence which poisoned our hearts, a brighter sense of His goodness and the clear consciousness that all His dealings with us were prompted by emotions of benevolence. Redemption means that God had interposed to rescue this world from the malignity of the devil, dispelling the illusions which spirits of evil had gathered in fatal enchantment around the souls of men, and sending larger armies of helping spirits to minister to the heirs of salvation. Redemption means that while we deserved to be regarded as enemies, having chosen that attitude, and not choosing to make solemn and bold profession of any more loving allegiance, God has been pleased to shower upon us the favors of friendship, to pity our false and ruinous position—to forbear when a breath would destroy—to forgive when we persisted in sin—to throw the light around us when we were too proud to ask for it, and to send the. Spirit into our hearts, day by day, while we grieved and resisted and refused His blessed aid. Redemption takes hold upon our eternal prospects. It signifies that the work is done for us forever—that God has sealed an everlasting covenant, and that there is nothing needed for our salvation while the woes of earth shall last or the bliss of heaven can grow, which is not made over to man by the bond sealed and delivered to Jesus, "in whom we have redemption through His blood, even the forgiveness of our sins."

I am not, my brethren, unconscious of the answer which our self-vindication renders to this Divine appeal. We plead that the enjoyment of these rich benefits does not come necessarily and inevitably, but upon conditions which we must fulfill, conditions that grind against our wills and provoke resistance. We plead that the very perversity of our nature, which must be forgiven by a holy Judge, renders us averse to the conditions of forgiveness, and sets heaven no nearer to us though our Great Redeemer hath opened the door.

My beloved brother, in this contamination of sin—my exalted brother, in this splendid redemption, I feel the power of this plea for the sinner. It is the voice of my own heart. Infirmity echoes it every day. God would confound me as a hypocrite if I disguised what this sinful nature must confess. Let us be just to ourselves, and own that this is our plea of extenuation. But let us not be unjust to our Father, our Saviour, our God.

Is there any perverseness in our nature which God does not assist us, does not enable us to overcome? Is not that ample forgiveness, which is written in Christ's bond, intended to cover just those deficiencies which lurk around our work, when we have made the effort and shown that there was in us, at least, sincerity and resolution?

Conditions! Yes, there are conditions. Blessed be God! He has not shut us up in a doleful certainty. It is a blessed promise that allures us. No uncertain decree of His secret will is suspended over us. He willeth not that any should perish. But He does define conditions that test our acceptance of His gracious trusts. He begins with the least, but His design is to give us the utmost. And the daily condition with which we must comply is merely this, to use the little that we have that we may be entrusted with the more.

Could there be simpler or easier conditions? Measure the difficulty well, my brother, and then deal justly with your God. Can there be a heaven, that is not absurd, which contains elements not desiring to be free from sin? Can there be a home with God for the master and the delight, where the will of God is refused obedience? And do you suppose the infinite wisdom of God would make such an incalculable expenditure of labor and suffering and prophecy and miracle to save man when, after all, there was to be in man nothing to be saved, no will, no exertion, no power of loving God, no disposition for heaven, no condition that lay in himself to fulfill?

All that heaven requires of us amounts to no more than our exhibition of the desire to be blest of heaven. Redemption brings us all the rest. Surrender to the love of God, and the love of God surrenders everything to thee.

If there had been no compliance to be evinced by our own nature—if man was not to be persuaded to work out his own salvation—if the glory of God was not to be promoted, and the joys of millions of heavenly beings enhanced by the return of this lost humanity to the obedience of a child, to the attitude and act of religious submission—then that long drama of redemption might have been abridged into a single act, and this hidden among the secret transactions of God. Eden was needless, and Sinai was superfluous, and Jerusalem was built in vain, and Calvary was stained with useless blood, and the Church has struggled through a fruitless fight. One instantaneous fiat of the Almighty would have accomplished all. Penitence was wasted effort. The sighs of devotion would be but whispers against the tempest. The painful piety of saints becomes a hopeless struggle against the edict of Omnipotence. Such a desolate dominion of arbitrary power is not the lot of man. Thanks to God! His redemption teaches us that everytning which has transpired to move the heart of man is but the addition of arguments inducing us to flee to those conditions which bind our souls with that Saviour of the world, "in whom we have redemption through his blood, even the forgiveness of our sins."

Our Christian duty derives illustration from the sentiments of the hour. We are patriots in our recollections and our hopes. What the hand of God wrought for our feeble colonies resolved to be free and independent States, and what was enacted by the patience and the daring of men so like ourselves, these are the themes that teem upon our memories. It was a political redemption, achieved by blood. Gratitude recalls its heroes. Patriotism applauds its success. We glow with the recital of the grand principles of liberty and humanity vindicated and maintained by the redemption of those days of virtue and valor. And when the heat of momentary excitement presumes to brand us with some epithet that stigmatizes our patriotism, is it manly resentment, or is it holy indignation that mantles our cheek and repels the reproachful term? Alas! we burn with shame when some distant allusion charges us with cold disregard for our country's redemption and our nation's claims. But neither the sigh of remorse nor the tinge of shame attests some faint awakenings of gratitude when eternal redemption is the theme, and the claim is His who loves us more than we can love our native land. The blood of brave men consecrates our nation's claim. But the precious blood of redemption consecrates the claim of Christ and His Church—of Christ who purchased each one of us and has the right to claim a thousand-fold more than we render to our country's cause—of His Church which claims our vows of citizenship, claims our submission to its sanctifying laws; for the kingdoms of this world shall perish, the empires of the East shall decay, this Grand Republic of the West in vain shall dip its wing in either ocean and smile upon a gladdened and a free people redeemed from every social enthralment, for in the lapse of ages it shall dissolve, but the Church of the redeemed, undissolving and undecayed, shall live on forever, and through the arches of eternity shall ring her heavenly anthem, "ten thousand times ten thousand, and thousands of thousands, saying, with a loud voice, Worthy is the Lamb that was slain to receive power, and riches, and wisdom, and strength, and honour, and glory and blessing."

XVI.

GLORY.

JEREMIAH, ix. 23, 24.

"Thus saith the Lord, Let not the wise man glory in his wisdom, neither let the mighty man glory in his might, let not the rich man glory in his riches:

"But let him that glorieth, glory in this, that he understandeth and knoweth me, that I am the Lord which exercise loving-kindness, judgment, and righteousness, in the earth: for in these things I delight, saith the Lord.

THE text reveals the fact of human experience that glory and boastfulness are near of kin. Merit and dignity and greatness may be our unconscious possession. But glory is the resplendence of those qualities and those acts in which we put our excellence and upon which we stake our merit. There is something personal, appropriated, and incommunicable in the nature of glory. Imagery represents it as a halo that lingers around a person or a deed. It is the glare which comes out from a brilliant exploit, or from the presence of the illustrious man. His glory is the showing out of all the splendor that belongs to him. Carrying up this sense to the exalted perfections of Deity, our Lord's prayer terminates with a doxology, a giving of glory, and we ascribe the summit and the source of all that is illustrious in creation, to God's own original and underived glory. And in the like use of the term, as signifying the exclusive and personal excellencies of His nature, the Almighty protests by the mouth of His Prophet, "My glory will I not give to another."

We may regard it, then, as the shining forth of an individual excellence so as to attract attention and direct it upon the source of the glory.

There is accordingly a close relationship between this possession of glory, and the boastfulness of a conscious eminence. The real splendor of character, and the dreamy conceit of brilliancy, are of the same aspect, and so far as the man himself is concerned it matters little whether he is glorious in reality, or glorious only in his own eyes.

It is only in a secondary sense, therefore, that man can be said to glorify his Maker. God is indeed glorified by all the mirrors and reflections of His riches and might and wisdom. Though they be the minute atoms of creation, yet does the light of His intelligence and power and bounty shine from them. As through the smallest crevice the prospect of a vast space may be transmitted, and with the slender reeds of a telescope the beauty of the heavens may be comprised; so the glory of the Infinite is seen, and for the purpose of being seen is contained in the smallest fabric of His skill and goodness. It is so with the character of a man. In great emergencies and under the broad gaze of ample observation, he may put on the features and the manner of nobleness, but if he be truly glorious and excellent, intrinsically and thoroughly what he then seems, the least of his actions and the most retired of his ways will be touched with the hues of excellence. It was symbolized in that pervading energy of Christ, which sent a virtue of beneficence and health to the hem of His garment. It was not necessary to draw the virtue from the gaze or from the words of Jesus. He was anointed with power from on high, and the efficacy was with his person. We say, then, that God by creating the reflections of His wise and good will makes Himself in the face of creation to be glorified. "The heavens thus declare the glory of God." And inasmuch as His law is superior to the gross form which it governs, and the holy will of God is better than any and every other image and reflection of Himself, man has the means of glorifying God above the whole visible universe by doing His will and delighting in His will, and conforming to that will, and pronouncing that will wise and just and glorious. Is it any stretch of exaggeration to say that this man's glorifying God is more acceptable, more to the honor of his Maker, than the whole system of creation? Is it too much to say that this immortal spirit, putting on the graces and the nobilities of the new creation, is in His sight and in his angels' sight, more glorious than the whole beauty of the sky? And instead of praying for the greater emanations of creative splendor, is it not the consummation of all prayer, "Thy will be done on earth, as it is in heaven?" And is there not something more rapturous, more ecstatic, more thrilling, than the glory of God in creation, when a man rises up to glorify his Father in heaven—a surge of joy stirring that ocean above when one sinner repenteth?

Man is therefore glorifying God, when the will of God is the object of his knowledge and the occasion of his delight. He is entering into a possession of glory by reflecting and mirroring from his soul the perfect law of God. There is an intrinsic and superlative excellence passed upon his nature, for it is not only glorious as a creature being the crown of the material world, the image of God, but it is glorious as an agent, as a possessor and accomplisher of a self-chosen character, resplendent and excellent by its own effort.

For I need scarcely discuss the question, whether glory is that which is thrust upon a man without his own will and consent and seeking, or that which is acquired and earned and made the appetite and prize of his soul. Which is the glory, to have been born the heir of a rich estate, or to have wrestled with poverty and vanquished idleness and commanded success, and come into the possession which birth and the world and our own passions would have denied us? And which is the glory, to have struck by guess upon some piece of good fortune and to have seemed wise when it was an accident that befriended us, or to have stored away experience and caught at the straws of wisdom and made ourselves wiser by the assiduity and patience of learning, by the habit and discipline of wisdom? And which is glory, the temporary possession of some envied success, or the name of having deserved it, and of having been in ourselves far better than the fortune which was allotted us? It is not, then, the glare of what we have, which constitutes a genuine glory; it is the excellence and honour, the splendor and the nobleness of what we were. If the show of the possession was the glory, Nero was master of a more opulent empire than Augustus, and Judas was the most glorious of all the Apostles. No, there is a secret contempt which a man must have for himself when the means of his success carry no hallucination of merit, and the shame of enjoying what one does not deserve is more bitter than the sense of defeat. Glory may follow reverse, and no passing cloud extinguishes though it may obscure and dim the light of a character natively glorious.

Well have we said that it is not the passing of great trusts and favors upon us by Providence, but our reflections of that will which Providence reads and interprets to us, which constitutes the glory of man. And well has the Prophet epitomized the whole lesson in the one sentence, "Let him that glorieth, glory in this, that he knoweth and understandeth Me, that I am the Lord which exercise loving-kindness, judgment and righteousness in the earth; for in these things I delight, saith the Lord."

Now I take it to be here implied that the more a man commits himself to Providence, the more he expects all rewards and all penalties to be administered by God, the more he so lives and shapes his character so as to be in league with God's overruling, all-inspecting and righteous Providence, the more lustre gathers upon his soul, and the more he has to glory in what he is. The sentiment is a paradox. It is like the contradiction of the Apostle, " When I am weak, then am I strong." It is the putting of our glory in the hand of God, that it may be more surely ours. It is the disclaiming of our own power, that we may claim the power of God to be ours. It is the putting all excellence and beauty in Providence, that Providence may keep it for ourselves. So then " he that glorieth, let him glory in the Lord."

In this topic we discover a twofold suggestion, the one, that we should not mistake a Providential trust for an evidence of glory ; the other, that we should recognize a real glory in the humble office of working with Providence.

For the first, let the Prophet speak : " Let not the wise man glory in his wisdom, neither let the mighty man glory in his might ; let not the rich man glory in his riches." Now I have no idea that this is meant for a protest against the haughtiness which sometimes possesses a man more than all he possesses. I consider it a warning against the delusion of conceit and self-satisfaction which wisdom and power and riches are so apt to beget and to cherish. They come to us with a kind of persuasion that we have really been superior to the thousands who want them. They may not make us supercilious, or fantastic, or proud. That is only the weak and foolish phase of these possessions. They may not tempt us into gaudy displays of ill-mannered affectation, or gross assumption. But they have a strange spell over our consciousness. They blind us most wonderfully to the real ambitions and aspirations of our nature. They decoy a man into the farthest idolatries of himself, of his wit and craft and sagacity and art, while he supposes himself untainted and free. The man of the world, as the phrase is, keeps his eye upon the main chance, shuns the disreputable deeds which his own class denounce, hates above all things to be outwitted or put down in society, plumes himself upon the standing which he contrives to keep in the world, and laughs at the enthusiasm of the mere scholar or the niggardliness of the miser, or the singularity of the serious man of religion. He makes it a sort of glory to be of the world, up to its mark, expert in its fashions, glib in its phrases, great in its ambitions, and successful in its appearances. He ridicules pretension, and scorns awkwardness, and so he creeps or dashes or struts up to a degree of saintship in the diptychs of the world. There is no suspicion in his mind that all the glory of his achievement is but the reflection of that hollow display, that flimsy glitter, that inglorious mockery of nobility, the fashion of the world. He claims a stock of peculiar qualities on his part by which he contrives to make himself shine, and be the envy or the gossip of a circle. And he measures the amount of his glory by the dimensions of his importance in this imaginary sphere. Poor wreck of a man! or rather ugly distortion of what was meant for a man! He had a Providential trust of wit, of manner, of perceptions, and he mistook the possession for an evidence of glory, when all the glory was to be in his way of using and honoring what he had.

Another man is the Providential Trustee of power. God has given him, we will say, the sacred trust of the priesthood. He has a position of influence and of labor. The elements of might are in his hand. There is a rampart of official eminence before him. The confidence of men has entrusted him, and the confidence of men will allow him to speak with positiveness and weight. He moves men with the leverage of his trust. There is a willingness of tribute to his character. His opinions carry their force. Impelled and bewitched with the idea of his influence, he devotes it to the ends of prejudice and party; not to his trust of making men better, but to his fancy of making them like himself; not to the glory of drawing them towards God, but to the glory of warming them with his fancies and singularities and opinions. He glories in his might. He glories not in the execution of his trust, but in the aggrandizement of his personal position. Such a priesthood was foreboded as honoring the God of forces. Such a priesthood puts its glory in the Providential trust, and not in the holy exercise of the trust.

My brethren the illustration skims over your hearts, and alights upon him who for the reason of his trust and his weakness is always the mark of suspicion. But if neither the sacred trust deters a man from such vain-glory, nor the reproofs of his own discourse warn him, nor the engagements of his life protect him, how much more does the secular heart stand in danger of a deeper delusion, glorying in wisdom, or in might, or in riches.

Our second suggestion is opportune, that we should recognize a real glory in the humble office of working with Providence.

There are two facts which seem to me conclusive supports of this suggestion.

In the first place, there is no other mode of life so independent, so thoroughly calculated to bring out the real, honest elements of a man, as that agricultural life which is a plain, daily, open working with Providence, and in sight of it. Such a life transports the most of a man's thoughts, business, hopes, meditations, and by consequence his desires, from the region of conflict with man to the region of contact with Providence. It may look homespun, and have less of the manner and polish of the world upon its surface. But it looks into the eye of Providence, it converses with the clouds and the skies, it meets the daily footsteps of God, it has a glory of His hand to explore in every rood of soil it touches and in every bud that swells before its eye. It works, and has the blessed strength and wholesomeness of the vigorous man; but it works constantly and gladly with Providence, ready to see how God directs, and ready to second what he originates. And if it has no false and specious splendors upon it, yet it has the double glory of being useful in the highest degree—useful to man, and independent, for it is taught, along its whole tread of labor, to glory in the Lord. I take this to be a demonstration printed upon the necessities of man, printed upon the first page of nature, a demonstration that the glory of a man arises out of his working with Providence, making that his study, his ambition, his delight.

There is one other fact which claims our observation. It is the mood and temper to which a life truly glorious always brings a man. It never inflates him with the thought of great power or great resources in himself. He is lost in the grandeur of Providence. His genius is felt to be the inspiration of God.

His glory is received as the answer of God to a life that trusted in Him. The sense of strength in working with God's hands, is the paramount sense of a soul thus schooled in the education of glory. Pride retreats as glory enters. The lowly and the meek man is discovered to the soul more and more as the rightful king of glory. Working with Providence, as Providence calls us, with the means Providence gives, let us not fear it, let us not stand aloof as if it were the nursing of pride; its anthem will be, "Not unto us, O, Lord, not unto us, but unto Thy name give the glory."

XVII.

REPENTANCE.

PSALMS li. 4.

"Against thee, thee only have I sinned, and done this evil in thy sight; that thou mightest be justified when thou speakest, and clear when thou judgest."

IT is David's confession. The guilty king, anguish-torn, and heart-sick, with the black atrocity of his deeds photographed before his conscience, groans in penitential shame and distress. He disguises not the perverseness and the guiltiness of his heart. And not contenting himself with making amends to the persons he had wronged, to the kingdom he had dishonored, to the social feeling he had sullied, to the prophet he had provoked, and the station he had degraded, he carries the whole enormity up to the ear of God, and prostrates himself in the acknowledgment that the worst feature of all his yieldings to temptation and passion was that thereby "he sinned against the Lord." In this was the genuineness of his repentance; in this the possibility of his restoration.

The principle remains the same. It is intrinsically the same on our side; unchangeably the same on God's side. The mercy that soothed the lacerated spirit of the blood-guilty king is the same Fatherly pity against which our sin-laden bosoms must lean. And if the crimes of David be not ours, yet in us is the resemblance of propensity, is the recollection of a guiltiness that needs the same forgiving remedy from heaven, the same penitential confession.

What we need is to trample down that self-excusing, self-justifying habit which disqualifies us for any gospel born of God, and throws our hearts into a fatal contrast with the language that befits a sinner, "That thou mightest be justified when thou speakest, and clear when thou judgest."

If true penitence and real faith were nothing more than an acknowledgment of conduct inconsistent with the Divine law, all would be penitent believers; for we could hardly find an individual acquainted with the rule set for man to walk by, who should yet pretend that he had continued "in all the things which are written in the law to do them."

But it is one thing to confess that *we have transgressed;* and another thing to confess, at least to feel in our hearts, that *we are justly condemned for our transgressions.*

On this humiliation, this inward sense of sinfulness, all depends. Yes, eternity depends upon it; more than I can describe, or you conceive. The *ruin*, or the salvation of the soul depends not on our repeating it in a creed or a catechism, not on our subscribing to it as an article of religion; for then I might quote a few sentences from the Liturgy in which you have this day joined, and have done. But it must be felt, not declared, acknowledged in our hearts and evidenced in our lives. A person does not feel *guilty*, merely because he has been proved to have *offended.* He must be persuaded in his heart not only that he has transgressed a law, but that it was a law which he ought to have obeyed. It is easy for me to affirm that "the Scripture has concluded all under sin," and you may bow to the authority of Scripture, and have nothing to reply; but no good is done, till you confess the *justice* as well as the authority of Scripture; till you are touched in your hearts, and exclaim with the repentant king, "I have sinned against the Lord." When the Holy Spirit has brought conscience to this conviction, Jesus and His Gospel are welcome to the repentant heart, and no yoke that mercy assigns to the returning sinner deters him from grasping the "exceeding great and precious promises" "which are by faith in Jesus Christ to them that believe."

I ventured the observation—most men readily allow that they have not lived up to the perfect Law of God. But they do not so readily allow the sinfulness of this; they have *some excuse* in reserve behind which to shelter themselves. They may have *offended,* but they are not *guilty;* in other words, it would be unjust in the Almighty to condemn them.

God ought to be vindicated. We ought to be saved. Neither is He justified, nor are we rescued,—unless we measure the worthlessness of these excuses. Will you accompany me, then, with your candor and your attention, while we probe these excuses and detect their hollowness?

I. One excuse, by which men palliate to their own minds their neglect of the Divine Law, is the *corrupt nature which was born with them.* God, they think, knows their frailty, their corrupt propensities, their rebellious passions; they derive their being from Him; and will He severely notice what is wrong in the creatures which He has made?

I enter not upon the inquiry, how far this very corrupt nature is in itself the occasion of condemnation. I descend from that high ground, and say, that the force of the excuse depends entirely upon what you have done to amend this corrupt nature; whether you have contended against it, resisted it to the utmost of your power; whether you have made it the subject of continual endeavor that your evil dispositions might be reformed and renewed. Instead of this, can you lay your hand upon your heart and say that you have never given willing way to it? Never indulged in wickedness from which you could have abstained? Never encouraged passion? Never pampered appetite? Never placed yourself within the reach of temptation? A prudent man, who has some disorder inherent in his bodily constitution, does not argue that it is useless for him to take care of his health, because of his constitutional weakness, but by reason of it he takes unusual care,—he avoids exposing himself, he shuns fatigue, he abstains from risks which a stronger might encounter without injury. Have we acted as the prudent man, with this corruption infecting our nature? Look back to the beginnings of sin, and trace the facts, whether we have yielded when we ought to have resisted, whether we have encouraged evil desires and pursued evil habits till their strength became more than a danger, grew into a tyrannical mastery.

In order to understand the Scriptural representation of man's state, it is unnecessary to believe that any one will be finally condemned for sin which he could not have avoided. When the veil is removed which is now spread over the conscience, every impenitent transgressor will perceive that he had daily made his nature worse by "hardness of heart and contempt of God's word," and that he had used no pains to correct and purify it; that if he had inclination to sin, he had also power to resist that inclination, unless he has persisted in breaking the bonds of restraint and provoked God to withdraw the grieved and insulted Spirit, and leave him to his worst enemy, his wayward heart. The man that truly repents, confesses that he has truly sinned and deserved to be rejected. He cries out with no affectation of sorrow or of humility—"Make me a clean heart, O God! Cast me not away from Thy presence." He hates the sins that cast dishonor on his Lord. He rises up to battle with the degeneracy of his nature. He writhes under the venom that taints his soul. And he disdains those ungenerous excuses which acquit himself by accusing God.

II. Another excuse behind which irreligious example shelters itself, is that of want of knowledge. It is not the way of men to pronounce themselves ignorant on religious subjects. They are more likely to assume the air and the tone of great shrewdness, and of very criticising penetration. But they are none the less prompt to repel the entreaties of theologians, and of God's own inspired words by pleading a kind of defect in religious knowledge. The subject comes to us in this age, must come if is suitably presented, with much of the result of study and scholarship. And men will reply that their scholarship has not run in such abstruse directions, and is not equal to these obscure controversies; that the kind of knowledge which would make them versed in Scripture is not theirs, and God will not expect to reap where He has not sown.

But that very ignorance which some plead as their excuse, is, perhaps, an aggravation of their sin. An evil heart betrays itself, from the beginning of life, by an unwillingness to study spiritual things, and to attend upon what might prove a restraint upon corrupt inclinations. Look back upon your early days. Did you take pains to acquire knowledge? Did you always listen to those who were willing to teach? Did you never turn away from warning and instruction, as if it were an evil rather than a good? Did you never misemploy the leisure of the Lord's day, and look for amusement instead of information? Even when present at the worship of God, did you seek after "knowledge of the truth?" Did you reflect upon what you heard? Did you study it, meditate upon it? Did you deem it a pleasure and a benefit when religious instruction came to you in such forms that you must be earnest about it, and attentive and revolve it in your mind, or the truth would escape you? In a word, did you act upon the subject of religion, as you act upon every other subject concerning which you are interested and desire to be informed?

If you have not done this, do not believe that the plea of ignorance will avail. If you have done this, we may venture to affirm you will have no ignorance to plead.

God has put this matter of practical and sufficient religious knowledge under such an explicit promise as He seldom gives on any subject. "If thou wilt receive my words, and hide my commandments with thee; so that thou incline thine ear unto wisdom, and apply thine heart to understanding; yea, if thou criest after knowledge and liftest up thy voice for understanding; if thou seekest her as silver and searchest for her as for hid treasures; then shalt thou understand the fear of the Lord and find the knowledge of God." Nay, there is more than a promise; there is regular provision made for encouraging us and for fulfilling the promise. God hath set apart one-seventh of our time for the acquirement of religious knowledge. A seventh part of time is sufficient for learning anything relating to this present world. But God's will is learned with special assistance, and the effort is success, for "the Lord giveth wisdom."

I speak as if addressing those of less advanced intelligence. But that is not the fact. I speak to those of great advantages, and of enviable attainments. It can scarcely be otherwise where our beautiful worship is frequented. It will attract intelligence.

But if men, in whatever rank or situation, neglect the means which God has placed in their hands; if they reckon anything better worth seeking for, than the way of eternal life; if they take that season which God has destined for the concerns of the soul and devote it to amusement, or idleness, or to worldly cares; then, indeed, they may, they must be doubtful and deluded,—ignorant of their spiritual needs and uncertain of the remedies; but let them not bring forth this wanton ignorance as the cloak for their sin. He that promised has also threatened, and the penalty is as doleful as the promise is cheering—"They shall seek me early, but shall not find me, for that they hated knowledge and did not choose the fear of the Lord."

III. Another shelter which we find against the attacks of conscience, is the excuse of *evil association;* men plead the influence of thoughtless or dissolute companions among whom their lot has been cast from early youth, or the corrupting examples that surround them, examples of inveterate vice, examples of venerable years refusing prayer and sacrament, examples of vain conduct or malicious motive or treacherous vacillation on the part of those professing more worthy lives. The retarding and the perverting influence of such wretched examples is not to be dismissed as of no account. It is painful to reflect on the power of evil example, on the immense evil one ungodly man is able to effect, on the mountain of obstruction which one grave and plausible instance of prosperous resistance to the humbling duties of religion will erect to check and defy the stream of better instruction. But whatever the acceptance of this excuse among men, it will not abide the searching inquiry of God. Before you can plead it there, you must prove that your own will was not a party in the evil which you joined, that you have not neglected prayer, and shunned instruction, and closed your eyes to Scripture, and rushed upon the dangers of indulgence. Did example ever lead you to that which you loathed? Did you not submit to be the captive, before one link of the chain was riveted? Did you not discard and discredit the good and the safe examples, because in your secret desire, in your heart's preference, the irreligious and the worldly example was the unresisted fascination?

Ah! there is another aspect of these charms when sickness brings better thoughts, and the face of God is contrasted with "the course of this world." The miserable imitator of ruinous examples will find his vain excuse dissolved, when the secrets of the heart shall be judged, and thou that scornfully quotest these guides of destruction shall not be justified in thy plea.

IV. I will speak of one more excuse by which many lull their consciences to sleep, and palliate the guilt of a life without religion; they are *active-*

ly employed in the business of the world; its affairs lie heavy upon them; they are constantly occupied in their calling, and have little time for prayer or Scripture, for God or their souls. Neither is this excuse confined to those whose every hour is precious to the subsistence of their families; it is equally the argument of artisan and statesman, of physician and merchant, of her that has literary leisure, and her that toils for weary hours.

The answer is obvious. None in any condition or occupation has the right to be thus immersed in the world. It is not possible where the heart is right. Many situations give little leisure; but none legitimately debars us from "working out our own salvation." If there be such a situation, the question of duty is instantly solved,—let a man leave it,—abandon this moment a calling in which you cannot "abide with God." What! you will say, abandon worldly hopes, flattering prospects, a position of success? I do not make the calculation. Your Saviour makes it. He brings in all the powers of heaven to decide this balance of advantages, and promises for every comfort thus forsaken, "manifold more in this present time," a huge interest on this investment in God's everlasting bond. "I have been young, and now am old," says David, the penitent David, "and yet saw I never the righteous forsaken, nor his seed begging their bread."

I do not deny that there are some vocations for which the real reward is in another world, not among these mysteries of iniquity, not amid this tribulation that gives such glorious examples of patience and inflexibility. And I do not stand upon the old Hebrew hope of seeing all of God's righteousness in this life. But this lends no virtue to the shallow excuse for sin, that we have preferred the world that perisheth to the world that fadeth not away.

My brethren, the subject is not pleasing. It is difficult to present it without appearances of harshness and of language that is invidious in its tone of superiority, and ill-befitting one sinner pleading with another. But neither you nor I must shrink from duties because they cost.

Consider then, with yourselves, you that have lived, and are still living such a life as the Scriptures condemn. If you ever look forward to that judgment which the Scriptures reveal, what plea are you preparing to offer there? Is it that you are naturally corrupt? This will avail nothing, unless you have resisted your corruption and sought God's appointed remedy.

Will you plead the want of religious knowledge? Neither will this avail, if you have ever missed or failed to seek the opportunities of learning.

Have you been deceived by scorners, and enticed by other sinners? Neither will this palliate the sin to which your heart rushed, and in which your consent was the great aggravation.

Has this present world, "its cares, its pleasures, or its riches" engrossed your mind? Behold, death and life were before you, which to choose; and if you have chosen the evil and refused the good, if "for one morsel of meat you have sold your birthright," can you complain of it hereafter, if, like Esau, you shall "be rejected, when you would inherit the blessing?"

See, then, in time the vanity of your pleas; accept the Saviour's offer; "take his yoke upon you, and learn from him the only way of everlasting life, and you shall find rest, true rest unto your souls."

If, indeed, I could prove only the disease, and point out no remedy, I had better, perhaps, be silent. But I prove the disease, in order that you may joyfully and thankfully embrace the remedy; and I sound no note of condemnation, no echo of alarm, without pointing to the most glorious of remedies, the Son of God sent into the world not to condemn, but that the world through Him might be saved.

You cannot but know whether you have renounced alike all unscriptural excuses, and all unscriptural grounds of confidence, and are relying on the merits of Christ Jesus, made over to those who believe in Him and are sanctified by Him. To them the pledge is given, "to them there is no condemnation."

XVIII.

MOSES CHASTENED ON THE MOUNT.

DEUT. xxxiv. part of verse 4.

"I have caused thee to see it with thine eyes, but thou shalt not go over thither."

THE scene to which this passage introduces us, is familiar to every one who has perused the Bible. Coupled in our minds, as *Christian* readers, with the emblematic significance of the objects, the elevation of Pisgah taken for the stand-point of far-seeing piety—the undimned eye of the lawgiver representing the clarity of vision peculiar to faith, and Canaan itself being the hieroglyphic of *heaven*—coupled, also, with the idea of Moses's solitary death, with the announcement of his burial by the Lord and the secrecy of his sepulchre, with the revelation of Michael the archangel and Satan wrestling over the body of the prophet, and with the *re*-appearance of his body in audible interview with Christ and Elias, and in the lustre of the transfiguration—a convergence of light seems to be thrown upon Pisgah from type and from miracle, from the promises of the old dispensation and the splendors of Christ—from the face of God, and the sparkling wings of the angel champion.

And were it not that ditty and ode have degraded the subject—that spurious devotion and gross imagination have polluted the sacred theme, our Christian feelings would concentrate, as the Scriptural light converges towards the lawgiver upon the mount of vision.

The carnal Israelite was forbidden to stand with the prophet upon this height, and to witness the events of his death. We understand that angels approached with the lowliness of ministers, rather than the curiosity of spectators. Let us approach reverently, as spiritual Israelites. Let us draw nigh, as angels came, bending over the grave of the lawgiver.

In our recent consideration of this subject, we analyzed the aggravations of the sin, whose penalty was this premature death of the prophet. We alluded, also, to the moral furnished by the retribution upon so meek, so noble, so eminent a man.

We return to the view of his intercourse with God upon the summit of Pisgah. We behold, with him, the desert of his life's weary experience stretched in the distance—the dull, leaden waters of the Lake of Sodom, and the deep, winding bed of Jordan before us, and the land of beauty reaching on to the verge of the west. Pleasantly do its hills and slopes contrast with the remembered plains of the Nile, and the brick-kilns of the land of bondage. How cheering to the eye that had gazed for forty years on sterile deserts and massive rocks, to behold the land of vineyards and fountains, the land flowing with milk and honey! It was, to the patient breast of Moses, an awakening from a dream of famine. It was the viewing, in its luxuriance, of what he had by faith promised to others. It threw the glow of certainty back upon the messages he had faithfully proclaimed. It was age realizing the castles of youth's fancy. More than this, the territory in view was the patrimony to whose borders he had led his beloved people, and whose possession they should soon conquer. The bannered army were to celebrate in this inheritance their festival of peace. And if we could imagine the inspired joy with which some war-beaten patriot would behold his ravaged country suddenly changed to a landscape of fertility and peace, we may have some image of the delight with which Moses feasted on the prospect.

But, to complete the picture, we must bring the higher coloring from heaven. His religious emotions were stirred at the sight. The strongest and the loftiest affections of the soul were drawn into exercise. The evidence was spread before him, that his trust in God brought its recompense. His constancy in virtue had preserved him for this gladdening sight. His courage and his meek submission to the guiding hand had ensured the reward. And from the privilege of forecasting the future, which he had now attained, he was assured that mercy and loving-kindness had watched over his path of trials. Rejoicing and recompensed servant of God! What rays broke now upon thy soul from the dark passages of Providence! It was not in vain that the burdens of office bruised thy submissive shoulder. A refractory people had murmured against thee, but the Almighty had never withdrawn His friendship. And now conscience, that master power within, soothed thy wayworn spirit, and listened for the approving voice of God—" I have caused thee to see it with thine eyes."

The scene of Pisgah is, accordingly, a blending of recompense and chastisement—the meeting upon one conspicuous spot of the comforts and the woes of life. The summit of the mountain gleams in the sunlight, as the prophet kneels upon it, viewing the verdure of the west, and making melody in his heart to the Hebrews' faithful God. A threatening cloud rolls its shadow up the height, and enveloped in its shroud the lawgiver sinks before the frown of heaven, and vanishes from the view of men.

It is the mixture of rewarding and chastening that obscures the meaning of this scene. And it is the disregard of this complexity in the event that produces such misapplication of its instruction, concealing its moral bearings, and debasing its use as a type.

We are not warranted in separating the blessing and the penalty of Pisgah. They are the twin creatures that manifest the work of God. Moses is eminently blessed while he is eminently punished. He earns the vision of Canaan, while he receives his deserved fate. It is the lot of a righteous man, which he exemplifies, but of the righteous under the rod of correction. Had he been cut off for his ungodly and passionate words, without ascending to this view of Canaan, we should have seen righteousness chastened, but not cheered—corrected in justice, but not gladdened with mercies. Had disease invaded his frame and stolen his life at the foot of Abarim, we should have heard of pomp and woe among the tents of Israel, and a lamentation because the mediator had died. But there would have existed no conspicuous proof that the righteous lawgiver tasted of his reward. Had a bolt of punishment smitten him with sudden death upon the plains of Moab, there would have been signal retribution for his public offence to terrify the camp. But this would have destroyed the testimony of his favor with God, and of his departure in the joy and peace of the righteous.

He appears in the closing scene of his life, separated from the appendages of earthly station, secluded from the gaze and the admiration of his people, conducted into solitudes to meet with God, and to experience both the earthly gains of his persevering righteousness, and the chastening for his example of sin.

We deduce, therefore, from the actual accompaniments of the prophet's death, a moral instruction in the methods of Divine chastisement. We read in distinct characters, as we mount the peak of Pisgah, the handwriting from heaven, that God prepares the righteous to rejoice in their chastenings. He would not correct his Hebrew servant till He had showed him the goodly land. He would not dim the eye of the faithful prophet till it had gained the prospect of the promised reward.

The necessity of correction runs parallel with the certainty of our waywardness, and imfirmity, and surprise by sin. Moral government must be suspended, and holiness must be the result of arbitrary power rather than gracious discipline, or the chastisement of heaven must visit the righteous. The natural eye can have this insight into the wisdom of the Divine judgments.

But to the spiritual eye, to the righteous beholding the face of a reconciled Father, there is a vision of higher things. It discerns a merciful method in the course of chastenings. It anticipates the recompense, before it feels the temptation. It tastes the powers of the world to come, before it quivers at the fetid breathings of hell. We are clothed with the panoply of God, before the destroyer is permitted to come in his onset. Like Moses preparing for his punishment, we gaze upon an animating scene, and are elevated in soul to receive the kiss of the Lord before sin approaches to wrestle.

The blessed volume is emblazoned with the illustrations of this consoling doctrine. The very pages of nature are adorned with the charming pictures of this Divine method. We may not unfold all these testimonies. Let us cull instances.

You will have thought, before I speak, of Jacob surprised in his dream with the vision of the angels, and the ladder standing between himself and the gates of glory. You will have recalled the dreams of Joseph, and the interpretation given by his father's prophetic spirit. And that I need mention no more, you will connect with the name of the lawgiver, the vision of Christ's body transformed, and of His majesty and His conversation with the buried patriarch and the translated prophet, before the disciples understood that their Master should die, and that they should be, like Him, baptized in blood. For how could Peter have risen again from his fall, if he had not seen those splendors on the mount? Or how could he have made that confession, which was the Rock of foundation to the Church, unless he had entered with his Saviour into the cloud of glory? The vision of faith preceded the trial of faith. Men were ready to bear the horrors of darkness, who had occupied their minds with visions of light.

How is it with the great processes of Divine discipline now? Look at the uniform history of a soul bearing the life of God within it. Is it planted at once in the thickest of the fight? Does it know at once the severity of temptation? Far from it. Its early experience is joyous. It is feasted as a returning prodigal. It feels the craving of new appetites, and tastes the bounty of supply. It is a child in grace, and the very tenderness of its life brings it into the calm retreats and pleasant engagements of youth. In after years, in the hard duties of perseverance and hope against hope, amid the insurrections of passion, and among the disheartening scenes of defection and apostacy, it has need of these early joys, these fresh visions of relief and satisfaction, to stay its purpose, and keep it alive for heaven.

Or take an illustration from the universal discipline imposed upon the conscience. We speak now of experience which comes within the range of every one of us. Think, then, of the alluring visions, the beckoning hopes, which uniformly exhilarate the hearts of the young. Think of the peaceful conscience, the healthful, happy innocence of childhood, which tinge the future with the beauties of Canaan, and open to the unsuspecting heart a far-reaching land of promise. This is the discipline by which God leads us towards years of temptation. The youthful conscience stands upon the Pisgah of preparation for the hour of trial.

And when in age and years of care, sins have defiled our conscience, and guilt shuts from view the prospect of a brilliant future, whither does the soul flee? Where and how does it gather encouragement for the efforts of repentant and restoring virtue? Oh! it is the conscience of youth, the day-dreams and the night-visions of hope and trust, the resolutions of an unfaltering sincerity, and the aspirations of an undefiled spirit—it is these that come back afresh upon the pinions of memory, and draw the heart up to innocence and heaven.

Take away the visions of childhood, fling an immortal spirit into the conflict of life without the discipline that trains the youthful heart, all astare in this new strange world, and you may have prodigious energy—strong, resistless purpose ; but it will be the strength of a monster, not of a man—it will be heartless, unrelenting, adamantine solidity—a flesh and blood machine, that crushes along its way, and not a thing of soul that grows wiser and better in its trials.

We are bold, then, to assert that the whole economy of God teems with illustrations of the truth, that God prepares His servants by hopes and promises and visions of delight for the seasons of correction. And the lawgiver is but a figure of our own experience, when he ascends the mount of observation to satisfy his hopes and die—to come in glad familiarity near his God and meet the blended kiss and curse—"I have caused thee to see it with thine eyes, but thou shalt not go over thither."

Fix this encouragement upon thy heart, O mortal man ! From the sportive joys of childhood to the stooping woes of age, thou art under the discipline of thy heavenly Father. He foresees thy ways, and blesses thy perseverance and thy fidelity to Him, even while He visits thine offences with a rod, and thy sin with scourges.

Be persuaded by His own words to put thy whole trust in Him. Be persuaded by the examples of His Providence, to rejoice in the certainties of deliverance. Be persuaded by the chastenings He has inflicted on the righteous, that He will by no means clear the guilty. If the unadvised speech of Moses must be so signally punished, what woes must chase our transgressions in word and deed! If one sin was so remembered by the justice of heaven, what memories of terror may we expect! There are cheering words echoed from Pisgah to the patient and struggling servant of God. But the alarms to our impenitence and indevotion are muttered from that height. The body of the righteous man is prostrated there, the victim of a single sin. Years of eminent holiness could not avert the death. Angels that blushed at the fall of the meek man, could not spread their wings between him and his penalty. Virtues that had kept their habitation in his heart through every assault, could not screen him from the chastening shaft.

Where, then, is the hope of the profane, the prayerless, the unbelieving? What mercy shall interpose for them, when the patient and earnest child of God must feel the scourge of God? If the diseased and tortured souls, who flee to the Almighty Helper, are but spared from death, and drawn into heaven by the discipline of pain, what shall become of the hopeless and the helpless impenitent? "If the righteous scarcely be saved, where shall the ungodly and the sinner appear?"

Let us be moved, while we may be moved, by the persuasions and the commands of God. He utters it with irreversible truth, "The soul that sinneth, it shall die." The righteous shall die within the very sight of Canaan, but the resisting creature of God shall be forever dead. "If judgment begin at the house of God, what shall the end be of them that obey not the gospel of God?"

Turn to that scene of death upon the mountain of Moab, ye that groan waiting for the redemption of your body. It is wounded and crucified to the world. It is weighed with the oppressions of life. But it shall not perish. It shall not meet the fires of vengeance, though it is touched with the woes of correction.

> " Snatched sudden from th' avenging rod,
> Safe in the bosom of thy God,
> How wilt thou then look back, and smile
> And bless the pangs that made thee see
> This was no world of rest for thee !"

XIX.

AUTUMN HOMILY.

GENESIS viii. 22.

"While the earth remaineth, seed-time and harvest, and cold and heat, and summer and winter, and day and night shall not cease."

THE waters of the deluge are subsided. Into the crevices and caverns of the globe, the huge waves have crept. The drifted ark, that had breasted for a year the boundless flood, lies an empted monster upon the sides of Ararat. A cleansed earth is repeopled with the tenants of that floating church. The patriarch rears at once the altar, fit symbol that the first labor of man, in the new world rescued from curse, should be in the offices of religion. With the smoke of the offerings curling aloft from the plains of Armenia, ascended the more grateful odor of man's thanksgiving and prayer. "Are these fields to be desolated again for the sins of man?" asks the suppliant patriarch, with his spared household before the altar. "Are the fountains of the deep, and the windows of heaven again to pour out the depopulating streams of wrath? Shall the seasons, broken with the deluge, resume their pleasant circuit?

Shall the husbandman plant again in hope, and the harvestman reap in joy? Shall the regarnished earth be the happy home which successive toil and rest shall bless?"

And the Lord smelled the sweet savor, when earth's restored face was consecrated anew by the altar and the prayer, and the bow of mercy spanned the baptized globe with the response of promise—"While the earth remaineth, seed-time and harvest, and cold and heat, and summer and winter, and day and night shall not cease."

It is possible that in this sixfold division of the year, reference was had to the diversities of climate upon the earth. The post-diluvian seasons in the region of Armenia, where this promise was received, may have required this number of divisions. Most European nations have adopted the division into four seasons, transmitted to us, and easily applicable to our western climate. But there is scarce a tyro in geography who cannot tell us where the year is distinguished only by summer and winter, or only by seed-time and harvest, or only by alternating cold and heat, and where, again, besides the four regular seasons, intermediate periods of rain or parching heat annually recur. And where the same divisions are observed, yet the order is inverted, the seed-time of Palestine coming with the autumnal equinox, and the harvest falling in March, while an almost contiguous people, the Copts, have the same seasons as ourselves, with the only variation of beginning them at the middle of the respective months.

The import of the promise, therefore, is not the assurance of either order in the seasons, but that these alternations shall occur. Especially shall those seasons most needful to man, and necessary to vegetation, never cease. The seed-time may be less propitious, but never wanting; the harvest may be smitten, but its period shall come. Seasons may advance mantled with that uncertainty which bids us lean on God, yet moving in that order which shows the power and the benignity of God.

"Mysterious round! What skill, what force Divine,
Deep felt, in these appear! A simple train,
Yet so delightful mix'd, with such kind art,
Such beauty and beneficence combined;
Shade, unperceived, so softening into shade;
And all so forming an harmonious whole;
That as they still succeed, they ravish still."

"The rolling year is full of Thee."

This diversity has its influence upon man. As the varieties of landscape, the multiplied changes of natural scenery, the aspect of the earth, and the movements of the rivers, and the very shapes and colors of the clouds, have modified the tastes and dispositions of men, so still more does the order of seasons affect the traits of nations. The dweller under perpetual suns is languid, but inflammable—a very beast in his idle luxury, and a paragon of saints in his endurance of fasts and hermitage. The robust Laplander is, by sheer necessity, frugal. Ockley in his history of the Saracens, tells us that most of the Arab traits are to be referred to the influences of climate and habit, and the productions of their territory. Where nature rolls her car of profusion, and decks herself in all the varied beauty of the seasons—where the provident insect has taught industry, and the skies have given men lessons in colors — where inspiration seems to float upon the air—in Egypt with her uncorrupting atmosphere, in Assyria with her plethora of fertility, in Greece with her shaded vales and streams and sounding shores and sunny hills, under the tinted skies of Italy, this side the heaven-climbing Alps, among the mingled rigors and blandness of the British Isles, and here in our own all-sustaining garden-land, the arts, the refinements, the inventions of men have found their culture, belting the more genial and diversified regions of the earth with civilization. It is not chance that has steered the progress of human development, but Providence; and Providence works with no mightier machinery than the steady influences of nature.

It accords with our belief in the original unity of the human races, to assign many of the types of mankind now existing upon this earth to climatic causes. We are not, indeed, to suppose that the same plastic power exists in all ages, that the European would now become a red man by acclimation in America, any more than we are to suppose that a full-grown man is to recover the developing power that works so constantly in childhood. The human system may grow beyond the influence of climatic causes, and man, when fully developed in body and soul, may live in such electric, instantaneous connection with his brother man—space and time may be so annihilated, that all people shall see eye to eye; but the interval fills the earth with diversities corresponding with the diversities of the seasons.

Our purpose, however, is not to dilate on the periodical changes which have in perpetual succession ensued upon the Divine promise.

We would rather take wisdom on the wing, and hearken to her voice as she passes by clothed in the sad raiment of the present season. The autumnal season is, in many respects, peculiar to our land. Those who have traversed the globe, pronounce it the glory of this western world. There is a tinting thrown by nature over our forests, a haze enveloping our horizon, a drapery in our clouds, and a brilliancy in the sunsets peculiar to the season and the territory. Autumn is a lingering and marked portion of our year. It slowly impresses upon us the philosophy of its teachings. It reluctantly leaves us to the rude assaults of winter. Its discipline is like that of wisdom itself, preparing us for the future, bracing us against shocks to come, warning and encouraging, besetting us with storms, and yet tempering them to our tenderness. There are those who are charmed with the bursting life and struggling promise of the spring. It is eloquent of resurrection and the putting on of glory. But the heart, after all, feels dissatisfied with its mockery. It fails to realize eternity. Men spring up to work with it hopeful but fearing. We look for some higher teacher than nature, when things supernatural are studied. We ask some more brilliant type of the resurrection than the perishing flower or the bloom of the fruit-tree. But autumn is full of realities. It teaches what nature is adapted to teach, and no more. It is full of those things which correspond with man's present position midway between birth and joy, and death and gloom.

Autumn has its moral aspects. As nature is a parable of God, the season of dying nature is the parable of man's transitoriness as a creature of God. The fall of the leaf, from which this season derives a name, is the natural symbol of man's frail hold upon life. He flutters through a deciduous existence. On all the garniture of his life decay is written. The grave-yard gates are opened daily to admonish him of this. His senses fail, his friends are dead, his grand schemes are blasted. The seasons are to roll on, the livery of verdure is to clothe the earth, the gay mantle is to be thrown over hills and valleys, but not for him. The seed-time of the corruptible is at hand. Like the acorn swinging on the strong oak he must drop, a helpless thing; and the dust shall overlay him, and the winds of winter shall gather their wreaths of glittering fleetness above, and the grass shall spring, and the wild flower shall waste its fragrance above him; but his winter turns to no spring, his seed-time yields not to the harvest till the seasons shall grow weary of their round.

The myriad leaves that go trembling to their

autumnal grave are monitors to us all. Do we discern the signs of the times? Do we see what our lives must be, were there no resurrection promised? Our lives sparkle for a season, but their very memory shall soon be gone. Our autumn is at hand. The winter of oblivion hastens on behind it. To what shall we liken our mortal life? What image shall we find in nature?

'Tis like

> "To snow that falls upon a river,
> A moment white—then gone forever."

We must not pause with this melancholy view of the season. Its own dismal days are too apt to fill us with these oppressive thoughts. Sadness without a promise and a duty to relieve it, is never a blessing, and ought never by us to be cherished. Those pleasant reveries of grief are the bane of the soul, unless they are cheered by promises and thoughts of duty. The autumn has other messages than those of sure decay. It is the garnering season of industry. Its burdened fields bowing to the reaper—its ripened fruits regaling the eye—its sum of gains poured into the contented heart of toiling men—these are the lessons printed on the autumnal leaf of nature. The harvest-home fills up with joy the cup of industry. Rewards to them that work, to the laborer his hire, to the persevering husbandman his abundance and his rest—these are the maxims echoed from the breast of the harvest-field. There may have been days of anxiety, days of panting toil, days of discontent and reluctant industry, but the harvest is come, the work is recompensed, and so far as human infirmity will allow, industry is satisfied with its rewards. It has not been in vain that the plowman turned the early furrow, that the planter sprinkled his fortune over the kindly earth, that the laborer watched, and the sickle or the cradle was swung, and the patient beast dragged God's bounties to the granaries of man. All people wait for these fruits of industry. On these rewards of the laborer, all nations are built.

How plainly does the recompense of autumn discourse to man that the hand of the diligent maketh rich. The fields themselves proclaim, "As a man soweth, so shall he reap." It was but little that was scattered, but it was ventured in the hands of God, it was tended by the hand of industry, and it hath come to much. In other labors Providence is disguised; but here the harvest is the result of that wisdom which controls the heavens and made the earth, and man feels that he comes close up to the Omnipotent, and that, with the fruits He gives, He says—"Work while the day lasts, for the night cometh when no man can work."

The returns of autumn have their moral influence. The voices of the fields are heard in workshops, in all the laboratories of art, in every nook where man finds his chance to toil; and these oracles that come each year, like nature's apostles clothed with riches, bid men to labor in hope that they may reap—to sow for the incorruptible, that, when the harvest comes, they may have not the shame of the sluggard, but the joy of the immortal reaper.

We cannot picture to ourselves the teeming fields of autumn without recalling the words of bounty it proclaims, "He that soweth sparingly, shall reap sparingly." For His own glory, God sowed the seeds of vegetation over the face of the earth, and every season now tells of His goodness. Be it ours to fix this axiom in our heart, "He that soweth sparingly, shall reap sparingly." Autumn is the season of bounty. It feeds the millions of animated beings that must perish without its liberal hand. It does not live for itself. Its existence is lengthened to another harvest by the liberality with which it dispenses to the beasts and fowls that toil not nor gather into barns. It makes no complaint that the numbers dependent on it are so many. The harvest-field waits for the gleaner as well as the reaper.

> "Be not too narrow, husbandman! but fling
> From the full sheaf, with charitable stealth
> The liberal handful."

The bounty that always rolls in upon one's self, that, like the gulf of hell, is always receiving and never returning, has no use upon earth. When it is gone, it is not missed. The bounty of autumn survives its own departure. It is the symbol of that Fatherly hand which

> "Spreads a common feast for all that lives."

Autumn writes also its monitions in letters of light across the sky. In this season, as the verdure of nature is yielding to the advance of desolation, the heavens themselves are brightened with those meteoric wonders which so brilliantly betoken the consummation of this earthly scene. The wide expanse of the universe is seen to be thronged with material existences that may sweep in devastating showers of fire over this earth. For though the promise be true that the seasons shall wait as handmaids of mercy upon the rolling earth, yet the promise is linked with a warning that the earth shall not always remain. The elements that vivify shall themselves melt with fervent heat. This teeming depository of God's wisdom shall be rolled together as a scroll. On earth angels shall write an epitaph, when beneath its ashes shall be buried the hopes of the wicked; while a home more gorgeous in its pavement and in its roof, more plentiful in its comforts, more unsullied in its pleasures, shall receive the righteous to eternal recompense.

My brethren, in every season of the annual round, to the discerning soul of the God-fearing and the Christ-believing and the man-loving Christian, is verified the allegory that leads the pilgrim to the "House of the Interpreter."

Hoarse winter pipes through rattling reeds his plaintive cry, "*Memento mori*," "Thou must die." The warbling notes of spring thrill us with the cheerful bidding to arise, and look upward and *hope*. Summer-tide swells the acclaim of nature, and shouts from laden boughs and exuberant fields—"Praise the Lord, for he is gracious, and his tender mercy is over all his works. But the soothing season of the year, that bends the fervid sun askance, preaches the calmer lesson of content. It rehearses the annual mercies of "Him who doeth all things well." And by its very drapery of gloom, as by its brilliancies of changing leaf or meteoric sky, it pictures sermons on the happiness of sweet content.

"Some murmur, when their sky is clear
And wholly bright to view,
If one small speck of dark appear
In their great heaven of blue.

"And some with thankful love are fill'd
If but one streak of light,
One ray of God's good mercy gild
The darkness of their night.

"In *palaces* are hearts that ask
In discontent and pride,
Why life is such a dreary task,
And all good things denied.

"And hearts in poorest huts admire,
How love has in their aid
(Love that not ever seems to tire),
Such rich provision made."

XX.

THE GLORY OF THE LATTER HOUSE.

PHIL. iii. 21.

" Who shall change our vile body, that it may be fashioned like unto His glorious body, according to the working whereby He is able even to subdue all things unto Himself."

THE mighty working of Christ! The achievement of the Omnipotent! He that was like us, putting forth the energy of Divinity, that we may be like Him! Is this our hope, our destiny, the end of God's hidden designs with this soul-bearing flesh? Then, argues the Apostle, our home is not in this banishment of suffering, our citizenship is in the country of God's uncovered glories. But with what body shall we come? The same that here executed the will of God, or here lived for the gratification of self. The same that was here abandoned of its immortal partner, and left to the dishonour of perfect helplessness, as the clod of the ground; the same that was buried amid the woes of afflicted hearts and the pompous ceremonials that signified the respect or the flattery or the hopes of men; the same body that was corrupted in the grave, or dispersed by the winds, or swallowed in the waters. No difficulties can be alleged against this, which do not disparage the power and the truth of God, which do not in fact leave man the sport of nature and the victim of arbitrary and contradictory powers. But if the restored body be the same as that which here perishes, is it not loaded with infirmities, perishing, and gross, obstructed with disease, exhausted in weakness, and filled with pain? Must not the same energies revive, and the same want of energies continue? Must not the same necessities oblige it by the same laws for sustenance, for relief, for health and strength? Must we not come up again from the grave destined to the same decay, or else lingering in a frame that sinks perpetually in an ocean of miseries, and never reaches bottom? These questions, arising out of the identity of the present and the future body, are those which now demand our attention. And yet we are aware that we are trenching upon subjects which transcend the understanding of man, much more the ability of our powers. Curiosity has loved to pursue with the maddened brain of the Italian the phantoms of Paradise, and the glittering forms of heaven. An oriental fancy has prepared for the Mussulman his resting-place of sensual delights. There are the angels, "many of whom have seventy thousand heads, each head with seventy thousand faces, each face with seventy thousand mouths, and each mouth with seventy thousand tongues, each of which praises Allah in seventy thousand languages." Such are the monsters of exaggerated qualities, which imposture and hallucination have framed in the imaginations of half imbruted minds for the tenantry of a huge palace of luxuries. The savage hunter, that once chased his prey over these evangelized regions of civilization, painted for himself a rest in the warriors' land of triumph, where the red-man was still the hunter and the savage, and the war-song of his barbaric delight was the anthem of his everlasting praise to the Great Spirit. Thus has each phase of human character descried for itself the landmarks of a congenial Paradise. We must beware that we walk not in the same tracks of dreams and conjecture, and design for ourselves the architecture of a new home for this unforsaken spirit. Consider, if you will, the temerity of such attempts. We know little of the body, as it now exists. Centuries upon centuries have rolled upon men, organized with the same constitution, conformed to the same original model, and possessing precisely the same physical powers, and yet the simplest principles of anatomy, the most ordinary laws of our physical system, the very palpable fact of a circulation of the blood—such common facts of the body's present nature have been unknown until the last century. And we have reason to believe that principles equally simple are yet to be ascertained as regulating the ordinary functions of the nervous system. The seemingly supernatural results of mesmeric influence, authenticated as they are by the wonder of all ages, by the recorded confusion of philosophy, and by the unaccountable fickleness of human attraction and repulsion, are so many indications of subtle principles pervading our flesh, which delight in exhibiting themselves to our amazement, and concealing themselves from our scrutiny. Is not the confession of science amid all its progresses in discovering the mysteries of the human organization, a confession of imperfection? Does not the triumph of disease and agony witness that the body, so well known in its features and its weakness, is yet in its capacities and its possible energies unknown? Has not the Almighty in writing the decree of death upon the door-posts of this earthly tabernacle, written there also the decree of imperfection in our knowledge of its attainable endowments? What, then, have we to hope as to our unaided and conjectural framing of a newly-endowed body? Temerity alone could rush into such explorations of the future. As God hath drawn aside the veil, we may gaze upon the image of the glorious body, but where He has curtained the scene, we may not venture—ignorant and baffled adventurers as we are, in this vessel of a vile body—we may not venture to imagine the nature of the glorified body. Such particulars as are furnished for our instruction and incitement will be presented under these three points. First, the contrasted endowments and qualities of the present and the new body. Second, the objections to the mode of treating the subject we have adopted. And third, the practical reflections suggested by these considerations.

The degree of change that is to pass upon this flesh, is sufficiently intimated by the comparison which the Apostle presents between the present body of our humiliation, as the original strictly may be expressed, and the body conformed to the glory of Christ. The contrast has been elsewhere exhibited in four particulars, which may be regarded as the guides of our study, and the limits of our curiosity. This present condition of suffering, of pain and dissolution, has been contrasted with a future exemption from these distresses; "it is sown in corruption, it is raised in incorruption." Our present heritage of deformed or disgraced bodies, of shame and immodesty, of degradation to the fellowship of brutes and reptiles and animals that walk this lower earth, of humiliation to dwell in tabernacles which express almost nothing of our true character and our excellence, is to be exchanged for an inheritance undefiled, for a body no longer deformed by the maiming consequences of sin, but reformed after the image of perfection; for a state of conscious purity and dignity, for the company of the unblemished and the undissolving, and for a frame that by its clarity and the impression of the Divine seal without, shall express the secrets of Divine favor and the beauty of the soul's virtues recorded and living within; "it is sown in dishonor, it is raised in glory." Our energies here repressed, our capacities now limited, our subjection to hampering bonds of infirmity, are to yield to the acquisitions of new power, power commensurate with our wills; "it is sown in weakness, it is raised in power." Our present animal body, likened in its necessities to the beast, depending for its support upon food and sleep and the unobstructed movements of the breath, is contrasted with a body of a different nature, exempt from these necessities, and adapted to the wants and the undertakings of the tenanting spirit; "it is sown a natural body, it is raised a spiritual body." Study the contrasts, as marked as the contrasts between this inert globe, and the overarching canopy of heaven. For the new bodies, that like Christ's have once suffered for sin, are no more exposed to pains and grief and tears. They are forever impassible. Patience, here the crown of virtues, because here the virtue that grows out of our humiliation—patience has had her perfect work, and is there superseded by the exhilarating virtue of a happy activity. We suffer in this present land of groanings as prisoners upon the rack, knowing that only by suffering is our penalty to be completed, and that an extremity of agony carrying us down upon the point of the lance of death to lie with the vermin or to feed the fishes of the sea, is to be the end of these bodily afflictions. The glorified body has none of these miseries to endure, and no future struggle, no couch of loathsomeness and corruption to dread. Even in the season of animated spirits and robust health, there is ever in this life some joint displaced, some nerve uneasy, some muscle strained, some oppressive weariness, an ache or a twinge or a languor, or a restlessness that disturbs and mangles the integrity of our pleasure; or, at the best, there is a fly in the ointment, there is a doom of dissolution and putrescence stamped on the clear front and the sturdy limbs of health. In the glorified body not a vestige remains of this doom, of these broken joints, and shattered nerves, and desperate diseases.

Contrast again, as God has summoned us to do, the dull uncomeliness of the present frame, with the clarity and the beauty of the glorified body. The change has been feebly represented in the apparitions of angels, in the appalling splendors of the upper world, in the transfiguration of the Redeemer's body again restored to its destiny of humiliation, in the visions of the rapt evangelist, in the brightness above midday which prostrated the bloody Saul, and in the prophetic promises of a lustre like the brightness of the firmament. Among the scenes of heavenly reality, there was a sign in heaven, "a woman clothed with the sun, and the moon under her feet, and upon her head a crown of twelve stars." But this is to the glory of the saints, as twilight is to the glare of the sun. For the excellent ornaments of the woman were the borrowed splendors of other creatures, like the costly brilliancy of a queen's robe and diadem. But the lustre of the glorified body shall be intrinsically its own, carrying the light of seven suns wherever it moves, and attended with the shining of the stars, as if the sun were making a pageant with a supplement of torches. In vain does imagination lift its wing to look over the battlements of heaven upon those forms of splendor. We cannot picture to ourselves the comeliness and the loveliness, the sweetness and the dignity, the mildness of aspect and the awfulness of majesty which every saintly body shall then assume. "From dishonor to glory" is the most that language can compass, from the earth and the worm to the pavement of gold and the music of angels is the extent of the contrast. I represent to myself my ideal of bodily perfection, the most exact symmetry, a complexion more pleasant than the light and the gayest combinations of art and nature, clothed with the clustered beauties of the visible universe, and surrounded with all that could please the senses or charm the fancy, and yet I am imagining a clod instead of a saint, and representing a sunbeam that darts from world to world by a mere stroke upon the canvas. Could we once catch the vision of the glorified body, we should even blush at our imaginings, we should sink confounded as Moses must even look through a rock to behold the fringes of such glory, we should imitate the idolatry of St. Peter and be building tabernacles of worship for such a personage, we should bow in the act of St. John worshipping the ministering angel. Contrast again the natural weakness of this vile body, with the natural powers of the glorified body. Here it wrestles with the obstacles of physical and visible nature; there it commands every energy which its will would possess. Here it is dependent upon daily refreshments, and the restorations of quiet, and the protections of ingenuity and law; there it is too vigorous to need recreation, and too mighty to be subject to any external injury. All power is in covenant with it, all weakness is in humiliation beneath it. We shall fail to gauge the bounds of this power.

We shall look at it only to see it extending beyond our imagination. For instance, you observe what the power of God exerted upon this inert earth does already effect. Why, the power that He hides in the dust is the agency of all that reason can calculate. It heaves up its constant successions of vegetation. It throws out its myriad upon myriad forms of ephemeral life. It brings up from its magic receptacle the food of millions. It hurls the waters from its embrace. It rends the ribs of rock, as the withes upon a Samson, and vomits from its basaltic throat the burning streams of desolation. This torpid earth is such a vehicle of power. And who is the reasoner that could not be forced by logic to admit that each atom of dust must, for ought we know, contain within itself the principles of all these powers? When we urge upon you these powers of matter, you begin your philosophical analysis, and speak of assimilations and combinations and resultant forces. But resultant forces are always products and not new creations. A resultant force in one direction requires still greater forces in other directions. And so your divisions and combinations and concretions of powers, instead of diminishing the adaptations of matter, only serve to exhibit the fact that each grain, each least element of matter may be by God's appointment the bed of repose for all imaginable power. Think then of a body built of this dust, with these atoms most skilfully and mysteriously arranged, in the very shape which angels choose and which God Himself wears in their midst for them to adore; think of this body raised from this condition of restraints and impotence to a condition of freedom and power, where the recondite energies of matter may all be developed, nay where the adoption is the redemption of this body, and the marvel is the creature's emerging into glorious liberty and the manifestation of the sons of God, and what limit shall we dare assign to the unencumbered powers of the dust awaking from its sleep! The whole doctrine of the resurrection implies that as it is the body and not the soul which sleeps and rises, and as even in this slumber of the body its elements are enacting wonders, those same elements when awaked, and their powers elicited, must possess energies transcending all the reckoning of the human mind. It must be the fulfilment of the anticipated power, which shall make nature our handmaid as she is the instrument of God, when the Divine power of the human body shall change our vile body that it may be fashioned like unto His glorious body according to the working whereby He is able to subdue all things unto Himself.

Contrast, finally, the present nature of the body, animal, sensual, growing and decaying by the laws of nature, with its future nature as a spiritual body, whether by this be meant the constant indwelling and possession of the risen frame by the Holy Ghost, as an everlasting temple of God, or rather be meant by it the enduing upon the flesh of such qualities as we attribute to spirit. No doubt both these senses are included, and the latter because of the former. A spiritual body! No longer chained to this earthly ball, but free to range the climates of successive glory. A spiritual body! Not such as drags its form from scene to scene, or holds its perilous speed over the waters or after the vaporous charioteer of man's enlistment, but more agile even than the electric power which man would now in his weakness harness to his service. For this gift of agility, this spirituality of the body, shall make it move as quick as thought, the perfect instrument of the soul, traversing in the twinkling of an eye the remotest heavens, and observing in one moment the wreck of this shattered sepulchre and the beauty of the empyrean. A spiritual body! Light, and subtle, and wafted upon the air. No element shall obstruct its motions. It ascends upon the clouds, like the glorious body. It walks upon the waters like the glorious body. It stands in the midst while the doors remain shut, like the glorious body. It emerges from the tomb, before the stone is rolled away, like the glorious body. It vanishes in a moment from human sight, like the glorious body. It walks invisible in the midst, where two or three are met together, like the glorious body. It communicates its power, while it lives undiminished, like the glorious body. A spiritual body, like that which here hides itself under the symbols of matter, to convey the pledge and the means of everlasting life, the bread to signify the power of the risen body, the wine to signify the cleansing of the poured blood, both received into both body and soul, both entering into the mortal and corruptible frame, as the seed of resurrection and immortality and incorruption, as the sacrament of His omnipotence, who shall change our vile body, that it may be fashioned like unto His glorious body according to the mighty working whereby He is able to subdue all things unto Himself.

XXI.

THE WHOLE DUTY OF MAN.

ECCLESIASTES xii. 13.

"Let us hear the conclusion of the whole matter: Fear God, and keep his commandments: for this is the whole duty of man."

IF in anything pertaining to ethics, Pagan philosophy became "elevated and magnificent,"— if in anything uninspired reason, while doing greatest honor to itself, fell far below the sublime anticipations and the terse solidity of Scripture, it was in the effort to work out the problem whose result the preacher has here condensed into a pithy proposition. What is man's sovereign good? What is his ultimate happiness? What precept, or what law, or what object shall he set before him that will not mislead, and shall not fail to conduct him into true satisfaction? These were the questions on which human wisdom expended its strength, reaching no clear and undisputed conclusion. Even the divine Plato staggers beneath the task, and covers his defeat with pompous words and wild speculations. The solution of these momentous questions was beyond the unaided ability of man.

The Epicurean confounded pleasure with happiness, and teaching men to please themselves, contradicted his own theory by showing that pleasure was only a relative term, and that man must, after all, be instructed how to discern the sources of a true and permanent pleasure. If he pleased the clamorous appetites of nature, he incurred calamity. If he sought the higher pleasures of intellect, he was happy only by self-denial. The philosophy might be true that we were to make pleasure the aim of our life,—but the question was still revolved, What is the source of most enduring pleasure? What is the sovereign good that eclipses all others?

Then came up the Stoic, telling us that virtue was its own reward, and that virtue was to live indifferent to all pains and pleasures. I would not represent stoicism as the sublime absurdity it is sometimes described. It came near to the beautiful patience of Christ. It was a lofty flight for Pagan ethics. But after all it was a wretched failure. It put all virtue in the conformity of actions to reason. The consequences were not to be considered. Antecedent reason must decide what conformed to nature, and that must be chosen as excellent in itself.

Mark the struggles for a law that should define the sources of true happiness. How captivating the theory that virtue is to be chosen for itself, and that without regarding sensations of pain or pleasure we must conform to reason. Still the profounder suggestion ensued,—What makes reason for us, but the law and the true end of our being? Philosophy proved itself inadequate to the inquiry it had commenced. Human reason was not independent, or self-originated, and it must look to the relations in which our nature stands. Stoicism was solitary and egotistic. Reason must be the exponent of our relations with our fellow-creatures and with God. Philosophy might analyze, might propound inquiries, might consider wants, might unfold page upon page of human feeling. Philosophy was but the servitor of reason. Religion was our need—religion to answer the interrogatories of the troubled soul—religion to manifest the law and the end of our being.

One who had sounded all the depths and shoals of ambition,—one who had sought for happiness in every resource of epicurean delight,—one who had collated all the testimonies of diversified experience, sums up the maxim which philosophy had fruitlessly attempted to frame, "Fear God, and keep His commandments, for this is the whole duty of man."

It appears to be the conclusion of the wise man, that our happiness (I say happiness, for he only speaks of duty as conducive to this end)—our happiness is determined by our religion. It is not dependent upon any degree of prosperity,—upon any amount of earthly power,—upon any proportion between our desires and enjoyments; but upon our religion. I am not speaking now of the Christian religion exclusively. I am only approaching the conclusion of all experience; that the reality and the quality of our happiness must be graduated by our religion. If this be pure, and steadfast, and aspiring after God and the godlike, we shall be treasuring to ourselves where neither the worm nor the thief can come, the most of the best pleasure. If our religion is of lower aim, and of meaner desire, our happiness will be depreciated, and its permanence entirely forfeited.

Now what do we mean, when we speak of a man's religion? Certainly we do not mean that of which he has the most, or makes the most. It is often an uneasy appendage to his life. It is often left to odd moments, or marked occasions. It is often a flat contradiction to the bulk of his character,—neutralized by acts more significant of the real man within. One's religion is not known by his prayers,—is not apparent on the surface of his life. It belongs to the principles that govern him. It is the secret sense of power and majesty to be feared,—the secret sense of a will and a law to be obeyed, that originates our religion. The thought of happiness hugs this religious sense. They are twin children of the heart, and in the heart they clasp each other in promise of mutual defence. Every man, therefore, has his religion. He cannot escape responsibility by claiming that he makes no Christian profession. There is in his mind, unless thoroughly idiotic, a religious sense of power and law. There is in his mind a sort of allegiance to some one object of supreme honor and supreme desire. There is some idol, some deified image that receives his secret homage, and seems to smile or frown upon his prostrations of soul. Happily for us, conscience is the unsilenced monitor who with terrible whispers recalls the true object of all reverence and all submission. But conscience is not always admonishing, and conscience may disturb without nullifying our religion.

Let us bring out to view some of the manifold forms of religion which may thus be enlisting our homage, and laying limits to our happiness.

I may be allowed to place in the foreground what appears the most innocent, and the most nearly genuine. It is almost ludicrously true that some souls are betrayed into the error of putting all their religion in the fact of feeling *happy*. The twins are confounded by them. The religious feeling and the happy feeling are with them identical. Whatever exercise of religion has brought them into this ecstatic frame of mind is the highest act and the best gain to which they can devote themselves. With them it is not so much happy to be religious, as it is religious to be devotionally happy. From some period when this transfusion of ecstacy poured across the soul, they date their getting of religion. In the return to some such condition of devotional excitement, and relief from dull common-place, they are to find the renewals of their lapsed religion.

The object of fear is not the majestic purity of Jehovah, burning into the crisped writhings of consternation and remorse the guilty spirit,—not the offended glories of the Divine holiness, but the languid inertness of the wearied and unthrilled soul. They fear the paroxysms of their own nature, and are not aware that the very dread which they call religious is in distrust and dishonor of God. He asks for our reasonable service, and He gives happiness not that we may make it our religion, but that our religion may be commended by its fruits.

Fantastic piety tracks the path which this religion of ecstacy has opened. With it Loyola stood upon the steps of the church of St. Dominic, at Mauresa, and wept aloud, because he beheld the mystery of the Trinity visibly revealed to him at that moment, under the figure of three keys of a musical instrument. He got religion, as he thought, when sitting one day beside a stream and watching the running water, while on its surface played the symbols of the Christian faith, and the Popish dogmas. He was great, and he had visions which decoyed him on to an earthly glory.

But, alas! neither his Jesuitism nor his fanaticism have perished with his greatness. Little souls have as huge visions, and the imagination which could never dream so much as he acted, has sucked in the intoxications of happiness through the same channels. So nearly genuine, and so nearly false a religion has always enlisted, will always enlist the homage of our vitiated nature,—has always begotten, will always beget the sneer and the opposition of men.

At a remote distance from this class, kneeling devotees pay their homage around the shrine of wealth. Note the throng that press to the offices of this mammon religion. They are not only clad in silks and bedizened with jewels, but from every rank of life appears a representative at this worship of wealth. Some that possess it, and some that hope for it, and some that count upon legacies, and some that wonder why the rich righteous are not withdrawn by a good Providence from this scene of temptation. Money is of all things the most natural, and yet the most paltry of gods. Was there not a moral in it, when the people who rejected Jehovah, made a golden calf? And was it strange that Moses should have a congregation before him worshipping the golden god, when even Christian precept cannot obliterate this idolatry? "Covetousness is idolatry," on the authority of an Apostle. And the moral law which began by denouncing idols ends with condemning covetousness, the last vestige of idolatry which will linger through every commandment to pollute the soul of man.

Wealth is not so strictly an idol, as an effigy. It wears the clothes of a living God, but it is powerless to act the part of Deity. It neither allays a fear, nor utters a worthy law. And among the votaries of this religion, it is impossible to discover one soul that derives any solid happiness from his homage.

Here, for instance, is Sir Mammon Money-Bags. He is one of those strong-minded men that bar the heart against the whimpering approaches of piety, and grasp with most heroic fortitude the better side of a bargain. He has a career of most glorious success. His investments are answered as if they were prayers. He chants in his heart a daily anthem, and the chorus is compound interest and ten per cent. He becomes the lion of a new prey at every turn. This baffled speculator envies him. This honest bankrupt dreads him. This poor man votes for him. This priest tells him that he is generous, and accosts him as an influential brother. On all sides, he feels the rising tide of fortune. But rich Sir Mammon is a poor, miserably poor man. His taxes are enormous. Everything is expected of him. He has to eat his god, and distribute his god, and exchange his god, and pay for two religions at once. He is Achilles, but the spear is in his heel. And because he makes the having money his only ambition, and the fear of its loss his haunting terror, he is like the troubled sea, whose waters cannot rest. He lives complaining of poverty, he loses and is wretched, he trembles at the shaking of stocks as a reed shaken with the wind, and he dies more forsaken of his God, and more destitute of all in which he trusted, than the beggar who thanked him and God for the crumbs.

Under the shadow of this plethoric child of fortune creeps to his daily devotions in the worship of riches, a shrivelled form of meanness, too earthly-minded to carry the head erect, too abject in his homage to ever fling away the look of baseness and cunning. He is the tool of others' covetousness. By him the very foibles of the rich are flattered. He humbles himself that the congregations of the poor may fall into the hands of his captains. All his suavity and obsequiousnes,—all his honeyed words and courtesies,—all his airs and manners are but tribute to the image of wealth on whose excellency he dotes. Plausible where a favor is to be earned from this power, he is rude and heartless towards the defenceless and the crippled sons of want. He beholds in every man a brother, if as a brother he can be of any profit. Men whom the rich patronize, he courts. Men who can help him to the magic power which he supposes to lie behind the care of earthly substance,—and little stratagems that can endear him to this Plutus,—and costly civilities that make him one of the favorites of this power,—these are his study,—these the lessons he reads in every manifestation of human character. At last carried away with the fervor of his religious devotion to the homage of wealth, he scouts all religion but this, and pronounces the power he has idolized to be the master-force in every human breast. Pity mourns for the bartered soul with the plaintive elegy, "Ephraim is joined to his idols; let him alone."

Another form catches our eye, mantled in the costly ensigns of wealth,—a feminine gentleness buried under the too evident display of an ungraceful pride. The head is bowed before a Saviour's cross, but the wandering eye searches for the gaze of admiration and the leer of envy. With disdain she shuns the crowd who ape her finery, and looks for the recompenses of her religion not among the cheered and comforted hearts of earthly trial and want, but among the welcomes and the compliments of those who would rival her own power of display.

No dread so unconquerable with her, as that of losing the name of wealth. No sacrifice so eagerly offered, as that of riches and pains to wield the power of reputed wealth. With a complete infatuation, she chases this imaginary power. Ignorant of the pity that warms many a heart she crushes, and of the contempt that repays her hollow civilities, she worships a power that is forever deceiving her, and lingers into an old age of tawdry uselessness, or of ridiculous conceit. We leave her with the hands clasped in mimicry of prayer, while the eye steals around for tributes to her gay importance,—and the sigh of her heart is a fear not of Jehovah's searching eye, but of the greatest evil, to bear the unflattered trials of poverty,—unfit for the ministries of feminine mercy,—unfit for the offices of love to Jesus,—unfit for the purifying assiduities of a sister's affection,—unfit for the winning modesty of a wife,—unfit for the charities of heaven.

Time forbids us to pursue these delineations of human character exhibiting a religious devotion, that loses its sacrifices, and wastes its substance before the imagined power of wealth. Wealth is at the best an instrument, endowed with power only to serve the cause of God—worse than lost when abused to be either feared or trusted. It is our trial to need it, and our trial to have it. Its use is to make us instrumental in pleasing God and profiting men by bounty and charity—by managing in honesty and in mercy—by neither dreading its loss, nor coveting its possession—by neither expending in wasteful luxury, nor hoarding in distrust of Providence, and in love of power.

"If riches increase, set not your heart upon them.

"God hath spoken once; twice have I heard this; that power belongeth unto God."

From this power comes our true misery—from this must our real happiness come. Its greatness challenges our awe—its anger shakes our souls—its favor beams upon us the dawning of a clear satisfaction here, and a brilliant inheritance among the saints in light. "Let us hear the conclusion of the whole matter. Fear God and keep His commandments, for this is the whole duty of man."

XXII.

THE ASCENT OF THE ARK.

1 Chronicles xv. 29.

"And it came to pass, as the ark of the covenant of the Lord came to the city of David, that Michal the daughter of Saul, looking out at a window, saw King David dancing and playing; and she despised him in her heart."

YOU will find a verse very similar to this in another account of this transaction, in the sixth chapter of the second Book of Samuel. You will observe, also, that the history of the ark of God shows how intimately it was connected with the tokens of the Divine presence. Kept and bandied from city to city by the profane Philistines, the manifest strokes of Divine indignation followed those who dishonored the sacred emblem. Reclaimed from the Philistines, or, more strictly, dismissed by them, as too heavy with curses for such ungodly hands, it was harbored by the house of Abinadab in Kirjath-jearim. For twenty years it was left in a state next to sacrilegious neglect. David, who had risen above the indifference of the times, thought it not good to leave the ark of God in Gibeah, but designed to bring it into his own city to secure there the blessing. With piety that looked around for occasions of zeal and service, he prepares a new tent for the awful symbol. Conrad thinks that the tabernacle of Moses was ruinous, and that, on this account, the king substituted a new tent for the ark. In removing the token of Divine presence, a hand of presumption was put forth to stay the tottering carriage, and the invaded majesty of God flamed forth the sign of the trespass in a death-stroke upon Uzzah. Alarmed at this interposition of Providence, David arrests the march of the company, and lodges the ark in the house of Obed-edom, "and the Lord blessed Obed-edom and his household." With more deliberate preparations, with every arrangement of honor and decency, with the proper officers assigned to each part of the duty, the covenant-treasury committed to the shoulders on which God had placed it, with human devices of security entirely abandoned, and human methods of respect and praise most ingeniously accumulated, the royal penitent proceeds to complete his design. "And David was clothed with a robe of fine linen, and all the Levites that bare the ark, and the singers, and Chenaniah the master of the song with the singers: David also had upon him an ephod of linen." Not that the king assumed the sacerdotal dress, but that as all the singers, so he who rejoiced with them put on robes such as the child Samuel wore, and Levites wore, differing from the fine linen ephod of the priests, and not, like theirs, commanded of God. And this explains the taunt of Michal, that the king uncovered himself; for so to her pride it was, when, for honoring the presence of God, he put off his royal apparel, and was no better than the commonest of the people. "Thus all Israel brought up the ark of the covenant of the Lord with shouting, and with sound of the cornet, and with trumpets, and with cymbals, making a noise with psalteries and harps." It was at this time that the scene occurred which is described in our text. David so lowered in his dress—so overcome with joy as to sport in childish exultation (so it seemed to the irreverent spectator)—so transported as to mingle himself with the crowd and share in their rejoicings, was an object of contempt to Michal.

In explanation of this occurrence, it is to be noted that "this sort of rejoicing is at this day used by the Abyssinians in the evening of our Lord's resurrection, when men and women clap their hands and dance to several instruments of music, till morning light, and all this in their churches; which in all likelihood came from the Jews, who still dance in some of their festivals." These dances in sacred worship were universal in early and barbarous times. The Lacedæmonians had their choirs of boys and their choirs of old men, whose songs of obscure terrors or joys were accompanied with the measured movements of a dance. The savage of America was never so inspired with the solemn impressions of his terrific religion, or so subdued by and absorbed in his expectations of a future, as when the dance around the medicine-man witnessed the wild yearnings of a benighted conscience within him. Callimachus tells us of the youths that danced around the altars of Apollo, and Plato witnesses that among the Egyptians all kinds of music and songs and dances were consecrated to their gods. The methods of homage, and especially the acts of jubilee, are determined by the times and the customs of a people. You expect different solemnities as you pass among people in different degrees of civilization. Their faith is venerable, so far as it is true; but their manner of expressing joy or reverence will depend upon their habits in other particulars. Nero and Caligula went out into the streets of Rome and publicly displayed themselves in the dance, to their great dishonor and the disparagement of imperial majesty, without any counterbalancing impression of veneration for the Supreme. With them it was puerile; but David expressed his joy and thankfulness in a way best calculated to exhibit his earnestness, most significant of the honor due to God, and conformable to the customs of the times. The twenty-fourth and forty-seventh Psalms of David were probably composed for this occasion. Any one who peruses them will perceive how solemn and majestic the joy that glowed on this occasion. The language of mere human exultation never abounds with such severe expressions of reverence as are found in these Psalms. And when royalty laid aside its appendages of earthly dignity, and, clad in the garments of a servant, expressed at once its awe and its rapture, nothing could more fully demonstrate the king's sense of the Divine presence with the ark, and the Divine blessing upon the place of its abode.

We must remember, however, that this transaction was not in itself all that was intended by these words. The opening of everlasting doors—the lifting up of the gates for the entrance of the King of glory, expressed far more than the song of joy as the ark of the covenant approached to its new tabernacle. To catch the spirit of the Psalm we must suppose the procession moving with solemn steps from Obed-edom to Zion. A serious acknowledgment of God's universal dominion stays the beginnings of levity—a recital of the qualifications for those who would walk in the procession of praise toward the upper courts of God, is added to this solemn acknowledgment; and as the guarded ark ascends the hill to the height of its sacred deposit, joyfully and with animation the cry rises from a happy multitude, "Lift up your heads, O ye gates; and be ye lift up, ye everlasting doors; and the King of glory shall come in." The shadow only was this of the substance that we commemorate. Jesus Christ is the true ark of the covenant. He was the angel of the covenant, whose presence led the people of Israel; and the cherubim whose wings overshadowed the mercy-seat, were but signs of His angelic attendants. In Him the promises of God are yea and amen. He is the mediator of a new and better covenant, that takes into its reconciling terms heaven and earth, angels and men, the remotest Gentile and the God of all. By His presence in the church, and by it alone, is it the kingdom of God, the sanctuary of blessing, and the guide of salvation. As the ark was enshrined within the sanctuary, so is Jesus Christ enshrined within the sanctuary of the church, embracing the living and the dead, and so is He set forth as enshrined within the symbolic sanctuary of the Christian temple. If we have any promises to plead, they are contained in the ark of the covenant, in Jesus Christ revealed to us. The Father is manifested in Him, and He that hath seen Him hath seen the express image of God, so far as God can be manifest to mortal sense. The cloud of Divine glory was, as it were, coffered in the incarnate Christ, and the covenant is laid up in the power of Christ. To whom He will He giveth life, and whoso entereth into everlasting life does it by believing in this only-begotten Son of God, and reverencing in Him the very presence of Deity. He, ascending to the tabernacle of celestial fabric, was so welcomed as we shall see Him come again. As, with the voice of an archangel, with the sound of a trump, with thousands of His saints, in the glory of His holy angels, shall he appear—with these attendants must He have been exalted to the right hand of the Father. No splendor of earthly triumph can equal the scene which must then have been presented to the spectators in the spiritual world. To see on the one side a throne prepared for man in very union with the seat of Deity Himself—to see the ranks of the brilliant and mighty apparelling themselves with the tokens of human innocence, in white garments, and descending to the clouds of earth—to see a Conqueror stained with no blood but His own, trampling upon a chief adversary and million potentates that had defied both man and angel—to see a Saviour carrying the pledge of mercy to a ruined world in His compassionate hand—to see the ark of the covenant going up from this country of Philistines, through the Kirjath-jearim of the grave whither sacrilegious hands hurried Him—by the house of Paradise, which He blessed as Obed-edom by His sojourn—to see the fellowship between spirits and flesh restored by this Reconciler of things visible and invisible, and all weaknesses of earth divested, and the dull blemishes of transitory glory all omitted in this triumph—this was it that drew from the chanting angels that buoyed up the cloud to heaven, the shout—"Be ye lift up, ye everlasting doors, and the King of glory shall come in." Ye iron doors, that barred the face of man from scenes of heaven, burst before the Conqueror that broke the grates of death. Ye gates that shut against the banished pair, and hung immovable, pressed with the burden of presumptuous sin, and bolted with the curse of God, lift up, for the sin is borne away upon the Conqueror's shoulder, and the bolt of the curse is riven by the omnipotence of the covenant.

Such was the true import of the songs which David was inspired to prepare for the removal of the ark to its resting-place. And as around the ark thus exalted, the son of David, the heir of all human wisdom, was moved and enabled to build afterwards a gorgeous temple, adorning it with every beauty that nature could furnish or art could fabricate; so around the body of Christ gathers the lofty structure of men built up as lively stones into a spiritual temple, showing some of the foundations here upon earth, but resplendent and completed in that upper world. Whether the Psalmist foresaw all this, we cannot decide. We have reason to suppose that the resurrection was, as it were, present to his mind. His graphic description of the ascension, fuller even than the simple narrative of the gospel, looks like the enraptured language of one who beheld afar off the achievement of this triumph. Possessed with such hopes, if not with such visions, David strips himself of a monarch's attire, and walks with high and low as a servant of God. He rejoices in the procession, and stimulates the people to exult in the approach of so great a blessing as the Divine presence in the ark.

"But Michal despised him in her heart." She was of that caste which were nursed in the days of Saul. They had not much reality in their religion, except when they were frightened to it, and then a witch or a prophet—sacrificing with their own hands, or impatience at God's commands—either was the resource, as the mood was.

When Saul was ruling, the ark was not inquired of—the tabernacle at Gibeon was enough, any place of worship, though God was not there in His covenant presence. Michal was a woman nursed in the lap of such religion, at her father's house. The covenant presence of God, in a peculiar manner, did not suit her philosophy. She was very glad to see the king honor religion, but not to make so much of it, not to see him such an enthusiast—to see him forgetting his painted royalty, and abusing himself to honor a gilded chest. She thought meanly of him, and expressed her contempt of his superstition, showing the root of her feelings in the language of pride. So was it when the Ark of the Covenant went up to the tabernacle and the holy place where angels dwell. Apostles were emboldened and thrilled by the gifts of this ascension, and the mockers despised them in their heart, and said, "These men are full of new wine." Paul is obliged to vindicate himself, because he spoke of the resurrection, and to declare to those who despised him in their heart, "I am not mad." The kingdom of the covenant spreads, and the historian records it with contempt, as the diffusion of "a pestilent superstition." And the same feeling that nerved the Pagan against Christianity, now swells the bosom of many who despise the Church in their heart. They can acknowledge a state religion, but they cannot honor the ark of the covenant. Such spirits are Jeffrey in the Scotch Court of Sessions, and Hobbes in the school of philosophers, and Macaulay in the list of state-religionists, and the hundred echoes from this land of Sauls.

It is, too, true that the same feeling has overspread even the Church itself. You will observe that, by the appointment of the Church, this is one of the principal festivals in the year; it is made equal with Christmas in every respect — special psalms, special lessons, special days of preparation—the festival joy carried through many days and impressed upon the Sunday that follows, and the communion expected to be administered in its celebration. But just in proportion as the Divine presence in the Church has been forgotten, just so far has this day been neglected. I know no name for such Christianity, but to call it the faith of Michal, which was the unbelief of Saul. It was the direct antagonist of David's faith. Saul was no more strictly the enemy of David, nor David more strictly the preserver of Saul, than the religion of the day is the contemner of holy places and sacred events, and the Church is the maintainer of Christian religion in the world. The ascension of Christ, to be at one and the same time present in heaven for us, and present with us by covenant, is virtually lost from doctrine. Common Christianity is but common morality. Reverence for holy places decays. Observance of Christian events diminishes. Knowledge of Christian truth vanishes. It is no shame to be an unbaptized Gentile. It is no terror to hear that he who believeth not shall be damned. It is no persuasion to hear that "except one be born of water and the Spirit, he cannot see the kingdom of God," and to hear the answer of Jesus to our delays and doubts and wanderings, "He that cometh unto me, I will in no wise cast out."

Upon us rests the hallowing of these days—the commemoration of these cardinal facts. Let us be elated with joy and animated to all diligence in the praise of God, for our Saviour is in heaven, and here with us. He comes among the two or three, as cheerfully as He ascends among the throngs of angels. "O clap your hands all ye people; shout unto God with the voice of triumph!"

A king is gone up to possess the empire of the universe, and we are heirs with Him. Death is vanquished, and the doors of heaven opened to all believers, and we are followers by the same pathway. Sin, that binds and tortures, and drags to earth, and howls and jeers around us, that is now the voice of a multitude to intimidate, and now the voice of enchantment to allure—sin, that rages and triumphs around and struggles within us, that makes hasty words and bitter thoughts, that cools our affections and obstructs our prayers—that threatens our salvation, and intercepts the view of the recompense—sin is carried to the gates of heaven in bondage, "captivity captive."

"Chains of my heart—Avaunt! I say.
I will arise, and in the strength of love,
Pursue the bright track, ere it fade away—
My Saviour's pathway to His home above."

XXIII.

THE PISGAH BURIAL.

DEUT. 34, part of 4th verse.

"I have caused thee to see it with thine eyes, but thou shalt not go over thither."

PRE-EMINENT among the evidences of accuracy in the Sacred Scriptures, and among the admonitions of Divine retribution, are the inspired records of infirmities and sins charged upon the heroes and exemplars of the narrative, and of punishments surely and severally ensuing. The great legislator of the Hebrews, the miraculously preserved and guided liberator of his nation, the hero of one hundred and twenty eventful years, is dismissed from our view, ascending the craggy heights of Abarim to behold along the western horizon the promised domain towards which his life of pilgrimage had panted, and gifted only with the glimpse, to lie down and die. Nor is this represented as a mere parable, preaching human disappointment, effort struggling through life only to reach the vision of unattained objects. It is the retribution of heaven, and not the calamity of earth. The hero stands upon Pisgah, a monument stationed upon that height, to commemorate not success, but defeat,—not the advance of the tabernacle displacing the barbarities of Canaan, but the baffling of hope and energy and merit by the sinfulness of man. Upon the plain at the foot of Nebo was spread out the camp of the covenant. The hopes of mankind,— the promises which cheered philanthropy, were deposited in that camp. Within its shelter were oracles published by the great Creator,—lessons which were to transmit principles of wisdom to all ages,—histories that contained the facts of twenty-five centuries, and traced the motions of the finger of God from the building of a world to His last guidance of this wandering people. Imagine the emotions of such a man as the Hebrew Prophet, forsaking this people at the borders of Canaan, and mounting the steep of Pisgah to descry in the distance the land of their future rest, while he must now part with them, and in the solitudes of the mountain find his burial. If there be such an impulse as disinterested patriotism, (and who can dispute it without betraying his own incapacity for it?)—if patriotism can take root and grow in the human soul, he must have felt its power. If sympathies and gentle affections are formed between old and tried friends, and the participation in the fortunes of a neighborhood fastens links of attachment upon the familiars of a quarter century, with what intensity must affections have glowed in a man so pure, so meek, so compassionate, towards the intimates of forty years, partners in a weary journey through a strange land.

In many a sorrow, they had grieved together. They had witnessed, as groaning brethren, the haughty insults of Egypt. In periods of alarm they had trembled as one frame, and over victories achieved by Omnipotence for them, they had chanted as one voice, their hymns of thanksgiving. Their leader out of bondage had been their protector from the hour of escape. He had averted destruction, and drawn them to himself, as the purchase of his own intercession. They were, to human view, his people, saved by his patriotism, indebted to his mediation, dependent upon his direction, sustained by his encouragements, and restored by his patience and firmness.

Why, then, could he not be spared to pass with his trust over Jordan? Why must he leave them at the threshold of their habitation?

There is no cloud of death upon his eye,—no ravage in his frame, to make desirable a release from his misery. Decrepitude has not disabled him for the marches of the army, nor timidity disturbed his purpose. "His eye was not dim, nor his natural force abated."

In the midst of his vigor, God summons him to die. The voice, which had conducted him through so many deaths, bids him take his farewell of life, and within sight of the delightful home for his people, to surrender his soul to his Maker. He treads the acclivities of Abarim; the tents of Israel are stretched upon the plain below; no human sorrows dim his eye; heroic through life, he dares to be composed in death; the thought of

Hor and of his brother who went up its sides never to return, comes upon him, and it revives the memory of the sin in which they both partook, and for which he, like Aaron, must die in the mount. But an earthly reward and pleasure are still before him. The land he may not enter, he is to behold. The inheritance not possessed, he is yet by vision to enjoy. With alacrity he climbs the farthest peaks of the ridge, and from the summit of Pisgah, gifted perhaps like Christ, on the pinnacle of temptation, with new powers of vision, he surveys the length and breadth of Canaan. "And the Lord said unto him, This is the land which I sware unto Abraham, unto Isaac, and unto Jacob, saying, I will give it unto thy seed: I have caused thee to see it with thine eyes, but thou shalt not go over thither."

His earthly recompense was ended. The eyes, regaled with this glance at the fields of promise, closed upon the scenes of earth. He was alone with God, rapt in the memories of the past, in the prospects of a brilliant future, and the soul eager to hide itself from fellowships of sin, and bury itself in glory, was carried to its God. It is said, that angels waited upon the obsequies due to his body. His sepulchre was never violated by the hand of idle curiosity. We read, that the Lord buried him. Perhaps it was that angel of the covenant, the Lord, manifest in these latter days, on whose transfigured body in the mount Moses was an attendant,—perhaps it was this Son of God, who then appeared in his human form to solemnize the rite of burial, and honor as a Saviour the lifeless flesh of the lawgiver. I would not pause, however, to unravel the conjectures respecting this event. It is enough to leave the great man to his rest, with the instruction derived from the pious and harmless gloss of the Rabbins. The record is that he died "at the mouth of the Lord," which the Chaldee paraphrast renders, "by a kiss of the Word of Jehovah," and which the Jews interpret, "that God embraced Moses, and drew his soul out of his body by a kiss," as it were, charming his soul out of the body in unutterable raptures, such as Paul experienced, transporting visions of God, and of the Canaan where no sorrow comes. He saw the better land, and his soul went over thither.

The occasion of his death at this time is no secret to us. He was forewarned of his disappointment, and instructed to regard it as the retribution pursuing a public and aggravated offence.

To obtain such a view of his transgression, as he must have found in the moments of repentance, we must retrace the last forty years of his life. We must behold him just emerging from the scene of deliverance at the Red Sea, and conducting a degenerate and rebellious people through the parched and terrible wilderness. Drought oppresses them. A madness spreads among the thirsting multitude. A horrid death stares upon them. In alarm and vexation, they accuse the daring man, who had led them from the graves of Egypt to the heats and thirst and maddened death of the desert.

God bids him strike with the rod of so many miracles the granite side of Horeb.

> "From its disparted side
> Adown the mount the gushing torrent ran."

It was the typical Christ,—the fountain opened in the desert for him that thirsts for righteousness. Moses was by the act reinstated in the confidence of his people. On this miracle, his power to supply in any exigency was established. For forty years, amid their murmurings, no renewal of this miracle was needed. Finally, as their tedious circuits brought them nearer to their rest, and the last year of wandering was begun, in waiting upon the funereal honors for Miriam, at Kadesh-barnea, there was no water for the congregation. Rebellion was muttered from their faithless hearts. They knew not that the same Rock followed them, which poured forth its refreshing stream at Rephidim. Moses and Aaron are bidden again to speak to the rock in Meribah, and behold the perpetual fountains of Divine forbearance.

The lawgiver was for once transported with passion. His meekness forsook him, and with the raging eloquence of pride and disdain and anger, he addresses the people as "rebels,"—he flings out a vaunt of his miracle at Horeb,—he assumes the power of commanding the streams from the rock at his own option, and smites it once and again, when bidden to speak to the rock. Alas! The mighty is fallen. The meekest man is the public spectacle of proud, and irreverent, and presumptuous passion. The lustres which had illumined his face, were obscured. The man who had spoken with God upon Sinai, and came down burnished with the lingering splendors of his Divine communion, was overtaken by infirmity when he dealt with man, and the cloud of human woes gathered over him from this sin at Meribah. And this sin shrouded him with its penalties. It was the barrier, more formidable than the flood of Jordan, which excluded him from the promised land. It was the enemy that robbed him of his brother, and buried the companion of his whole career upon the heights of Hor. It was the avenger that chased him to the mountain-top, and as he gazed upon the landscape of Canaan and the home of peace and abundance provided for his people, laid the fatal rod upon him, and left his body in the dust of Moab.

Because he had not sanctified the Lord in the presence of the people,—because he had substituted his own indignation for the denunciations of the Almighty,—because, as inspiration notes it, "he spake unadvisedly with his lips," his sin pursued him, and with the object of his earthly hopes before him, his sin appeared to baffle and upbraid. The voice, whose utterances had been encouragement and might to his harassed spirit, came at last like the cruelties of remorse, "I have caused thee to see it with thine eyes, but thou shalt not go over thither."

Let us view this infliction, then, in its moral bearing, and in its uses as a type or figure of our lot under Providence.

We are to regard this Hebrew lawgiver as a man actuated by exalted motives. His whole history is a living verification of this remark. He was an example of most eminent virtue. With unsullied character he broke from the charms of the Pharaonic court, and with most generous and persevering philanthropy and piety, he espoused the cause and shared the reverses of the people of God. We challenge the instance of such virtue beyond the pale of Christian grace. He rose out of a world of festering corruption, in an age when nothing was to be borrowed from the past, nothing of the present to be imitated, and he displayed a system before which the institutes of man sink to puerility and fable, and a character which Minos and Lycurgus, Solon and Zaleucus may have striven to emulate, but could not eclipse. His aim was not to found a religion, but to lay the foundations of virtue. He would have erected no empire, but that of allegiance to the author of wisdom and of holiness. "Sparta formed soldiers; Rome, conquerors; Carthage, merchants and navigators;" but Moses would have formed saints. We pronounce him, in a mere worldly view, the most celebrated and the most beneficent lawgiver, that preceded the grace of Christ.

We see him aiming to conduct his charge into the land of Canaan. We see him preserved through manifold perils, and more invulnerable than the charmed favorites of poetic fable. His purpose is almost accomplished. We look to see his entrance of triumph into the land beyond the

Jordan. A single act dashes from his hand the possession he had almost grasped. He died, with his work unfinished. That is the moral of his life, and of his punishment. He wrought well, but he did not attain his end. He moved in the paths of piety and of hope, but he reached not the promise. Virtue was his, and victory, and communion with God, and a glimpse of Canaan, and the kiss of Jehovah, and the tranquil sleep of holiness, and angels to fill his grave, and clusters of rewards waiting his soul beyond the Jordan of death, but in this life he was baffled. He was taken away in the midst of his days. The Son of man came, while the garments of the prophet were laid aside for work.

And this was the penalty of his unadvised speech. He could foresee, as every heroic philanthropist can foresee, the desirable object yet to be attained, but he cannot taste the fruits of his journeyings in the abode of rest. Happier far was his repose in the cemetery of the patriarchs' souls. But his earthly aim was left unsecured.

For our admonition are these things written,—not for wrestlings over the conjectural passages of the narrative, but for profit by its moral.

Holy and beneficent though our purpose be,—ardently and courageously though we pursue it,—discomfited and thwarted though we appear,—we must not yield to the tempter. We may mourn in the ears of God, but we must not rail before men. A single offence breaks the cord of blessings, and dismisses us from earth with our work undone.

There is, unquestionably, before every soul that liveth, a certain task-work within its capacity, and, by the help of God, within its reach. "To one five talents, to another two, and to another one; to *every man* according to his *several* ability." — S. Matt. xxv : 15. We are protected through infancy, and nurtured in virtue, and endowed by grace, for the purpose of directing us to this work. And if the eye could be kept single, so that the whole body should be full of light,—that is, if our conscience could be kept pure so that beams of illumination could shine from the Spirit upon our understanding, we should proceed directly to our desired task, and accomplish it manfully. But so many indulged passions, so many earthly interests, so many untamed desires swerve us from rectitude, that our doom is disappointment. And what is the result? How does it affect the termination of our career? Alas! we read the answer in the announcement of departing souls, — they are summoned away in peace, but they groan under an oppressive consciousness that their work is not finished. And the thought that comes, as they look off from Pisgah, is that they needed not the wisdom of age, but the conscience of innocence. The folly that leaves its sting, is the want of uprightness, and not the want of craft. If we would depart in the sublime confidence of Christ, "I have finished the work which thou gavest me to do,"—we must with cleansed conscience sanctify the Lord in our hearts, and fling away the wilfulness and vexation that betrayed and slew the meekest man. Our perseverance will bring us to a mountain-height, whence we may descry the inheritance of the people of God,—but the vigilant,—the consistent Christian shall here on earth taste the vintage of Canaan,—he shall experience the calm that betokens an eternal rest, and while in death angels caress his released soul, he will find no chilly Jordan to cross; but exchange the Canaan of an earthly reward for the surrounding delights, the descending raptures of his heavenly rest.

Now, my brethren, is the season of preparation for this happy event, Mock not at the entreaties of God. He would draw you towards the fields of promise. Hearken to His voice, and you will find it decoying you from pleasure to pleasure, and from glory to glory. It is a Father that speaks.

Does not your heart echo to the poet's wish?

> " O, that without a lingering groan
> I may the welcome word receive;
> My *body* with my *charge* lay down,
> And cease at once to *work* and *live*."

Choose with Moses, rather to suffer affliction with the people of God, than to enjoy the pleasures of sin for a season,—and a home with which earth's comforts are as dust compared with the stars, shall open to your vision,—open to your admission,—He shall cause thee to see it with thine eyes, and to go over thither.

XXIV.

TIMID WOMEN.

ST. MARK xvi. 5, 6, 8.

"And entering into the sepulchre, they saw a young man sitting on the right side, clothed in a long white garment; and they were affrighted.

"And he saith unto them, Be not affrighted: Ye seek Jesus of Nazareth, which was crucified; he is risen. . . . .

"And they went out quickly, and fled from the sepulchre; for they trembled and were amazed; neither said they anything to any man; for they were afraid."

LANGUAGE seems here to accumulate itself in the effort to express timidity. Other evangelists brighten up the coloring by throwing a streak of joy along the margin of alarm, when the women fled from the sepulchre to announce the angel's message of resurrection. But St. Mark obviously aims at giving prominence and emphasis to the fact that these morning visitants at the birth-place of our triumph were agitated with fear, and that this timorous, startled, unnerved condition of mind prevailed over all other feelings. This commotion in their minds was produced by two facts, either of which would occasion some trepidation; and was increased by the surprise that met them with new wonders at every step. One needs habitual presence of mind, and he needs a good degree of strength of character to be always well-balanced and secure against a tremulous feeling under abrupt and repeated surprises. Mere goodness that keeps the conscience quiet—or mere ardor of affection, throwing all the emotions into the one posture of excited affection, will not secure one against a timidity under surprise.

Had these women been schooled in self-possession, however, two alarming facts woke their reasonable fears.

The body of their Redeemer was missing from the tomb. They supposed that rancor had exhausted itself in consigning Him to death, and in placing the soldierly watch around His sepulchre. What new indignities for this harmless majesty had been devised? Was not even love to be permitted to express its sorrow? If they could not screen the living, are they to be forbidden to bemoan the dead?

Unconscious of any rescue for that inanimate body, their only hope was that the intensity of their grief would so far be respected as to admit the last offices to the lifeless, for which their spices and ointments had been prepared. With all their thoughts concentrated upon this duty, and without a film of doubt to change the direction of their feelings, they discover an utter disappointment, so unaccountable, so confounding with its obscurity, so crushing to the last foothold on which their hearts had stood, that there could be no emotion left for them but vague alarm—that frightened, shattered state of soul when all is excitement, and danger is known to be on every side, but how and when it shall fall upon us, or how disastrous it may become, the howling darkness will not tell.

The narrative introduces another circumstance that agitated these mourning women. Within the rocky cavern where they sought to embalm the beloved dead, they find a living stranger. The linen shroud of the buried is not upon him,—the napkin that covered the head of Jesus is folded and carefully laid aside, as if there had been no haste and no perturbation in conquering that rigidity of death; but, sitting calmly there, was the "young man, clothed in a long white garment," whose presence gave occasion to a new whirlwind of fears.

We that know the magnificence of the event can see a propriety in such angelic attendants waiting around the tomb of a heavenly Master, and we find no difficulty in the alarm of the women at this strange apparition, because we have already imagined the scene of the breaking twilight, when the angel came upon the wings of the morning, shaking the earth with his footsteps, flashing terror from his eyes that prostrated the armed soldiers, and with the touch of his hand snapping the clasp upon the stone and rolling its huge mass from the mouth of the sepulchre. When the vision made those sworn and vigilant keepers to shrink and swoon like dying men, is it wonderful that two timid women should have been startled into fright? We admit that there was no such portent in the quiet object before them, as in the giant power which had felled the guards before the tomb. But the visitation was on the same errand and from the same source. It was the ministry of angels that was so terrific to men who confessed no fear, and so mild to timid women who made no concealment of their fright.

And herein is a great part of the mystery, and the greater part of the moral.

Thus it was mysterious that a set of armed, hireling, dare-devil men should be hurled shuddering to the earth by the mere glance of that angelic eye, and yet that the placid features and the soothing tongue of a similar being should simply have affrighted women who were already smitten with panic. I say, that this is unaccountable except upon the principle of God's presence, and conscience realizing that appeal—the inward nature of the men feeling that power " which makes cowards of us all," and the natural timidity of the women not being eradicated by the power that was mildly revealed to comfort and cheer.

It was so surprising, as to be in a certain sense mysterious, also, that this angelic apparition should have been disclosed to the view of the women on three occasions at this sepulchre, but never once to the disciples. Sometimes it is two angels, "the one at the head and the other at the feet where the body of Jesus had lain," and again one sitting at the door; they seem to appear and to vanish at pleasure; Magdalen sees them both in the very spot where Peter and John discovered no one. And Magdalen at her first approach to the sepulchre had not beheld them. No hypothesis of a phantasm meets the case. The flitting phantom does not assume the ordinary human features, but here was always a guise which was neither lustrous nor horrid, as mere imagination would discern. The painted illusion of the mind does not wear the same form to both beholders, as this appeared to Mary and Salome. It does not speak to two hearers at once, as the young man soothed the startled women. And that was not imaginary, which was one form to the two spectators, and two forms to the Magdalen; which at one time says, "Be not afraid," and at another, "Why weepest thou?" addressing different emotions; which at no time suggests to the imagination that it may be the revived Jesus, and yet declares what hundreds of witnesses afterwards verified, that the form which imagination would have conjured at the tomb, should be seen upon the mountain in Galilee. The indications of a phantasm are not present. And yet the heavenly messenger announces the resurrection of Jesus, sends special messages by the women to the disciples, proves by his very language that he comes from the source of revelation, and then leaves disciples to take this triumphant gospel from the lips of women.

Is there any mystery here to confound our reason? Nay, it rather accords with our expectation when we read by the light of a compensating Providence. She that showed forth the glory of her sex by being "last at the cross and first at the sepulchre," was rewarded by the first hearing of the gospel in its victory, and that from the lips of a heavenly preacher. She that lent her ear to the breath of the evil angel, and imported death by her tongue, listens first to the good angel and conveys upon her lips the sweet message of eternal life. She that began our woes by not fearing the wily stranger, crowns our joys by trembling at the presence of the innocent angel. Or if we fling from our hands these threads of allusion that bind together the grave yawning in Eden and the tomb unlocked by Christ, yet we cannot dismiss the physical fact that so much of heaven appeared to the affection of women, which was denied to the harder and more critical disposition of disciples that were men. It is the Easter parable, taken from the traits of our sexes. It puts the seal of the resurrection on the fact that there are elemental differences of soul in the sexes, and that heaven addresses itself differently to them here on earth, and may comfort them with just as marked diversities after the resurrection. Some have adopted an interpretation still more derogatory to man, or rather showing why he is adapted to a dominion among the earthly elements which may be his no more among the heavenly.

"Passionate sorrow, strong feeling, ardent devotion, these have eyes to gaze into the unseen world; while sounder or sterner sense and discerning judgment, that sees and weighs difficulties and human consequences, does not pass beyond the veil; the former qualities are more characteristic of women, the latter of men."

My brethren, it is not to be disputed that there is always this abundance of mystery, and of corresponding speculation, whenever the vaster and better universe droops into contact with our lower sphere. But there is a moral instruction intended always to reach us by this condescension of the higher intelligence. The greater humbles itself to instruct the less exalted. The mightier touches us to impart of its strength. Heaven comes to us not that we may tremble, but that we may learn. It is the method of things in the very order of the earthly elements. The blessings which would plant themselves in the ground, roll themselves first in mantles of the air. They harness the lightnings to their car. They yoke themselves with power, and brandish in the sky the tokens of swiftness and force. They come thundering and startling, but their object is to refresh, to fertilize, to show the springing up of blessings by this descent of wonderful power.

And herein is a symbol of what was proposed by that exertion of Divinity which met the timid women at the tomb.

It was power, superior heavenly power—the vague, the unmeasured, the boundless—which fell upon their view, and turned all their other strong emotions into fear. That was for the moment the prevailing sense, which excluded all other sensations.

And they received the gospel of resurrection, the consolation of Christ, only by first recognizing and trembling before a power adequate to this victory over the greedy grave.

The instruction thus looms upon us — first, to this effect; that the timidity of the women was nothing more or less than the usual effect of heaven revealing its presence to our human nature. Woman, as the weaker being, is presumed to be more naturally fearful, on the keener watch for danger; and, unless driven beyond herself by some other passion, the most subject to the sense of fear. And for this reason the heavenly power when revealed to woman, indulges her timidity and hides its majesty under gentler forms.

Fear is the tribute of our human nature to this superior grandeur. And fear is the posture in which the best and bravest of men have encountered heavenly visions.

You will think of Saul of Tarsus, a man of unblenched courage, quailing before the light and voice that threw a heavenly reproof into his soul, and left him trembling and astonished. You have admired the defiant bravery of Daniel, afraid of neither edict nor conspiracy, neither of the frowning monarch nor of the growling beast, but, with sinews hardened in prayer, withstanding terrors. But behold this unflinching champion, when the heavenly visitant drew near, and, as if he were but a timid woman, put on the form of the courteous gentleman. It was as the appearance of a man, and there was not even a sound to inspire terror—for he says, "it was a man's voice between the banks of Ulai;" yet he confesses "I was afraid, and fell upon my face, and I, Daniel, fainted and was astonished at the vision."

And this was the hero that challenged all Babylon to shake his nerves. This was the man that dared to decipher those letters which blanched the cheeks of Belshazzar, and dared to utter scornful messages to haughty and debauched monarchs.

How weak, how frightened, how womanly this man of prowess, when by the side of Hiddekel that heavenly angel re-appears, and the trembling prophet confesses his fear—"By the vision my sorrows are turned upon me, and I have retained no strength."

It is just as if the glorious heaven which first came near to breathe into us the living soul, could not again even by one of its deputies approach us without attracting that life into a shiver and a sigh. The three choicest Apostles converse with their heaven-descended Master day after day, and all his utterances, all his acts are wonderful, but there is no tremor in their hearts; they attend him up the mountain, where the heavenly origin of the man illuminates His transfigured body, and the ancient tenants of Paradise hold their permitted interview with Him that holds the keys of death and hell—and where are your intrepid Apostles? Trembling on the ground, afraid to speak, afraid to be silent, confounded in their speech, and disconcerted in every faculty. Years of experience roll on. Miracles have made the supernatural familiar to them. The risen Jesus has disarmed the grave of its terrors, and the ascending Jesus has made that heavenly home a welcome theme, an awaited refuge. You would expect the beloved John, the bosom Apostle, the eagle-eyed observer of heavenly things, to catch the view of that stupendous scenery without one nerve disordered, with no other thrill than the ecstasy of pleasure. Lo! he sees the gorgeous form in heaven; he sees his departed Master, no longer the weary man of sorrows, but with the grander life now owned by Him forever, and the paralyzed Apostle yields his breath in terror, and "falls at his feet as dead."

We cease to be surprised that the women meeting heaven at the sepulchre showed themselves timid. We are only assured that the heavenly apparition disguised its glory, and moderated its aspect into mildness, lest the womanly fear should have disqualified them for the heavenly announcement.

The ulterior, perhaps the ultimate instruction is the logical sequel of our course of thought—to this effect—that a certain degree of timidity is the preparative in a woman's disposition for the favors of heaven, and for more and more of that heavenly favor which beautifies her to the angels, and is better than life itself. She gains nothing truly, though she gains a platform or a ballot, when she loses this weaker grace of retirement and quietness. Her strength is in the attitude of soul which relies upon virtue and God. She is like the weakest of nations that may be the most invulnerable because its alliances are the strongest. We have called her timid, so that we may discriminate between her that shrinks from the shadow of danger, and "the bold bad woman" who is proverbially dangerous. Fortitude is no slight element in the pure womanly character. It is in some of its aspects more conspicuous in the weaker than in the master sex—more noted in her because she is weaker, less advantageously placed in society for exhibitions of bravery; but also more eminent in the serenely enduring woman, than in her vaunting, self-asserting, and enthusiastic but impatient and irritable partner. Man will nerve and solidify his masculine energy to breast the great evil which he is proud to resist, and deems it glorious to defy; but the meek, all-enduring, unexhausted fortitude of the woman sustains the fret, and charge, and perpetual sting of a thousand minute evils which would hector us out of our patience. And not the least of these evils for her helplessness is the fact which our manliness fails to appreciate, that she cannot help herself by assumption, and boldness, and self-assertion without forfeiting more than her arrogant victory will gain.

Perhaps we have departed from modern phrase, and from ancient precept, in commending feminine excellence because it is *timid.* We would describe that which in the phrase of the times, is patient but modest. We place a gulf between the strong-hearted and the strong-minded—a gulf like that which Lazarus could not cross, nor could the wearer of purple and fine linen cross to him.

We employ the most impressive term, and insist upon a virtue so opposite to the fashion of the day, that the false ambition for unsexing modesty would stigmatize our very virtue as timidity. We purposely fling our protest into the arena, when the scheme is to make the twenty-four hours neither daylight nor dark—to render society one huddled mass of virtues neither generously masculine, nor sweetly feminine—but all of life one even twilight, the witching hour for purblind bats, with neither courtesy nor modesty to elevate the honor of each sex.

The theme itself unwraps a series of valuable propositions for young women.

They will not so exceed in modesty as to deem nothing intended for them, when I speak for their benefit.

You ask me to expand my definition of the modest grace that is a heavenly cosmetic. Perhaps I shall speak prudently, though I speak as a man. It is to seek for wisdom from the experienced; in lowliness of mind to esteem others better than yourself; to flee the haunts of temptation; to repress the sallies of vanity; to nip affectation in the bud; to recoil from the voice of flattery; to turn a deaf ear to the persuasions of ambition; to hush the flippant voice which carps at the merits of others; to banish from the thoughts the syren that whispers elegant words of extravagance, and honeyed words of aspiration; to honor all men and dishonor no women; to make yourself the friend of the poor and the suffering, not by sentimental sighs over pathetic novels, but by good deeds that abridge your own finery and clothe the naked; to scorn the mean advantages of artfulness; and to uphold with due regard them that uphold the virtues of society. I am not a fanatic, I am not an inconsistent advocate of ostentatious plainness, when I ask for the outward tokens of feminine modesty in propriety and becoming simplicity of apparel. So pronounces St. Paul, when, in contradistinction to decorations consisting in "gold and pearls, and costly array," he directs that "women" should "adorn themselves with shamefacedness." You revolt against this sumptuary law of St. Paul. You deem him often severe against your sex, and transported by his own zeal against a gaudy world. Take then the counsel of St. Peter, modernized for the times: "Whose adorning let it not be that outward adorning of frizzing the hair, and of wearing of gold, or of putting on of apparel, but the ornament of a meek and quiet spirit,"—poor passports to the purlieus of pride, but beautiful jewels to win the admiration of angels, "in the sight of God of great price."

Why, my young friends, nothing can be plainer than that the Scriptures propose for the female sex a retiring character. To be "keepers at home," which means not only sufficiently staying within doors, but "keeping" the things that belong in doors; to "guide the house," which is something more than doing small talk in the drawing-room; to be "obedient to their husbands," if they have one, and if not, then obedient to some law of usefulness; to "bring up their children," and not wonder why the parson or the schoolmaster has not done it; to unite "fear," *i. e.*, modesty, and respect, and humility, with "chaste conversation;" *not to be* "idlers," nor "tattlers," nor "busybodies," nor "wanderers from house to house;"

these are the sharp outlines which Scripture draws.

"Against that character the prevailing system of modern education and modern proceedings declares war." "Adorning with shamefacedness," how old fashioned. The superior taste and breeding of a polished age have annulled this maxim. Derision hoots at the antiquated grace of "shamefacedness." The pupil who is unfortunate enough to betray symptoms of a tendency to exemplify it, hears her conformity to a scriptural model, her observance of a scriptural duty, pronounced vulgarity, and ignorance of the world; and is taught that the "adorning" which God has bestowed and enjoined, is, in the eyes of enlightened fashion, a blemish and disgrace. The leading concern of aspiring and misjudging guardians seems too often to be first to train up the pupil in accomplishments for the purpose of display; and afterwards to push her into situations contrived for display. Is it wonderful that effrontery comes to be termed politeness; that general and unabashed familiarity is misnamed ease and perfection of manners; that frivolous youth runs into insipid age; that womanly charms are the bold manners of unmanageable maidens and undomesticated wives.

Rise up, ye careless women, to behold the dignity which God and His angels see in the meek and quiet spirit.

Be ashamed of the fashionable customs—be ashamed of the social revolutions, which dethrone your modesty, and cast contempt upon your pure and holy fears.

"Be not ashamed when it concerneth thy soul. For there is a shame that bringeth sin; . . . and there is a shame which is glory and grace." "Be thou not ashamed of the law of the Most High."

It is that law which assigns you your place and your privileges in this society of earth, and shall allot you infinite rewards if God's will shall be with you paramount to every passion and every pride, every rubric of pretension, and every bye-law of despotic fashion. "Accept no person against thy soul; and let not the reverence of any man cause thee to fall."

Remember, above all things, that Christianity has been the rescue of woman from degradation and from shame—from bedizened debauchery and from sordid servility—and that woman never looks so magnanimous, and grateful, and brave, as when she bows at the feet of Jesus, and with the natural fervors of her piety confesses Him before man.

XXV.

THE DUTY AND MEANING OF REPENTANCE.

ACTS xvii. 30.

"God now commandeth all men everywhere to repent."

THE sun flashed upon the rock-ribbed hills of Athens. The splendor of his rays gleamed like a diadem from heaven upon the bald head of a preaching philosopher, Paul the aged. The ensigns of idolatry flaunted around him. He stands among the majestic temples, the costly altars, and the piled offerings, which the heart of a people had devoted to their unknown God. The learned of the earth were gathered beside him, the proud moralist was his hearer, the reckless epicurean and the iron stoic were listening for the terms of his new philosophy; from the eminence where the sunlight had found him, he glances out upon a land whose hills and vales and every acre were consecrated to the deities of a mythic religion, upon the monuments reared by pious hands over the graves of heathen virtue, and almost beneath his feet upon the rustling crowds that thronged the streets of Athens in their daily tasks and pleasures. What language shall he utter? Ages had hallowed the religious feeling that lay embosomed within this people. Mouldering rust had long gnawed upon the trophies, which hung as sacred charms, untouched by man, within those temples. How shall the preacher from Damascus open his message within this citadel of heathenism, fortified, and wise, and hallowed? There were eyes fastened upon him, that had danced in the glare of midnight revelry. There were hearts before him elated with the pride of success, and suspicious of some new design against their wealth and power. There were trained and disciplined intellects waiting for some syllable that should flatter their attainments, or for some doctrine on which the curse of novelty might be written, or the battle-ax of their censure might demolish. Ferocity and learning, craft and simplicity, power and servility, the array of human nature in its refined and debased forms was assembled around him. He directs his finger to the inscription of their own bewilderment "To the unknown God," he points to the witness within the breast of each that this God had been insulted and wronged, he stands upon the foundation of a spiritual philosophy that the Godhead is not like unto the graving of art and man's device, he asserts the lofty dignity of man as the child of the Almighty, and adduces the testimony of their own learned oracles; he recalls their long midnight of impiety and blindness, and concludes with the mercies and the message of this revealed God, "The times of this ignorance God winked at, but now commandeth all men everywhere to repent." It was useless to detail the precepts of Christ, it was useless to argue of grace and the motions of the Holy Spirit, it was worse than useless to delineate the beauty of holiness, unless the admonition of conscience was heard, and the voice of God was obeyed, commanding all men everywhere to repent.

A new destiny, O Athens, was thrust upon thy walls and hills and altars, when God commanded thee to repent. The word of life was the message of repentance. Centuries were waking from their dreams at the call from heaven which summoned them to repentance. Once along the margin of the Jordan it was a man in camel's hair, uttering to the people that were versed in the law, "Repent, for the kingdom of heaven is at hand." A prison and the ax of the headsman repay his boldness, and "from that time, Jesus began to preach, Repent, for the kingdom of heaven is at hand." The clouds receive Him, the gift descends in tongues of flame, and the answer to alarmed souls was, "Repent, and be baptized every one of you." An Apostle departing from Ephesus to his persecuted fate, leaves the warrant of his faithfulness in the declaration that he had kept back nothing which was profitable, "testifying both to the Jews and also to the Greeks, repentance towards God, and faith in our Lord Jesus Christ." Among the Jewish worshippers at Pentecost gathered from every land, to the corrupt magician assuming the garb of Christianity, to the centurion with his escort of mercenary followers, to the haughty denizens of imperial Rome, to the believers entangled with the crimes and pleasures of the luxurious Corinth, to the apostates in the churches of Asia, before the half-persuaded tetrarch of Galilee, and in the presence of the polished Athenians, the voice of the apostle was the gospel of his Master, "God now commandeth all men everywhere to repent." We need not therefore, insist upon the obligation of this duty under the gospel, that it is the aim of God's merciful dealings, the goodness of God being designed to lead thee to repentance; that it is the beginning of return to peace, the foundation of the gospel being "repentance from dead works;" that it is a universal duty, to the Jew with his ceremonies, the Gentile with his conscience, repentance towards God being testified; that it is an indispensable obligation, "Except ye repent ye shall all perish;" that it is a positive and imperative duty, "God commanding all men to repent;" that it is an awaited, a blessed, and a rewarded duty, the Father welcoming and "the angels of heaven rejoicing over one sinner that repenteth."

We pass on rather to consider, with the help of God, what is implied in this act of repentance, what is its value, and what the evil of its delay.

In expressing the act of repentance, the writers of the Scriptures have employed two species of terms, the one expressing a change of mind or intent, and implying a corresponding change of life, and the other expressing a change of feeling or concern, and implying an excited affection and a degree of affliction and oppression of spirit. These terms are applied indiscriminately to that repentance which is real and thorough and accepted, and to the partial and rejected counterfeit of the same, which bears the name of the genuine only from its designed resemblance.

As the whole of religion has ever been made the occasion of spurious pretences, of prejudiced misrepresentations, of corrupt counterfeits, of delusion and of hypocrisy, so especially that foundation of true religion, true repentance, has been misrepresented, pretended, perverted, and dishonored. Partly men have through ignorance mistaken the duty required, partly men have through bias feigned the spirit of repentance, partly men have through natural fear or shame displayed the compunctions while they lacked the pure desires of repentance, and the repentance of some has been the vain and desperate struggle to regain by sorrow a privilege that had been bartered and lost by sin. The tears of Esau fell like the droppings of the storm-cloud upon the ocean and upon the plain, swelling only the depths of his woe, but enriching the inheritance of his brother; "he found no place of repentance though he sought it carefully with tears." There is a natural degree of repentance, which can scarcely be called a virtue, because it is involuntary and universal, and yet it is a testimony to our moral capacity, inasmuch as it consists in a guilty reflection upon ourselves. For this reason, even heathen philosophy has pronounced repentance a human affection, a passion implanted in man, "a suffering of the soul which comes from being troubled at our former course." It is manifest, that when the gospel addresses itself to all, and enjoins upon all a positive act of repentance, it is not a requirement of this mere natural emotion, this inevitable and passionate sorrow, which the consequences of crime are sure sooner or later to bring, and which is rather the issue of recklessness in offending, and bitterness in suffering, than of change and tenderness in heart. The repentance of the gospel is sorrow for those things which the gospel condemns, and the change of mind and heart to the choice and pursuit of those things which the gospel approves. The repentance of nature is the power of memory allied with the shrinkings of the flesh. The repentance of nature fears suffering more than the law, and idolizes self without adoring the Maker. The repentance of nature is the weapon of justice, the repentance of the gospel is the instrument of mercy. The repentance of nature is the wound to the heart in the breaking of some link of natural affection, the repentance of the gospel heals where it bruises, and soothes where it tortures. The repentance of nature sinks towards the verge of despair, the repentance of the gospel rises upon the wings of peace and hope.

By observing some of the characters which a false and imperfect repentance possesses in common with that which is true and effectual, we shall be better able to distinguish the nature of this universal duty.

A change in one's habits is a feature of true repentance found also in that which is fallacious and imperfect. The escape from some domineering appetite, the rending of the shackles of habitual indolence, the devotion of one's energies to some newly-exciting employment, the change of association and purpose and manner of life are all compatible with a mere regard to one's interests in this life. A reputation to be retrieved, a wreck of a squandered fortune to be saved, the emoluments of industry and integrity to be secured, or the misery of a destitute life and an ignominious death to be shunned. These are sufficient inducements to restrain the habits of licentious indulgence, or to arouse the torpid limbs of idleness. They reach motives. They foster virtues. Habits are controlled, life is moulded, character is transformed by them. They are the badges of outward reformation. They are the key-notes of a moral change. Thanks to God that our race is not abandoned, that such repentance is vouchsafed to the victim of passion. But all this is not the substance of required repentance. To the Jew, far as he was removed from dissoluteness—to the Greek disciplined in the virtue of his schools, God's unmitigated command was *repentance*. A life reclaimed from a den of debauchery, and elevated to the posts of worldly honor, may yet spurn the name of Jesus, and linger through a career of blasphemy to the doom of impenitence. No, it is not the mere refusal of one sin, nor the mere reformation of certain lawless habits, the sum of the repentance which thousands ever attempt to attain; it is not this that is to win the blessings of the entire reformation comprised in the demand of Christian repentance. Another characteristic of imperfection in this duty, belonging equally to its proper discharge, is regret and sorrow for the past. What miserable victim of indulged vice does not lament the consequences of his crime, as they hang in clouds of distress around him? What abandoned drunkard does not drown the horrors of his soul in new draughts of drugged oblivion? The culprit curses at the gallows the infatuation of his youth, and weeps in anguish for the happy home he deserted and the confidence he betrayed. Oh! how often have we seen the hoary head of age pour forth the tears of sorrow over a misspent life, and yet descend without repentance into a hopeless grave. Encompass any soul with the penalties of its transgression, let pains and agony be laid upon itself and the body, awaken the reflection that these are the just issues of its own errors and crimes, abstract one by one the hopes of relief and rescue, and you are sure to behold the features of a fallacious repentance, the memories of the past odious and bitter, a heart harrowed with regrets, or steeped in desperate oblivion. Wrenched by such repentance, the soul of Judas rushed from the memory of his betrayed Lord to the release of violence.

And if his bloody fate testifies that a false repentance is filled with sorrows for the past, and that this remorse does not withhold the guilty soul from rushing on into dismal atrocities, it also instructs us that the mere sense of guilt is no assurance of accepted repentance. The confession is wrung from the guilty traitor, "I have sinned in that I have betrayed the innocent blood." Does the daring lip of perjury never tremble, as it covers guilt with guilt, and acknowledges its dread of the one by hiding it with the veil of another offence? Does the soul convicted of its guiltiness before God and startled into a momentary uneasiness amid the echoes of Divine warning, does that soul repent when it sees as in the midday the handwriting of its condemnation, and yet refuses to supplicate for the sinner's pardon? No, there is a deathless rankling of remorse, that confesses guilt, and never repents. There is a faithful conscience that rouses itself to reprove and to thunder its sentence of guilt, only to be mocked and crushed and silenced by the impenitence of the proud and obdurate heart. There is a voice that crieth to our souls, "Unclean, unclean;" that finds its echo here when it proclaims that God commandeth all men to repent; that comes with a fearful stillness in the season of recollection and sorrow, and whispers, "Guilty, guilty," but it is hushed into silence without completing its work of a saving repentance.

A false repentance will sometimes restore the fruits of sin, and disown its fraudulent gains. The thirty pieces ringing upon the pavement of the council chamber were the abandoned wages of iniquity, but the putrid corpse of the suicide was the condemning sequel of this repentance. Many an obstinate rejecter of God has purchased his recovery from the misery of his covetous choice if the restitution of the last hour can supersede the necessity of a new heart and a holy life.

The fear of punishment is also an ingredient in the cup of an imperfect repentance. It carries alarm to the soul of the sturdiest criminal. It pursues with its scorpion lash the profligate and oppressive. The fear of punishment lingers, when the tinge of shame has long faded from the face of crime. The fear of punishment brands its characters upon the countenance of the murderer, and seizes upon the hand that trembles to imbrue itself in blood. The fear of punishment hangs like a charmed chain upon the neck of the wicked, and penetrates with its dismal shudderings to the world where repentance is unknown, but the chained prisoners believe and tremble. Neither a mere change in habits, nor a sorrow for the past, nor a sense of guilt, nor a passionate effort at amendment and restitution, nor the foreboding of punishment, and the longing for impunity, make up the act on which the Holy One shall beam the smile of acceptable repentance. This implies a sense not only of guilt, but of a nature prone to sin, and by its very inclination and the corruption of its goodness, guilty; it implies a feeling of helplessness and utter abandonment, unless the Almighty interpose; it entertains no compromise with sin, but abhors and flees from its every form, and its subtle enticements; it rejoices in the service of God as our true allegiance and our only happiness; it resolves in dependence upon His might no more to break the bonds of His law and His love; it proportions its sorrow to the quality of its offences, and the stubborness of its resistance, and the former violence of passion, and the impetuosity of the tempers it would amend, and the magnitude of the mercies and deliverances it has despised. True repentance does not expend itself in alarm and tears, but in the revenges of self-denial and humiliation to our crested pride. True repentance leans, in shame of our disease and ingratitude, and with full trust in God's mercy, upon the staff of His methods. True repentance engages the affections, in its undertaking of amendment, and devotion. As the vapors from the ocean wander in capricious and fantastic forms to the distant mountains and the regions of perpetual storm, and then descend to their original home, sometimes in noisy rivulets, sometimes in deep, majestic rivers, so the souls that sprang from the will of creating Love, return to their home in the flowings of repentance, sometimes in swift and murmuring motion, and sometimes in the majesty of deep and overwhelming force.

I have seen one whose hairs were whitened in the compliances of sin, in the deliberate rejection of the gospel, in the courses of vice and profligacy. I have seen such a soul arrested in its madness, humbled in memory of a heedless and ungodly life, prostrated with grief, groaning for very affliction at its hardness and insensibility, and presenting the very picture of penitent wretchedness; but its emotions of compunction vanished without the promise of obedience and the resolution of surrender to the armament of grace, and an impenitent grave enclosed his last remains. I have seen another calmly resigning his soul to the vows of duty, visited with no tempest of grief, but patiently imploring the Divine help for his helplessness; awaiting no shock of Providence to alarm his slumbering soul, but seeking the gift of a sincere repentance; completing not his repentance with the first essay of amendment, but carrying it on from failing to failing till it should adjust and finish every virtue; I have seen him strengthening in his character, unfolding grace upon grace, and lying down in peace to wait for the consummation of glory.

Let us hear then the voice of the Almighty, as if he stood here addressing each one of us. God now proclaims His will, God now demands the acknowledgment of His goodness and His dominion. God now opens the avenue of return to everlasting life, commanding all men everywhere to repent. Who shall retort upon Him, that repentance is impossible—that repentance is shut up within the secrets of election, when He willeth that none should perish, but that all should come unto repentance? Who shall despise the riches of His forbearance, when He tenders salvation upon the condition of repentance? Is there anything in the act of repentance that can undo the past, that can restore the ruins strewn along the pathway of iniquity? Can repentance summon the victim of the murderer from his bloody grave? Can repentance recall a wasted youth, and regain for the enfeebled frame of age the vigor and the days of strength lost in lust and dissipation? Can repentance snatch the offender from the arm of justice, and reprieve the violator of his country's laws? Can repentance restore the blush to the cheek of violated innocence? Can it erase the lines of affliction that sin's desolating course hath marked upon the heart of the mourning wife, or the dishonored children of a guilty parent? Repentance cannot remand to the hope of salvation, the souls that have entered before it into their portion; it cannot reanimate the dust that was hastened by crime to the bed of corruption; it cannot recall the afflicted spirits of a parent whose reproof was despised, or a friend whose sympathy was touched and wounded; it cannot atone for the past, it cannot arrest the consequences of sin.

Yet God accepts it, " He visits oft the humble hallowed cell, and with the penitent who mourn, 'tis His delight to dwell." It is He that makes the atonement, it is we that follow the condition. It is He that blots out the record of condemnation; it is we that lament its long array. It is He that waiteth to be gracious; it is we that are to perfect holiness in the fear of God, enlarging our repentance as we increase our days.

It was the prayer of one in ancient days, who stood forth in his riper years as the champion of the faith and the agonized wrestler in repentance, whose youth had through the ambition of parents been furnished with all the brilliancy of learning and accomplishments, but whose body was polluted with the vilest excesses, and his soul corrupted into the most abhorrent blasphemies—it was his constant prayer, as the past rushed back upon his conscience, and the future was realized in its revealed terrors; it was his constant prayer, saint though he was, wise and learned as he was, victorious over temptations and over the oppositions of error as he was: "Give me, O Lord, give me the grace of tears."

XXVI.

SYMBOLISMS, AND THEIR SIGNIFICANCY.

EZRA VI : 11.

"Also I have made a decree, that whosoever shall alter this word, let timber be pulled down from his house, and being set up, let him be hanged thereon."

TO one who regards the edifice constructed by the piety of Israelites, and dedicated by the faith of Solomon, as itself the end and the object of all the care and solicitude of heaven, the result must appear entirely incommensurate with the Divine majesty interested, and the Divine vigilance exercised. Our estimate is entirely reversed when the Christian intent of the structure and of the Providence over it enlarges our sense of God's purposes and exalts each item of the fabric and of its history into a sign of spiritual and eternal things. It is beyond dispute that our Lord recognized this significance. He transferred the very name of the temple to His own body, and thus authenticated the Jewish idea that this structure, though doomed to demolition, was a consecrated residence of Divinity. Its designation to honor, however, was not occasioned solely by its being intended to typify something to come, which should be grander and more enduring. It was the repository of oracles which claim our veneration. It was the symbol of that religion which contained the transcript of Divine perfections. It was the centre of a worship more dignified and more purifying even in its moral effects than any nation by philosophy or by refinement had yet attained. The guardianship of God over it had not been that of mere preservation, but was the token of a sovereignty consulting moral ends, and not so much occupied with the sanctity of the place, as with the integrity of the religion and the perpetuation of the truth.

When man ventured to brutalize his own conceptions, and to make the sacredness of the Temple a protection for his perverseness, the Almighty beckoned to the remorseless devotee of Baal that he should invert this decayed sanctity, and prove that Providence was aiming at truth rather than magnificence, that God was authorizing what should elevate and glorify this human nature, rather than pollute and degrade this equivocal image of God.

But God's truth was vindicated when the seventy years of His frown had eradicated the last doubt concerning His jealousy. Under the auspices of Cyrus the search had been successfully made for the foundations of Solomon's structure, and the labor of re-erection had been initiated with the glowing zeal of the Jew, and with the countenance of the Great Empire of the East. Samaritan hostility contrived to impede this enterprise by machinations, bribes, menaces, and calumnies, until fifteen years of this struggle brought the restored Jew to the second year of Darius, and to his active and decided intervention.

We must not infer that these happy turns of events revolved only upon the axle of the royal will. God was touching those secluded agents in their arbitrary power. But was He not stirring the other earthly elements that contribute to His purposes? Does He ever accomplish any such reviving of the depressed piety of man without exerting that power of prophecy which is the token of God's presence?

Read those memorable words of Haggai,—terse and crisp and glowing, when, on Thursday, the 24th of August, he argued with a people who dared to call themselves covenant-keepers, while the cedar of Lebanon was carved to embellish their own homes and the house of God lay waste. Hear him again with the haste of prophecy that would not tarry, on the 13th of October, cheering the people who were roused to build, with those sharp outlines of a glory that should fill God's earthly temple, and be the desire of all nations. Or note those strange pictures in the gallery of Zechariah, who painted not ideals, but visions, and whose imagery was not the hot hopes of human ardor drawn out into color, but God's designs thrown into view.

These were the stimulants that inflamed the hearts which had faltered. With these testimonies of prophecy, these chidings to spur the nerveless, these incitements to animate the desponding, God himself inaugurated and furthered the temple work. The recovered zeal of the Jew was the signal for the renewed intrigue of the Samaritan. He whispered his malignant surmises into the ear of Tatnai, the deputed viceroy of Syria and Palestine. But the Governor, well interpreting the devices of Samaria, referred the question to the magnanimity of the monarch. Darius, partly influenced by his personal friendship for Zerubbabel, and still more by his regard for the memory of Cyrus, whose daughter he loved and married, ordered the edict of Cyrus to be produced from the archives, and confirmed it by a new decree. To every hinderer of the temple restoration he proclaimed his royal warning, "Let the work of this house of God alone." To his satraps he commanded that the Samaritan tribute which their bribery had diverted, should be restored to this sacred work. Upon his own revenue officers he enjoined liberal payments in aid of the Jews, and ample supply of all materials needed for their sacrifices. And that these injunctions might be not only ratified as irrepealable, but sealed with the invocation of Providence, he appends his prayer to the God who had placed His name in the house of Jerusalem, and fortifies one decree with another, denouncing this penalty, "Whosoever shall alter this word, let timber be pulled down from his house, and being set up, let him be hanged thereon."

To appreciate the actual stage of human civilization at the era of this favor from a Gentile king to the humiliated nation of God's covenant, we must cast our eye over those portions of the globe which have transmitted to us so ancient a history. Egypt, as representing all the cultivation of Northern Africa, was now a province of the Persian monarch. The vast Assyrian empire had for twenty years been a gem in the diadem of conquest which now graced the brow of Darius. The puerile fables and the gross traditions that had amused and debased the millions of the far east, were vanishing before the wonderful ethics and the high conceptions of the Chinese sage, Kong-fuh-chuh, who had just propagated a new philosophy, the elements of which are suspected to have been transported eastward by the scattered tribes of Israel. Towards the west, that Macedonian kingdom which Alexander two hundred years afterwards enlarged into a mammoth empire, was at this time tributary to Persia. The vaster Roman empire was then no more than an emporium upon the Tiber for a feeble Latin confederacy, not yet pretentious enough to invite the cupidity or match the strength of Carthage, although that was little more than New Jersey. Learning had reached its scientific climax at Athens, and deemed itself perfect because it had invented charts and guessed at globes. In one word, Darius was the master of civilization. His act was the tribute rendered by the possessor of supreme earthly authority to the majesty of God. His empire was, more than that of Cyrus, the summing up of Gentile forces. Everything else was too diminutive to be then alluring, or too barbarous to be capable of interpreting the spiritual system which the Hebrew's tenacity could not be forced to abandon.

This, then, is the moral of the facts. When the chance of saving God's Church, and the means for maintaining high spiritual truths appear to human calculation most desperate, then God shows that it is His hand which rescues, and His Spirit that moves the hearts of men. By the aged Daniel, uncorrupted by the caresses, as he had been unshaken by the cruelties of Babylon, the Almighty wins the homage of Cyrus. He sends prophetic fire from above into the souls of Haggai and Zechariah, and they warm the chilled hopes of the temple builders. He aggrandizes the dominion of Darius, and, at the same time, breathes into his soul the reverence which persuades the monarch to stand in awe of the Eternal One, who had avenged Himself upon Egypt, Nineveh and Babylon.

The language of Darius, when it concerns these topics of God's honor and spiritual worship, is no longer the voice of superstition. He speaks as an interpreter of Providence. He becomes like one of God's anointed. We hear him, as a potentate, addressing not his own generation only, but echoing through all the ages. It is the utmost of earthly power speaking to the last generation of earthly pride, and commanding it not to forfeit its earthly ambitions by impeding him that builds the house of God. It is the tone of prophecy blending with God's ordinance of power, and bidding the world abstain from hindering the sacred labor which pertains to the worship of God. It is the anticipation of the voice of Christ, proclaiming Himself the corner-stone of Providence, the foundation-stone of grace, and "on whomsoever it shall fall, it will grind him to powder."

The trumpet that sounds may be Persian, but God's breath fills it. The proclamation may fit that era and the temporary shrine of truth, but the principle of God's government is intended for all ages and for this *Christian* consummation of religion.

Put the spiritual interpretation upon it. Bring it out of the old shadows, and let it apply itself in this daylight of man's history. What is its voice to us? What is the offence it condemns? And if we thus offend, what is the penalty that justice denounces and pardon alone can avert?

Now, it is the property of all well-adjusted and perfected law, clearly to define offences. It scorns the ambiguity which entraps one in guilt unawares. There must be reasonable presumption that one knows his act to be criminal, and sufficient opportunity for him to shun it without a greater felony, or even-handed justice will be as blind to discover as she is impartial to adjudge upon the offence.

We must be equally just in admitting that the offence of obstructing God's temple work is to be measured not by the arbitrary demands of our prejudice, nor by the imaginary standards of our orthodoxy, but by the clear statutes of Divine authority. These statutes reach far and wide through the ranges of human action; they pursue the devices of the heart with a search that will not be baffled; they are so exceeding broad that no ingenuity can escape them; so minute in their penetration that no intent of our meanness can be too small for them to grasp. But when they treat of this everlasting temple which God constructs among men, there are four particulars concerning which our conscience cannot be at a loss, unless it has first guiltily plunged itself into the penalty of darkness, and hardness, and impenitence.

The decree of an unchangeable God describes His foundation of this work, defines the plan of its construction, appoints His agents to further it, and devotes it to His honor. Its foundation is Christ—"Other foundation can no man lay than that is laid;" its plan is the revealed word—"See thou make all things according to the pattern showed thee in the mount"—"Flesh and blood hath not revealed it unto thee, but my Father which is in heaven;" His agents, in its prosecution, are the ministry of Christ—"We, then, as workers together with Him beseech you;" its object is to erect a visible structure where God's presence is to be recognized, because His Spirit pervades and consecrates the work—"Ye are builded together for an habitation of God through the Spirit."

The statutes are unequivocal. They impose upon us the necessity of building all our character and all our hope upon that one foundation-stone, Christ

Jesus. They bid us banish theories, crush inventions, disdain substitutes, and pause from vain attempts to find another rock; for God Himself lays the foundation-stone, lays it in Zion, and seals it as elect and precious, on which time and eternity can find their true angle; God and man can build their united wall; justice and truth can meet together.

The statutes of the Lord presuppose the sufficiency and the unqualified obligation of the inspired Word. Pluck the heavenly marrow from the revelation of truth, and the statutes fall lifeless at the door of your heart. It is the living and powerful Word that smites the conscience. It is the Word out of heaven that interprets the Providence upon earth. It is the truth of the Word, superior to all our conjectures, as it is more soothing than all our consolations, which discloses the proportions of the temple we are summoned to build. If we offend at the foundation, when we reject Christ, so do we offend against Christ when we propose to do His work while spurning the Word of God.

But that Word affixes a permanence to the visible agency for erecting this earthly temple of God's praise. It declares, by the statute of the Saviour Himself, that He sends mortal men as the Father sent Him. While they come by His authority, speak His truth, minister His sacraments, proclaim His salvation, are building His Church—men do deride their message, men do turn from them with indifference; men allege that the foibles of this ministry repel them from fellowship, and justify the alienation of their hearts from the Church, of their tribute from the work of religion, of their lives from the obedience of Christ; but the edict of mercy charges them with attempting to alter the statutes of Christ, and replies to this most flimsy evasion—"He that is not with me is against me."

Let me assume, however, that I have in none of these things offended, that I cry out with purest steadfastness, "Christ only is my rock," that I live not by bread alone but by every word that proceedeth out of the mouth of the Lord, that I cling with the most exemplary consistency to the fellowship of Christ and His Apostles in the lineal Church; yet may I be amenable to the penalty of one who hinders the work of God. If upon my thoughts shall not be inscribed, "Holiness unto the Lord," I destroy what I had begun to build. If unholy angers tenant this breast, I grieve away the consecrating Spirit of God. If impure passions defile this heart, I resist the Holy Spirit of God. If days without thanks and nights without prayer roll over my worldly spirit—if the gains of filthy lucre engross my attention—if the fashion of this world dictates the precepts and maxims I observe, the glory deserts the inner temple, the voice of praise grows fainter and fainter in my soul, and so far as my immortality is concerned, I am quenching the Spirit of God.

But the penalty! What shall we pronounce that to be?

Why, like all moral enforcements, the sanction

of the law resides in the very crime. The consequence of violating moral law is moral degeneracy. There is no need of invoking outward nature. The offender is punished in himself. And all the war and league of outward things against him is but the echo of the sentence that is executing itself within him. He has not any consciousness of impunity. He affects such a dream. He attempts to produce such a philosophy. But there is a living protest against it in his own convictions. And this is the recoil of self-condemnation that falls upon the spirit that hinders the work of God's temple. It attempts to obstruct the work of God's house; it destroys its own house. That is the moral effect flung back into its own nature. It aims at the house of God and ruins its own. And the work of Providence corresponds with this result. No man can wilfully war against the Church without finding sooner or later that the retribution is in his own house. If his hostility proceeds beyond the mere neglect of his own religious duty—if it be the array of his craft or his influence or his power against the instruments of Christ, the open retort of God will be as manifest as the open defiance—the timbers of his house will be the instruments of his shame—his domestic affections will retaliate torture. The law of Darius was the prophecy of Providence.

But the prophecy of David is the law of grace—"Pray for the peace of Jerusalem; they shall prosper that love thee."

XXVII.

THE DAY OF THE LORD.

2 St. Pet. iii. 10.

"The day of the Lord will come as a thief in the night; in the which the heavens shall pass away with a great noise, and the elements shall melt with fervent heat, the earth also, and the works that are therein, shall be burned up."

THE calendar of Christianity expires not till time shall be no more. It throws solemnity over all our days by referring the result of what is daily transacted to the issues of that final judgment-day. God's wisdom could not content itself with holding forth some vague premonition that wrongs would eventually be righted, or that disguises must finally decay, and leave the realities of character exposed. But a positive, defined, and exact period has been determined and announced, within which this riot of wickedness shall be limited, and beyond which our trials and sufferings and uncertainties shall not extend. It is so intimately connected with the full and legitimate development of that government which our blessed Lord is conducting, that it shall appear as "the day of the Lord." It is to be so little indicated by precursors and portents, by addresses to the mere senses of those who darken their sight and corrupt their hearts by immorality and irreligion, that it cometh as a thief in the night. We are not so elated with conceit of our own sagacity as to presume that all the grand preparatives for that sublime conclusion of the world can be measured by our foresight, or depicted in the language of our aspiring fancy. The theme belongs to higher intellects. It asks angelic power to imagine the startling scenery. It demands a spotless purity to put the faithful colors upon the vast picture. We shrink from the temerity of portraying what is so transcendent.

The fact itself suffices for our faculties—the fact that this catastrophe of the globe is impressed upon our attention by Holy Scripture as the marked event, the signal date, the momentous day in our Christian calendar. To dismiss it from our thoughts is to divest all our earthly days of their value and their meaning. This is our day, this life of opportunity, this period of temptation, this lingering of gracious help, this waiting time for us and God; but the Saviour's glory shall be revealed, the triumph of faith shall be celebrated, the heavens and the earth shall be the parchment in the Redeemer's burning hand, and that shall be "the day of the Lord." For this the seasons hasten; for this the hidden fires roll their billows beneath us; for this the meteors display their myriad torches; for this the glorious sun treasures his unquenchable furnace, and the oceans hide their expansive and explosive forces in their cool waves. Earth has gone through its long strange cycles of diversified appearance before it was robed in such beauty and fruitfulness for the gratification of man ; it waits the change of purification that shall be ushered by no common day of volcano blistering an island, or flood cleansing a continent, but by the day eminent throughout all time that shall shrivel the skies and turn the seas into steaming clouds, and melt the mountains into streams of flame. Every revolving day, as it leads us towards, so it intimates this last of earth's days. Because it belongs to that order of nature which now gives us the "few and evil" days of mortality, it is put upon the record of man as a "day;" but in recognition of Him who makes it illustrious it is recorded as "the day of the Lord."

We shall enter with reverent research into the uses of this subject by considering the signification of this peculiar phrase, then its expressiveness, and, finally, the associations it is intended to suggest.

An inquiry is prompted in the mention of "the day," similar to that which has interrogated Moses as to his meaning in recounting the progresses of creation on *six* successive days. Whether both in the beginning and in the ending of this world's history, "the day" comprises merely our measurement of twenty-four hours, or is to be extended over a period of time varying as the subject varies, we may lawfully inquire. Let it be assumed, even, that the "days" of creation were no more than our work-day week, yet are we not thereby concluded to the same narrow sense when St. Peter mentions "the day of the Lord." There might be a presumption in favor of the same usage in both relations. But if we consult the whole description of the earth's conflagration, we shall find the Apostle pausing as soon as he alludes to the day of judgment and destruction, and interposing this cautious sentence: "Beloved, be not ignorant of this one thing, that one day is with the Lord as a thousand years, and a thousand years as one day." He uses it no doubt as a corrective to the impatience which frets at the slowness of God's promises and mocks at the delays of His justice. But it introduces an inspired idea concerning the methods of God's economy. It removes Divine things from our measurements. It leaves us to our dimensions of days because they best serve our moral benefit in this narrow span of life. But shall God be hampered with our short tether? Must He cut His great day to our cramped fashion? When the sun ceases to kindle, and the face of God makes the day; when the globe forgets her motion, and the light is seven-fold, all the glories of the creation being merged in the radiance of the Creator's appearance, our moments of hurried breath shall no longer define the time, but the grandeur of the occasion shall make the throbs of the universe take the place of our feeble pulses, and the movements of God's stupendous plan shall measure out the day. Expand your mind, says the Apostle, into some correspondence with that Eternal Being who scans a thousand years as if they were but one day, and in that elevation above these earthly views contemplate that coming "day of the Lord." There is one feature of this closing scene which will be instantaneous and in defiance of nature's slow course, for "we shall all be changed in a moment, in the twinkling of an eye." There is another act in this tragedy of humanity which moves like the slow torture of ages, when the mighty men hide themselves in dens and in the rocks of the mountains, and bid the mountains and the rocks "Fall on us and hide us from the face of Him that sitteth on the throne, and from the wrath of the Lamb; for the great day of His wrath is come."

The very description of that day by our Lord Himself expands it over a period of undisclosed duration. He seems to embrace within that day the season of panic and convulsion, when the powers of heaven shall be shaken, as the fig-tree trembles in the tempest, and when men's hearts shall be failing them for fear.

The most cursory reader of the Scriptures will recollect this as a favorite prophetic phrase. Its use began with that era of prophetic gifts which was opened about eight centuries before Christ, and it was continued in almost every prophetic announcement for three hundred and fifty years, being the central object in the last syllables of Malachi. Upon the lips of our Saviour it is phrased "the last day," or "the day of judgment," or "the Son of man's day." It reappears among the Apostles, retaining its prophetic significance with additions of sublimity and clearness.

In the olden era it was a prophetic term to denote some signal exhibition of God's presence to vindicate His own word and to display His resistless power. Christianity adopts it to express the same idea. Sometimes it may imply an allusion to that judgment-day which determined the fate of Jerusalem. But its full intent is not satisfied except by that great and dreadful day, of which the visitation upon Jerusalem was both an omen and a type. In the transition from a system of religion that was national to one that is catholic, this double signification was inevitable. The justice that doomed the privileged people was the same justice that should visit the whole earth when all nations had been privileged. And the shattering of all their trusts and all their strength, which was the Lord's coming in power and majesty to visit the people who rejected Him, must sometimes appear in prophetic words as their first and feeble meaning, when their great import is the gathering of all nations and the judgment upon quick and dead in the day of the Lord.

Its signification thus opens upon us from the harmonizing of all the Scriptures, as that time of manifestation when God will be vindicated and our fallacies shall end.

We have grasped the elemental idea in this phrase. We make our second inquiry—Is it not peculiarly expressive?

You perceive that it is almost identical with the name given to the sacred day of Christians, substituted for the Sabbath of the Jew. It accordingly carries along, and lifts into a prophetic importance, that primeval Sabbath of the Lord. It came as the sign that work was ended. It was God retiring from these scenes of unfolding beauty and utility to group all the occupants of heaven around Him, and pronounce judgment upon the product of His power. In the rest, not of blind slumber or useless inactivity, but in the rest of peace and of contemplation, He saw everything that He had made, and it was very good. So shall the work of all time be reviewed and pronounced upon, when the Son of Man shall come in the glory of His Father and the holy angels. Each sentence uttered by the lips of Jesus shall be the verdict applauded by the universe. The entire course of Providence, the whole scope of grace, shall be under the inspection of righteousness. Its work of patience and hope shall be ended. The product of this human heart shall be finished. The experiment of mortality shall be consummated. The week of sin and trial shall be over. It will be time to survey the scene, and to tell the sum of God's wonders and mercies. It will be the festival of recollection and praise. There will be no new experience of these conflicts between good and evil. The period of rest will have succeeded upon this long struggle. That original rest of God will show itself to have been the prophecy of His purpose. Those sacredly guarded Sabbaths of the law will reveal themselves as preparatives for the great event. And we shall understand why, with Christianity, the putting of holiness upon all our employments transferred the sanctity from a seventh day of mere restriction to a feast-day of religious delight; for the object from the beginning was not to sanctify the day, but to sanctify the man—not to cast disparagement upon labor, but to sweeten it by worship—not to picture heaven as the Paradise of idleness, but as the home of delight in serving God. It was the wisdom of the Lord of the Sabbath, therefore, which preserved the idea of rest within that perfect number of seven, but showed, by giving the sanctity to the first day, that in His majestic coming all days and all years would be but one prolonged "day of the Lord."

Is not the phrase of the prophets and apostles peculiarly expressive? It shows the end of time and the rest of righteousness. But its aptness is concluded from another view. That summoning of mankind to behold the Son of God in His majesty involves the stupendous exertion of His power in raising the generations of the dead. Each Lord's day reminds us that He burst the fetters of death, and, though breathless and lifeless, once emerged from the sepulchre with inconceivable power. Blessed encouragement to our quivering flesh is the memorial of the Redeemer's resurrection, as each Lord's day renews the sacred sign. Yet what are these but shadows and glimmerings in comparison with that emphatic day of the Lord when He shall summon the millions that have slept beneath the hillock of the grave-yard or in the deep cemeteries of the sea, and every human form that has breathed since man became a living soul shall appear upon that resurrection-day.

Some have expended learning in the proof that "the Lord's day," on which St. John was in the Spirit, was the annual Easter, and that, in this act, our sovereign Saviour, revealing heavenly things to His Apostle, put the highest honor upon His own day. But how shall we compare even these visions in Patmos, and that Easter which opened heaven to the Evangelist, with the magnificence that shall break upon our vision and the morning that shall awaken our dust, when all Sundays shall find their glorious fulfillment in the day of the Lord.

The expressiveness of the phrase beams upon us in the last and greatest of Sundays realizing universal resurrection. This does not exhaust the propriety of the phrase. The personal relation of that day to our heavenly Lord renders it eminently His. Until those hours of triumph shall come, His beauty and majesty and the gracious purposes of His dominion will be comparatively unknown. Glances at His glory have been permitted. Faint traces of His hidden excellence were discerned by astonished believers when He illustrated His mission by miracle, His destiny by transfiguration, His defiance of nature by walking over the waves, and His rightful residence by soaring into the skies. To a few eye-witnesses of His majesty were these indications of the Lord's inherent sublimity granted. By innumerable witnesses shall His glory be viewed in the coronation-day of the King of kings, when "thine eyes shall see the King in his beauty;" "when the Lord Jesus shall be revealed from heaven with his mighty angels, in flaming fire taking vengeance on them that know not God, and that obey not the gospel of our Lord Jesus Christ; who shall be punished with everlasting destruction from the presence of the Lord, and from the glory of his power; when he shall come to be glorified in his saints, and to be admired in all them that believe in that day." How could language be more explicit in pronouncing that day of manifestation to be the allotted time for bringing into view the attractions and the fearful splendors of Christ? And who so obtuse as not to perceive that this culmination of days inscribes itself by anticipation upon the whole "calendar of Christianity?"

It may seem to linger among the tardy triumphs of a forbearing God. It may seem to be vanishing into the distance of ages. It may weary the eagerness of the faithful Christian by its long delay. It may grieve our hearts with "hope deferred," and give occasion for the scoffing taunt, Where is the promise of His coming? Yet in the scheme of Providence it shall not tarry. If we could view all the events that promote this display of what is in man, and of what God's penetrating wisdom proposes, we might discern forbearance, we might be delighted with the exercise of His mercy, but we should never dream that there was any failure of His purposes, that there was any slow delay in working out the utmost for the joy of His chosen ones. His chariot of grace rolls upon vast wheels. We see the motion of some spot upon the rim, and to us there is no sign of rapidity. But the vehicle is grand. The circumference of its wheels reaches through remotest space. And as we stand upon this globe and feel not the velocity with which it rolls upon its centre and swings around its enormous orbit, so we heed not the speed with which time is rushing into the blaze of that day when time shall be no longer. It steals upon us, that day of the Lord, as a thief in the night. We are not unconscious of the instability that besets the solid ground, the strong-arched firmament. But we are ignorant of the processes that hasten their destruction. We are not unconscious of the law of dissolution that pervades the earthy fabric, as it wastes away the dust in which we live and crumble. But we are ignorant of the elements that fill the circuits of space, and may, at any moment, crush this shell of earth and send the shrieking missiles of a hundred blazing worlds into our beautiful canopy.

Not I, but the repenting Peter utters the exhortation—"Seeing, then, that all these things shall be dissolved, what manner of persons ought ye to be in all holy conversation and godliness, looking for and hastening unto the coming of the day of God, wherein the heavens being on fire shall be dissolved, and the elements shall melt with fervent heat?"

XXVIII.

HEAVEN.*

REV. xxii. 3-5.

"There shall be no more curse; but the throne of God and of the Lamb shall be in it; and His servants shall serve Him; and they shall see His face; and His name shall be in their foreheads. And there shall be no night there; and they need no candle, neither light of the sun; for the Lord God giveth them light, and they shall reign forever and ever."

IMMORTAL beings, here is the prize of your high calling! Here is the glorious recompense held out for your attainment. To assist you to gain this is the noble object of the Christian ministry. For this we are ambassadors of Christ to you. Do you help our arduous work? Does your whole heart, your unreserved confidence, your unqualified respect accept us as such helpers of your joy? May it never be our example that obstructs your attainment of this holy and eternal happiness. Let us fix our thoughts, then, for these few moments of this sacred day, on the theme so exalted,

* NOTE BY THE EDITOR.—There is evidence that this, and the following are among the last discourses that the Rev. Author ever prepared. If so, how appropriate that his last pastoral utterances should have been those touching the blessedness of the Heavenly City! J. G. W.

so far superior to our multitudinous cares, our petty ambitions. We are to elevate ourselves into some reverent contemplation of "the inheritance of the saints," "the things which God hath prepared for them that love Him." You ask yourself, Is such a pure and blissful state attainable by us, frail and tainted creatures? May I be welcomed in those happy regions? Answer yourself. Do you so desire it as to take God's pathway towards it? Will you sacrifice everything that obstructs your progress and your preparation? Then are you not only ready to march towards the better land, but are already tasting the flavor of its fruits. Oh! that the Holy Ghost would form within us all the desire, excite in us the ambition of being forever blessed in that heavenly home.

This blessedness comprises the entire removal of evil, the full possession of good, delightful occupation, the beatific vision, and perpetual glory. Let us view each element of this bliss in its order.

It is first realized in the entire removal of evil. Without this no happiness can be complete; there must be no root of bitterness to disturb and trouble the pure streams of enjoyment. This great feature of happiness presents itself under two terms, "No more curse," and, "No night there."

There will be no curse in that territory of peace, no remains of God's displeasure, not one frown on His brow. There will be nothing to occasion a curse; not one sin remaining, no temptation even to ruffle our tranquil minds; no conflict with indwelling corruption; no warfare with spiritual enemies. From that happy dwelling-place of the unenvying and the unembittered, every emissary of the wicked one is barred out forever.

Nor is there any remnant of remorse, or dread lest God's anger should waken against us. The soul adorned with the Redeemer's beauties, and enriched with the lovely graces of His Spirit, takes up the inspiring strain, "I will greatly rejoice in the Lord, my soul shall be joyful in my God; for He hath clothed me with the garments of salvation, He hath covered me with the robe of righteousness." And if some frightened memory of a past transgression should be startled by the scene, immediately the whole canopy of heaven would echo the soothing promise of God: "Their sins and iniquities will *I* remember no more." All those temporal sufferings which follow the curse, will also forever have terminated. "There is no pain there, nor hunger, nor thirst." The soul is beyond maladies, the body above suffering. It is raised in power. And the inhabitant of that land shall never say "I am sick." Now the Christian is vexed day by day with the filthy "conversation of the wicked;" he sees the God whom he serves dishonored, his laws trampled upon, his promises despised, his warnings defied, his day profaned, his ministry rejected, his church derided, and the ungodly triumphing; but no sinner shall "stand in the congregation of the righteous" there. *In hell* all curses meet, concentrate, and there are confined. But in heaven is nothing that defileth. How then are sinners, once touched with guilt, once wallowing in shame, now freed from sin and fear and shame, to dwell in those holy places? Ah! there is the mystery of the gracious gospel. They are "washed in the blood of the Lamb," they have "purified their consciences by faith," they have "renounced the hidden things of dishonesty," they have "loved not the world," they have cast themselves upon the mercy of our Lord Jesus Christ, and He hath kept them from falling. He has presented them "faultless before the presence of His glory with exceeding joy." "In Him, my soul, be cleansed from stain; in Him thy righteousness be found."

But the removal of evil is indicated by a second expression, "There shall be no night there." No absence from God, the true light, nor any of the evils consequent on that. If here we find the night as well as the day, a blessing, it is because we need its quiet and repose, it is on account of our infirmities. If perfectly happy and unwearied, night would only be an interruption, depriving us of a portion of our bliss.

Truly "the light is sweet;" it spreads beauty and glory in its track over regions which without it are all gloom and obscurity. But the brightest day on earth with all its lovely scenes, its waving grain, its verdant fields, its shaded slopes, its beautiful rivers glittering in the sun, and all the richness of the expanded prospect, beaming with light and sweet objects to regale the eye, are but as the dark night compared with the surpassing glory of that heavenly day. "The night is far spent, the day is at hand."

And truly there will be no occasion for night there. Our bodies will be too powerful and active and strong, either to admit of fatigue, or to require rest. We shall be too happy to desire for a moment cessation or change. They who are "before the throne of God and serve Him day and night in His temple," rest not from their blissful employment. Earthly delights fail, but heavenly delights are the sweeter in their use. The palate of sin hankers for poison and sickens with its pleasure, but there shall be no more death nor pain, for the former things are passed away.

The expression, "no night," seems more immediately to convey the idea of the absence of all evils incident to a state of darkness, whether spiritual or temporal. There will be no sinful ignorance, no error in our conception of things. There will be no guilt desiring darkness to veil its criminal conduct; no concealment requisite to hide anything from observation; no danger of deviating from the right path, nor reason to dread the approach of enemies to invade our tranquillity.

In the Divine dispensation on earth, there have been darker and brighter days. The Jewish dispensation, compared with the Gospel, was a period of shadows. The Middle Ages were dark ages in some senses. But in *all* dispensations, as contracted with the state of heavenly glory, "now we see through a glass darkly." In that glorious rest there is the brightness of one everlasting day, a cloudless and eternal lustre, with full capability of body and mind for all its glory. As in *hell* there is "the blackness of darkness," and all is night forever—horrid, fearful night, whose ghastly dreams have no morning to end them; so in heaven there is the noon-day blaze, and that forever; but a blaze that never wounds the eye and draws a tear, that never burns the painless body; for ignorance and sorrows alike are banished, where "God shall wipe away all tears, and the Lord giveth them light."

My brethren, is there nothing to awaken a desire, nothing to exhilarate a hope, even in this view of heaven, as an everlasting life from which every evil is entirely removed? Yet this is but a glimpse of the awaited blessedness. It comprises, secondly, the full possession of God.

Exquisite imagery symbolizes this transporting hope. For the sustenance of eternity is the communication of God to the godly. At one time it is the manna of angels that nourisheth; and what is that bread from heaven, but the Living One that is glorious in the perfections of the Son of God? At another time the figure of perpetual refreshment is "a pure river of water of life proceeding out of the throne of God and of the Lamb." And what is this but the fresh communication of the Holy Ghost, whose flood poured over the soul is life and peace and abundance of refreshment? Where the vision of God is a perpetual ecstasy, and where He gives us the utmost by nurturing our life, not with some productions of His hand, but with Himself imparted unto us, are we not in the highest degree heirs of God Himself, the giver and the gift?

Let the miser rejoice in the possession of an unsubstantial wealth; let the sensualist have his momentary joy; let the ambitious, or the men of science, or of human wisdom, pride themselves in the attainment of their several objects; oh! what is their happiness compared with that of him who has for his portion the God of true riches, of true glory, of true pleasures, and can bathe in that ocean of Divine fullness for ever and ever.

Two forms of language are employed to indicate what this possession of God becomes to the blessed. One figure denotes what they need not, the other signifies what they possess. "They need no candle, neither light of the sun." They need no borrowed or artificial light, invented to supply the absence of a better and greater. All human means are imperfect; all sensible things to supply our necessities, as they are but remedies for defects, so they are themselves defective. They waste themselves in serving us—the raiment we wear, the fire we kindle, the food we consume, the artificial light that cheers our darkness. When that which is perfect is come, these defective and perishing aids shall vanish away.

"They need no sun." No indirect light through the creations of God. We catch but glances of the glory of God; we know Him simply by touching the fringes of His garments. The heavens teach us, and the unseen beauties of the Creator are faintly sketched to us in the outlines of His work and of His Providence. But then we shall see Him as He is; and all the grandeur and beneficence which stare upon us now like the sun that makes our day, shall be but pale and dim shadows when God discloses His glory, and we have the faculties to behold it.

For this is what the blessed shall possess. The Lord giveth them light. We learn, we live, we are happy, not from these creations, rich as they are with knowledge, with nourishment, with contributions to our delight,—but from God Himself. "In Thy light shall we see light." Who, of mortals, shall presume to define the amount of this possession—this that waiteth to be ours. At least, it embraces knowledge, holiness and happiness.

Perfect knowledge shall be there. Now we know by faith—then by sight and by enjoyment; now we learn laboriously, slowly, imperfectly, climbing rugged tasks to know a little, and then beholding taller mountains and harder paths beyond, more convinced of our ignorance the more we learn, and compassing great attainments with means exhausted and health impaired. But there at a glance we shall take in more knowledge than years of study and experience can give the most laborious student here. We shall see the beauty of God's ways, the infinite wisdom and the boundless love displayed in our heaviest sorrows and severest trials. Oh, the glories of that history of histories, the developing and unfolding of the providential dispensations of God with his people, when each saint in glory will be as a mirror, reflecting another and another view of the graces and beauties of Immanuel!"

Perfect holiness will be our portion, when "we walk in the light as he is in the light." No sin left to defile, no habit laying its unholy bondage upon us, the last Egyptian dead upon the sea-shore, and degradation never more to pass upon our liberated and exultant spirit.

Is it strange that *perfect happiness* should be the sequel? With rapture does the prophet behold the glorious throng, though seen through distant ages. With pictures of untarnished brilliancy does he delineate to our admiring eyes the scene of perfect happiness when the redeemed come with singing unto Zion, when they shall *possess* gladness and joy, and "sorrow and mourning shall flee away."

And all this with no alloy of fear that the source of the blessedness may fail. It flows on like the grand movements of universal power, unchecked and unexhausted forever. For it is not the palpitating heart of man that has begotten this hope; it is not the wearying arm of some archangel that has lifted up the dejected soul, the corrupted body; "the Lord giveth them light."

Who, then, shall restrain that song of praise which tells of the rapture that fills those heavenly breasts? Dull and lifeless are our warmest strains when compared with the fervor of the heart that finds felicity its unceasing draught, and the Lord its everlasting fountain.

Could we hear but some echo of those songs

wherewith the heaven of heavens resounds, some remains of those voices wherewith the saints above triumph in the praises and the solemn adoration of the King of Spirits, how would it inflame our desires to be joined with them! "Blessed are they that dwell in Thy House—they will be always praising Thee."

O, that I could in any way stir up all earnestly and zealously to seek heaven! Sacrifice me, fling me aside as but the rubbish and scaffolding of the structure, if you will be yourselves built up into a temple of the Lord. Honestly and heartily turn your back on all that drags you away from heaven, and set your faces Zionward, and you shall reach those heavenly heights, and that blessed city whose "walls are salvation, and all her gates praise."

XXIX.

THE HEAVENLY BLESSEDNESS.

NO. II.

REVELATIONS xxii. 3–5.

"And there shall be no more curse; but the throne of God and of the Lamb shall be in it; and his servants shall serve him.

"And they shall see his face; and his name shall be in their foreheads.

"And there shall be no night there; and they need no candle, neither light of the sun; for the Lord God giveth them light; and they shall reign for ever and ever."

COULD heavenly happiness be seen in all its blessedness, there would be no room for the full exercises of faith, and comparatively little display of the excellency of Divine grace in the hope and patience and holiness of God's people. To exercise *faith*, it is only revealed in prospect; to excite hope, it is but partially developed, and it "doth not yet appear what we shall be." The brief delineation of our text suggests to us some features of the heavenly blessedness which we are warranted in contemplating. Two of those impressive particulars have occupied our attention.

That heavenly state addresses our desires as a condition from which *evil is entirely removed.* It captivates our imagination in being *the full posses-*

sion of good, of God Himself, and in Him of all knowledge, holiness and happiness. It now presents itself before us as a life of *delightful occupation.* Four words fasten this thought upon our hearts—"His servants shall serve Him."

Notice the glorious being who is served. No Gabriel or Ariel, that drew his being from another, and is resplendent and lovely simply by that which a greater hath bestowed. No potentate among the heavenly powers, who awes us by his majesty and puts us in jeopardy of yielding a service too humble or too ardent, leaves us dallying between his own demand and the claim of the Supreme and All-lovely. But it is the Mighty God, the Most High and the Most Lovely, to whom our every feeling, our every act will be well-pleasing homage. It is not clear whether St. John designed to refer to the Father or the Son; nor is it material. "He that honoreth the Son honoreth the Father also." The being served is He to whom all service is due. Created by His power, redeemed by His blood, sanctified by His Spirit, shall they not forever consecrate every power to Him whose they are, and to whom all they can render is infinitely due. To serve a noble cause is nobility to the servant. To serve with his regard and confidence some man of superior endowments and of lofty character is to imprint upon our own acts the merit of our exalted pattern and commander. What must it be to have the million tenants of millions of worlds pointing to us, and exclaiming—Lo, these are the chosen servants of the Master of us all!

But did they not serve God below? These frail, wayward sinners made to be the choice ministers of the universe! What is the difference between their serving Him here and their serving Him there? Here we soon weary; our spirits flag; we require rest. But there the mind is ever lively and awake; the body ever active and alive; the service is unwearied. Here our service is blotted and lame, amenable to criticism, and consciously imperfect; our faith is weak, our hope dull, our praises feeble—all is *disproportioned* and imperfect; there all is proportioned and perfect, the heart a burning altar, the tongue a living harp, the charity intense, the praise such as pleases every heavenly ear.

And that which gives the climax of completeness to our service above is the enjoyment there of a perfect communion with all our fellow-servants. Our own corruptions, and the infirmities of all God's servants here hinder full and entire union of heart; but there will be no alloy of this kind there. No envy or jealousy at each other's gifts and graces, happiness and glory. Just as the eye envies not the ear, and the hand envies not the foot; but all the members of the body are exalted in the happiness of each, so will it be there. The happiness of another will be mine in his possessing it. As the wife is exalted in the husband, and the child in the parent, so shall there be joy in the presence of the glorified servants of God in every joy that every servant possesses. What a home, what a nation, what a Church, when you shall be one of a happy company, where you have the full assurance that you love every individual there, and every individual loves you, and this not selfishly or hesitatingly, but purely, fervently, perfectly and forever! Glorious contrast with the tremulous attachments and the grim jealousies of this territory, where selfishness curdles our best affections, and treachery lurks amid the prayers and praises of the Christian Church.

Let us mount from this sorrowful world to contemplate another element of the heavenly blessedness—the beatific vision of God. "They shall see his face, and his name shall be in their foreheads."

The promise embraces two topics—the *nature* of that heavenly vision, and its *efficacy*. How tender and how delicate the organ of sight in this perishing frame! Perfectly affluent as it is in delights to pour upon the mind, gleaning exquisite discoveries from minutest specks, and ravishing the heart with beauties caught from the fleecy skies, drawn instantaneously from remotest stars, yet that starlight may smite it with pain, that faint speck may destroy it. But in the heavenly scenery it never shall be blind. Undazzled and uninjured it shall look even upon that origin of all charming hues and all flashing suns, "the face of God."

When Adam was innocent, he lived in the immediate presence of God. Expelled from Paradise, he lost the sight of God. The gospel is a process for man's recovering more than Adam lost. In order to this recovery, God gives His people the grace of faith, "the substance of things hoped for, the evidence of things not seen." We walk by faith, and in the exercise of faith have communion with God, but it is with many interruptions and much obscurity.

God is, indeed, everywhere throughout His infinite universe; higher than the heavens, deeper than hell, wider than the east from the west, indivisibly immense and eternal. But in what the Scriptures call the third heavens, He peculiarly manifests Himself to His creatures. There are the first heavens, the region of the air; the second heavens, the starry firmament; and the third heavens, the special residence of God.

O how glorious that Jerusalem above! With allusion to the brightest things here below, it is said to have a wall of jasper, buildings of gold, a foundation of precious stones, and gates of pearls; being clear as crystal, shining like unto glass, and transparent in brightness; and if the gates be of pearl and the pavement is of gold, what are the inner rooms?

But the chief glory is this—there God manifests His immediate presence. To see God perfectly, is often described as the special happiness of His people hereafter. "Blessed are the pure in heart, for they shall see God." "Now we see through a glass darkly, but then, face to face, we shall see him as he is."

It has been the high privilege of some to have such communion with God on earth, that they have been said to "see him face to face." Jacob wrestling with the angel, Moses in the mount, and the Israelites until they shrank appalled. All these, however, were limited views of God. When Moses asked to behold the glory, the answer was, "Thou canst not see my face, for there shall no man see me and live." In all these privileged interviews there was the voice, but not the vision of God. This is reserved for the heavenly faculty; the earthly weakness would quiver and dissolve. There "every eye shall see him," and the vision shall be the summing up of all that gives enchantment to the delighted eye, and sends through the eye whole deluges of light over the soul.

For this is that grander wonder of the blessedness, that the vision of God has such a *transforming effect.*

Few words describe it, "His name is on their foreheads."

That is, they become manifestly and obviously like the glorious God. Even this earthly and imperfect glimpse, given us in the Gospel, is assimilating and transforming. Our very look at that prism of love, God in Christ, sends heavenly colors into our affections, and heavenly likeness into our lives. "We all, with open face, beholding as in a glass the glory of the Lord, are changed into the same image, from glory to glory, even as by the Spirit of the Lord." Moses experienced it, when he descended from the mount with the brighter features. But with us in heaven the effect will be immensely greater. Then at last shall "the beauty of the Lord our God be upon us."

The name or character of God is even now visibly stamped upon the faithful Christian. Its token touches his forehead, when he begins the Christian vow, traced in that most loving language, the form of the cross, one upright mark betokening that the direct ray of love begins it, the transverse mark spanning the brow or crossing the breast to signify that every thought and every emotion is sacrificed upon that altar of love. And what we thus print with a single letter, imitating Him who puts in heaven a sacred sign upon the forehead, that the renewing and transforming power of God reveals as His gracious work, visible in the very lives of them who put on the new man, created after God in righteousness and true holiness—yet here, alas! how dimly discerned in ourselves or in others, amid manifold infirmities, under the shadows that hide our better motives. But in heaven the name of God will be distinct and legible. They will be "pure as He is pure," not one jarring note of discord, not one imagination of evil. And the incorruptible body, now the powerful vehicle of a spotless soul, "shall shine forth as the sun in the kingdom of the Father."

This mention of the kingdom conducts us at once to the final particular in the triumphant state of the blessed, "they shall reign forever and ever."

The endless dominion here described is by the very form of expression distinguished from any reign of a thousand years, and from any limited reward that might attach to this dissolving world. And yet the mind pauses before presuming to define the precise idea of this great allotment to the saints. Theirs indeed it is to reign; but it is in conjunction with the King of kings, and as the representatives of His supreme and indefeasible authority.

Conjecture may be lawful upon a theme which is purposely left obscure. It may be designed to rouse and expand the imagination, that the everlasting reign is clearly announced, but the region and conditions of the dominion are not defined. Certain it is that the elevation of us poor mortals to a royal dominion is continually displayed as the destiny that has always been intended by our Heavenly Father. The Great Judge of the universe embraces it in the verdict of His approval, "Come, ye blessed of My Father, inherit the kingdom prepared for you from the foundation of the world." And conspicuous among the figures that indicate the recompense to come is the crown which shall adorn the sovereign saint, "the crown of righteousness," "the crown of life," "the crown of glory." We cannot dismiss this idea of kingly dominion hereafter as a chance embellishment. It is a reality, which the earthly figure attempts to make vivid and impressive.

It implies authority, the unquestioned command over some department of the universe, the subjection of agents and instruments to our royal bidding, the rendering to us of honor and of tribute from powers and beings that take pleasure in our sway. In the moral throne we are to occupy, powers of intellect and emotions of the heart and unwearying muscles of the undecaying body are to be no more the rebellious and mutinous tortures of our better life, but willing and obsequious vassals in our holy realm. Immensity will furnish the million regions where the glorious reign of God shall be maintained with a redeemed and exulting sinner as the deputy of Omnipotence in each province of His love. As each star in the heavens now twinkles to show a separate globe where creation is wondrously exhibited, so each rejoicing monarch, saved from this coast of mortal wrecks, shall be a star in the more stupendous canopy of grace, and shine in royal lustre as one more trophy of redemption's victory, while all the blessed shall form that vast clustered constellation which beautifies the heaven of heavens as the Redeemer's crown.

And in that blissful height, with kingly power in their hands, and the blood of heavenly nobility in their veins, and hierarchies of the skies listening for their edicts, and all the elements of nature waiting upon these royal favorites, these ransomed children of the dust shall reign forever.

Aye, forever and ever, inconceivable and interminable perpetuity. So runs the sublime promise. Kings of the earth must perish. Dynasties may gleam for centuries, and then must sink to dust. The pure endearments of the earthly home hurry to their grave. Wealth cannot ransom from death, and the tongue of the learned is palsied silence, when life's fitful dream is o'er.

But on every throne, on every joy, on every

faculty which God imparts to His blessed, He places this indelible signet, "forever and ever."

How human happiness below trembles in the balance! Who knows that it can outlive the day? If we enjoy communion with God, how soon we lose the sense of His presence! If the light of His countenance shine upon us, it is but for a moment. But there it is wave after wave of joy that never ceases to bathe the peaceful soul. Oh, the glories of those words, "forever with the Lord!"

Here the agitated heart ever and anon is startled with the thought, "I may perish at the last." "What, if this never-dying soul should fail of heaven?"

Once enter there, and anxieties die at the threshold. Fear is banished, perfect love has cast it out. Oh, my God, shall the thought of losing Thee, through the million million ages of eternity, ever once for a moment fling its shadow over my tranquil breast? And He answers in the tenderest tones, "Never, no, never."

I speak to those who undertake no effort for the obtaining of this glory. Strange infatuation! How like to madness; how like to mournful, desperate folly! You drag these burdens of care, you chase these phantoms of pleasure, you gather these treasures which a breath blows from your grasp. But the realities, the eternities, the sublimities of heaven, languidly do you desire, recklessly do you neglect. Throw but a fraction of that eagerness which struggles for the earthly, into your pursuit of faith and holiness, and you will (most blessedly for yourself) be welcomed as meet for the inheritance of the saints in light.

And you, my beloved brethren, that live in the hope and prayer for this glory. Oh, why do we spend so few thoughts upon it! Why do we permit these sacred hours to pass, week after week, with such faint and infrequent meditation upon our heavenly portion? The wanderer dreams and lives in constant imaginings of his home. The lonely one keeps up sweet communings with the absent and the loved. Oh! let us think more perpetually of our Jerusalem, our Saviour, and our Father's house. Let us long to enter that city of the Great King, of which such glorious things are spoken; and since it is our chief good, our last home, the end of all our troubles, and the meeting-place for friends that never shall part and never shall feel the agony of distrust, let our affection be set upon it, our conversation be there already, and we, as strangers and pilgrims, pressing on, till through the gates we enter in, to dwell there forever.

XXX.

MIDIAN ROUTED.

JUDGES vii. 20.

"And the three companies blew the trumpets, and brake the pitchers, and held the lamps in their left hands, and the trumpets in their right hands to blow withal; and they cried, The sword of the Lord, and of Gideon."

IT might be anticipated that a people nursed by miracle could need no subsequent testimonies of Divine interposition to establish their faith in God. But with the same reason might we suppose that a good Providence sustaining the infancy of a people could not be forgotten in their days of strength, or repaid with ingratitude and impiety.

Need I say that the uplifting of this, the great Western, and the last empire upon the earth,—a nursling of propitious heaven,—a child whom civilization and faith in man were employed as governess and instructor to guide and teach; that the uplifting of this empire through the perils of infant infirmity has betrayed the same seated corruption in human nature. It seemed that wonder-working Heaven might grow quite weary of inventing miracles to persuade that chosen people in Palestine. In spite of the awe that lay upon their forefathers, they were a stubborn generation. Taught by the trembling piety of the pilgrim ancestor to venerate the Jehovah that dwelt invisible, and would have no image of His majesty upon earth, they carved the stone and hid their idols in the grove, and hewed out, like primitive politicians, only half devils, a bargain between God and Baal.

It was with them the pretence of being under a theocracy, when they really chose and served the government of cunning. They had hymns for God, and priests and tithes, but they kept up these as a kind of charm. What truly reigned in Israel was cunning, that bestial counterfeit of wisdom,—or, as Lord Bacon calls it, "wisdom's bastard brother."

And it is the same element that overreaches the honesty of the people in our own land, and, with its caucus rites deifying the means in the grove, it preaches the glories of democracy to the people. And we are all aware of this; and because we cannot help it, or because we are cunning, and give our hurrahs to grace a triumph, the aristocracy of cunning prevails.

The consequences to the people in Palestine were most righteous. They loved heathen gods, and they had the life of Gentiles,—desolation, dissension, war. They lost the ligament of duty, and their nation fell into fragments. They went hunting after their interests without inquiring of God, and their interests drove them back in dismay to the unity they had broken, and from that lawless and godless state in which every man lived by cunning, and did what was right in his own eyes.

In one of those revulsions the Midianites were the invaders. They came up from the south and east—the natural seed of Abraham, descendants of Keturah and Hagar, against the spiritual seed, the heirs of the promise. They were such as the Bedouin Arabs, that now inhabit the same territory—wanderers, reckless, marauding, looking to the harvest more than the slaughter. Over the fields of Israel these roving heathen poured their plundering hordes whenever the grain was ready for the sickle. Enervated because conscience was dead, and unresisting because union was sacrificed to selfishness, the industrious Israelites fled before the Midianites, and hid in dens and caves of the earth. For seven years these incursions had disheartened and impoverished the people. They were in virtual servitude to the spoiler, who came up at his pleasure to pillage.

At this juncture, Deity again descended among them. The Son of man, the angel of the covenant, appears to a laboring man, of the half tribe of Manasseh, while this poor man was hastening to thresh his wheat, and hide it from the Midianites. This person was the instrument selected by God for averting the dreaded incursion, and chastening a greedy race.

I need not detail what you have often read,—of Gideon visited by an angel at the threshing-floor; of the staff in the angel's hand touching the flesh and cakes of Gideon's repast, and fire out of the rock rising up to consume them; of God's commanding this prepared instrument to throw down the altar of Baal that his father had built, and to cut down the grove by it; of his remonstrance with the people of the city, and his call upon Baal to plead for himself as God had done, whence his name was changed to Jerub-baal; of the miracle of the fleece, and all the process by which God put this man in the school of temptation.

Inspired with courage, Gideon collects the forces of the Israelites. An army of thirty-two thousand men answered to his call. But the Lord orders him to dismiss the timid from his ranks. Only ten thousand remained to protect their territory. Again the trusty men are culled by the command of God. And only three hundred were selected to achieve the victory. A night attack was projected, and a stratagem was to render this successful. Three companies of one hundred each, came down upon different points of the enemies' camp, "and the three companies blew the trumpets, and brake the pitchers, and held the lamps in their left hands, and the trumpets in their right hands to blow withal; and they cried, The sword of the Lord, and of Gideon." Aroused from sleep with the clangor of arms, and the cry of forces rushing upon them from various quarters, the Midianites turned their weapons upon each other, and taking the flash of the torches for the signals of victory, and the trumpet of each man for the token of a column, they fled in confusion. Victory was easy. The reanimated Israelites rushed in from the adjacent region, and pursuing the Midianites captured their princes, and rejoiced in the trophies of a victory effected by the sword of the Lord, and of Gideon.

In the use to be made of this narrative, it is to be regarded, as *typical* of the *means* which God employs in His warfare with evil.

Regarding these events as types, we must connect with them the facts from which their typical value is derived.

And here let me make the remark that a type is no less to be expected in revelation, than in nature. And nature, we know, is a perfect complex of figures and images representing the spiritual.

On this principle rests the propriety of the parables, the genius of poetry, the expressiveness of art, the essential majesty of nature, the superiority of man as a discoverer and applier of these types.

It is an established fact that the chosen people brought from bondage into Canaan, were not only the existing Church of God, but were in their temporal and earthly lots types of the spiritual and catholic Church under the government of the Redeemer. St. Paul has amplified this fact in his epistle to the Corinthians, and has in his epistle to the Hebrews given us intimations of various types in the fortunes and the legal ceremonies of ancient Israel.

With this warrant, we may pronounce the temporal condition of the covenanted people in Canaan, as typical of our own spiritual state. Their vacillations and corruptions, their weakness and defeat in periods of discord, their triumph by means that seemed inadequate, their resistless progress when the banner of God was held aloft, their discomfiture when relying upon human policy or cowardly alliances; these notable facts in their temporal history are figures of the destiny awaiting our spiritual condition.

In this aspect, they appear before us in the days of Gideon, as types of a disunited, perplexed, and enfeebled Christendom. Keepers of the oracles of God, and dwellers among the riches of His promise, they were yet faint-hearted and distressed. Their harvests were reaped with the sword of the spoiler. Their possessions were invaded by the uncircumcised. Their Canaan was turned to a desolate region of violence and alarm. And the ravage was committed by brethren of the same ancestry, by a people boasting the lineage of Abraham.

If the Israelite was at this period a type of the Church spoiled and terrified, incapable of united effort, and paralyzed in many a member, then the Midianite is the type of those errors and half truths, those loose and plausible opinions, those doctrines of mingled Scripture and Satan, which resemble the truth, and boast of their origin in the word of God, and yet are hostile to the Church, hostile not with the design of ruining religion, but in their constant incursion upon the privileges of the Church.

Such is the doctrine, that religion consists in practice and not in believing. Such is the doctrine, that the Church depends upon no visible rites. Such is the doctrine, that sacraments are only empty ceremonies, and that their right use makes us no better than their disuse. Such is the doctrine, that the authority of a ministry is derived from the law of the land, independent of any other visible power. Such is the doctrine, that conscience is the true teacher, and nothing is to be received more than it requires. Such is the doctrine, that man can settle his own account with God and has no need of a Saviour. Such is the doctrine, that our wisdom is to make the most of this world and run as far in self-indulgence as we can without trespassing upon the *rights* of others. Such is the doctrine, that God will not observe our little sins, and will not call every secret thing into remembrance, but after all count us good enough for heaven. These doctrines are the Midianites that roll over the borders of the Church and sweep away the harvests.

In selecting the means of resistance, God does not adopt the schemes of men. He has a wonderful way of His own. We might expect the whole Church to be roused by such invasions and rallied to repel. Not so. The faint-hearted are released from the war. Inactive to resist, they only mourn the depredations of Midian.

And when ten thousand men who will not bow the knee to Baal, when a force of determined spirits remains, God reserves them till a chosen band have wrought, by His power, and opened the way of victory. It may be that the separation of these three hundred into three companies has some typical reference to the three orders in which it pleased the Apostles of Christ to arrange the ministry of the word. Certain it is that the Church of God has never repelled the invasions of false doctrine and saved itself in the integrity of true doctrine, except when it has followed the advance of these three companies.

But what are the weapons committed to these companies? What are we to understand by the pitchers and the lamps and the trumpets and the sword of the Lord and of Gideon? These are the types of strange means made mighty by God to the dismay of Midian and the subjection of earthly minds to the law of Christ. And as if carrying along this type in his mind, the Apostle describes the war in which he battled, "casting down imaginations and every high thing that exalteth itself against the knowledge of God, and bringing into captivity every thought to the obedience of Christ." The routing of the Midianites was not by the lance and the battle-ax, by the arrow and the javelin, but by the sound of the trumpet, and the glare of the torch, and the vehement shouting.

The trumpet signifies the herald. It was the sound of the trumpet that broke from the smoke and flame of Sinai and heralded the approach of God. The watchman stationed on the walls was warned by Ezekiel to sound the trumpet at the approach of danger, or the blood would be upon his own head. The entrance of the year of jubilee was proclaimed with the sound of the trumpet. The angels revealed to St. John, heralding the woes of earth, sounded the trumpet of alarm. And in the heralding of Christ's coming in judgment, the archangel's

> "trumpet shakes
> The mansions of the dead."

We may regard this portion of the stratagem as typifying the proclamation by the gospel heralds. And these trumpets in their right hands took the place of offensive weapons. Grace conquers by the sound of the trumpet. The gospel spreads its victories by boldly heralding the jubilee of release, the woes of earth, and the condescending power of heaven.

But the trumpet alone could not have availed, were it not for the brilliancy of the lamps in their left hands—apt symbols of that illumination which beams into and radiates from the souls of valiant Christians. Here was the type of that fire which descended at Pentecost with a sound from heaven, and which kindled a light to shine before men. And this beaming of the Holy Ghost is the dazzling light that confounds the enemies of Christ. This it is that gives success and makes the courage of a few more effective than the flickering cowardice of the whole army. One who experienced this success has recorded the secret of the power—"God, who commanded the light to shine out of darkness, hath shined in our hearts, to give the light of the knowledge of the glory of God in the face of Jesus Christ."

And these lamps were inclosed in pitchers, and

the breaking of the clay was the signal of victory, to typify that we have the Spirit of God in bodies of clay, that we have "this treasure in earthen vessels, that the excellency of the power may be of God and not of us;" and to foreshow that the breaking of the body only increased the lustre and insured the victory, that "the blood of the martyrs was the seed of the Church."

And the weapon whose force was invoked, and the appeal to which was a terror to the Midianite, was "the sword of the Lord and of Gideon," typifying "the sword of the Spirit, which is the word of God," and the sword of spiritual authority cutting off the members that offend. It is not a cunningly devised religion; it is not the hewing sword of arbitrary orthodoxy; it is not the armory of human wisdom, with any of its glitter or its keenness, that disperses error and conquers for God. It is the sword of the Lord and of Gideon—the word of God and the commission from God—the searching blade that cuts the heart, and the inflexible steel of indefeasible authority.

My brethren, these things happened for ensamples unto us. They were not recorded—they are not expounded for *entertainment*, but for instruction. Apply this type to the fortunes of Christianity. Has not the unaccountable victory been always granted to the three hundred men that lapped? Was it not so in the kindlings of apostolic zeal? Was it not so in the burnings of martyrdom? Was it not so in the ardors of missionary enterprise? Was it not so in the light and the trumpet of Reformation? Tell me, who have done most good upon earth, the warriors with their blood, or the missionaries of grace with their lamps and the battle-cry of the Lord of Hosts? Whose work shall tell upon the generations that tread upon our ashes, the glittering thousands that fear the Midianites and live in pleasure, or the three hundred that bear the trumpet in the right hand and the lamp of life in the left, heralds of the King of kings?

Let us remember, then, where the pledge of victory has been given from God. With a faithful sounding of the evangelic trumpet—with the light of the Spirit kindling rays of living holiness—with the word of God and the commission of authority, what matters it whether we be three hundred strong or banded thousands? The battle is not given to the strong. It is given to the companies that advance in the name of the Lord.

It is not numbers that we want; it is not the aid of a timid multitude; it is not human strength. Courage and faith—these are the charms that bespeak victory to each soul battling with evil. Courage and faith—these are the sinews which trembling, faltering Christians cannot possess. Courage and faith—these are the powers which put to flight the enemies of the Church. Courage and faith—these are the wise weapons that "put to silence the ignorance of foolish men." Courage and faith—these are the arguments that convince gainsayers—these, the giants that capture armies—these, the three hundred on whom all hope depends. Give me such leaven and I can leaven the lump. Give me such armor and I can be the champion of God. Give me the three hundred, such as consumed in the flames of the Reformation, and I can kindle a light that will burn up the dross of the Church and send its rays to remotest lands and ages long to come.

XXXI.

THE ULTIMATE REWARD.

ROMANS viii, 18.

"I reckon that the sufferings of this present time are not worthy to be compared with the glory which shall be revealed in us."

VIRTUES are sometimes distinguished into the two classes of *active* and *passive*, and between the two a comparison is sometimes instituted, as if it were in our power precisely to measure the dimensions, the power, and the value of a virtue. In fact, our moral nature is always tending towards the mechanical. We are morally strong, as a general rule, only by being mechanically habitual. And the apologist for his own delinquencies and vices, bases his excuse upon the mechanical principle of being tempted with some force superior to his judgment. And in spite of all that we profess, concerning faith and salvation by the merits of Christ, there is a perpetual leaning towards the mechanical measure of character. It is made up to us of combinations, a dignity here and a meanness there, the pared nail of a Pharisee on his finger end and the coarse provender of a Nebuchadnezzar between his teeth, scruples tender as the gout on this point and scruples as loose as a publican's in other respects, and we are willing to praise a character palpably defective, so long as it is not palpably corrupt. We take a mechanical measurement of souls, and they are righteous to us in proportion as they square with the fashions of our party, or weigh in the balances of a human opinion. The eye of God is no part of our calculation, or if it be, that eye is made to look with all our dimness and cloudiness of vision.

The tendency of this dynamic philosophy is apparent in the whole drift of our age. All ages of mankind have manifested it, but it floats upon the surface of society in an age of unparalleled physical development. What are termed the active virtues rise at this time into most conspicuous prominence, and character is decided more by what one does than what he *is*. The passive virtues, always least glorious among men, are at this time thrown into greater disparagement. When society is rude, and the selfishness of the world, unrefined and unglossed, is exposed in its natural ugliness, the active benevolence of the Christian becomes heroic, his integrity as a man, his ardor as a Christian, are staked upon the activity of his better qualities. He is superior to his age only by being goodness in living action. In such an exigency we look for a contrast in his energy and enterprise for the cause of God and his soul, which marks his consciousness of some high reward to be sought. But in the transformations of refinement, and above all, in the activities of Christian society, we look for the contrast of those passive virtues, which bloom amid the shadows of contented and patient suffering.

In an age when charity is denied, and sluggish sensuality engrosses the soul, the higher ambitions of the Christian are forced into action, into struggle. It is the season of fierce danger, when David wrestles with the lion, and the strength of his arm works the victory. But the time comes when the moody passions of Saul must be soothed, or the reproaches of the blaspheming Goliath must be silenced, and then it is the harp that gives him the victory, or the pebble from the brook that weighs down the boasts of the giant—the harp whose strings tremble in the peaceful sounds of private praise and melodious patience—the sling armed with the unwarlike virtue of trust in God. The *active* and *passive* virtues, twin-dwellers in the same soul, we may distinguish them, but how shall we separate them? They are but the two sides of the same object. And in their united excellence they form that glory which shall be revealed in us.

The sufferings of this present time are demands for both classes of virtue, and as the grace of God within us responds to the demand, we are prompted to adopt the reckoning of the Apostle, "that the sufferings of this present time are not worthy to be compared with the glory which shall be revealed in us." He excludes the mechanical by introducing the moral reckoning. There is no such idea as that of compensation admitted by him. The future is not measured by the proportion of the present. Righteousness and equity are the habitation of God. But when justice has pronounced its decree, and the subject is remitted to the hands of Infinite Love, then comparison loses its power. The work of grace exceeds the trial of virtue, as the work of the Creator surpasses the work of the creature. There may be some elements of resemblance, but in magnitude, comparison itself is forbidden.

The language of the Apostle takes a still higher range. The sufferings and the glory cannot be compared when their magnitude is taken into view. They cannot be compared, he adds, when our interest in them is considered. The glory is not some foreign possession, some chance inheritance which we may seize, or may miss. It is glory hidden away in the gift which we already possess; it is glory that resides in us, and belongs to the perfection of our nature, and shall be known and acknowledged of all beings as our own, when we come to be more perfectly ourselves. It is glory that shall be revealed in us. It waits for manifestation. *It* waits? Nay, the whole creation waiteth for the manifestation of the love of God. The glory that is in us struggles for its display; and the virtues which we by effort here maintain and here exhibit, are but the flashes of that glory which waiteth to be revealed. There is that passeth understanding in the gift of God to man. He communicates Himself. He tells us that we are made partakers of Himself. He calls us heirs of God—not of heaven, not of treasures that waste, but heirs of God, because He is Himself both the giver and the gift—both the Father and the inheritance. He promises that by the mere fidelity of our earthly patience, we shall be changed into His image from glory to glory.

On the contrary, how accidental, how foreign to ourselves, the sufferings of this present time. They come and depart, and they are no longer parts of ourselves. They are put on and off, like the raiment, not the substance of the soul; and let their impression upon us be the utmost they can give, yet it is not they, but we that remain. There is no uniformity in their effects; the soul it is that must decide their influence. Pharaoh was hardened where Israel was awed; and in Ephesus the same Apostle that comforted disciples disputed until divers were hardened. There is a spirit which will not receive correction, whose goodness is as a morning cloud and the early dew. And there is a spirit, how blessed in its sorrows, how affluent in its losses! which can petition heaven for a suffering, "Correct me, but with judgment, not in thine anger." My brethren, there are a thousand losses which seem to us in the prospect irreparable, but we may be assured that there is no calamity like his who loses the blessing of his losses. They must be counted among those transient elements which discipline the soul, and which are only of interest to ourselves, so far as they affect that immortality which cannot be disowned.

Here, then, is the alternative: a glory which is to be given us, to be the substance of our being, and to be eternal; or a suffering which is merely to touch us as it passes, which can only reach us under alleviations, and at the utmost is for a moment present, and then vanishes forever.

"I reckon that the sufferings of this present time are not worthy to be compared with the glory which shall be revealed in us."

The first deduction from this comparative value of the present suffering and the future glory, is that which it was the Apostle's main object to inculcate. He was fortifying a beseiged church against the invasions of suffering. What comes to us in scattered fragments of tribulation, was descending upon them in storms of persecution. The jealous empire of the world was rousing itself into hostility against the kingdom of God; the Apostle himself was soon to lay down his life as a sacrifice at the gates of the imperial city. Out of love to those disciples who had braved already the threatenings of power, he depicts, with the masterly hand of an experienced traveller, the perils and the fruits of the journey. There is no deception of concealment smoothing his discourse; but there is the fervor of genuine honesty in his language, as he throws the glow of assurance upon his convictions of the truth. Let no dread of the outer violence, let no cowardly surrender to an inward weakness, betray the immensity which rests within your trust. It takes a canopy full of worlds to declare the glory of God; and that glory is yours, shall be revealed in you, if you but withstand and hope to the end.

I know, he would seem to admit, that the sorrows of this life are surges that never cease to lisp along its coast, that suffering is in its very nature grievous to be borne, and seems to be the farthest from the happiness we desire. But there was another reality which he could not forget, and must not conceal; the life of suffering teemed with its own blessed fruits of patience, of humility, of weaning from the relish of this present bondage. I speak as Paul the aged. I speak as Paul the disputant with the Greek, the scholar of the Hebrews. My years, which have harvested blessings as they planted griefs, have been the chain of witnesses that the suffering here and the virtue revealed here bear no comparison. And when I wrestled with the wily Greek, my voice was but the echo of his own philosopher, his divine Plato, "that neither the happiness of good men nor the sufferings of the wicked, are in multitude or magnitude to be compared with that which awaits them both in another state." And the accents of Hebrew piety that float upon the memories of my boyhood are the testimonies of the suffering Apostle, "It is good for me that I have been in trouble. Before I was afflicted I went wrong, but now have I kept Thy statutes." But when above all this he mounted, a pilgrim to the land of promise; when he recalled the grace that had rescued him in Christ; when he realized what God had manifested to man in the sufferings of Jesus, what man had manifested in the new life that came by this Divine Jesus—was there any comparison possible between this brief moment of suffering, and that suffering a triumph through grace, and that untold and unspeakable glory? This was the man that had visions to glory in; this was the man that had gazed on the splendors of Paradise; this was the man that glanced across the fields of promise, and anticipated the knowledge which shall break upon our souls "out of the body." He testifies as one that had seen, he stands in the place of that parent whose spirit would speak to us from the regions of future glory, he stands in the place of that friend whose voice is divided from us by the dark curtains of the silent grave, and his language is a bold and sublime figure. The scale-beam of eternal justice is poised before him; angels heap into the balance their splendid trusts for the enriching and ennobling of man—man, the faithful, man the persevering, the angel-like. Upon the nearest balance of the beam, the fabled Pandora, lays her deceptive casket. Sufferings throng within it; woe lies upon the top of woe; maladies of the body and melancholies of the soul are gathered there. It is one vast receptacle of evil, such as the fable described. But Epimetheus discovers beneath them all the remedy, the healing balm of *hope*, and tasting of this heavenly gift of hope, the vision interprets itself in the encouraging conclusion that the sufferings of this present time are not worth weighing in the balance against the glory that is to be revealed in us.

XXXII.

RELIANCE UPON PROVIDENCE.

ST. MATTHEW vi 34.

"Take therefore no thought for the morrow: for the morrow shall take thought for the things of itself. Sufficient unto the day is the evil thereof."

THE plainness of the sermon from which this text is taken, forbids any other *kind* of sermon upon it. Before entering upon the simple truth taught us by these words, we cannot help pausing to notice how thoroughly doctrine and practice are mingled in the teachings of our Blessed Lord, how happily deep principles of religion are wrapt up in plain rules of life, and so the wisdom of heaven taught in the language of earth. So in the case before us, instead of discussing the cause of evil, or the vicissitudes of life, or the frailty and dependence of man; or instead of vindicating the schemes of Providence, and the goodness of God, He gathered them all together in a plain rule of duty with plain reasons for it, "Take therefore no thought for the morrow: for the morrow shall take thought for the things of itself. Sufficient unto the day is the evil thereof." Following the same course, let us learn to apply the rule our Divine Master has given, and to settle among our first principles, the reasons of that rule. We shall at this time enlarge on the meaning and application of the rule itself, without treating of the reasons which our Lord added to it.

I. "Take no thought for the morrow," was the Christian rule given to the first disciples. It is not to be understood from this, that no regard is to be had to the morrow, no heed taken of its probable demands, or its sure duties. Neither is it to be supposed that only the coming day with its prospects and concerns is embraced by this rule. The whole season of this short and uncertain life is to be awaited with the same patience and composure as we are bidden to observe in regard to the morrow. And the degree of our concern is expressed clearly enough in the original, which in its true force does not forbid the shaping of any plan with earnest attention to the future. It does not propose a duty so impossible to man as the entire neglect of wants and trials yet to come. This course would be as far from the blameless example of Him who uttered this holy precept, as it is from the plain sense of the words in the gospel. Our L od's declaration was, Trouble not yourselves, or, Ye may not trouble yourselves about the morrow. Burden not yourselves with its cares. The rule in any less sense would urge to its own breach, for the very effort, since effort it must be, the very effort to drive away all thought of the future would only unfold its dangers, startle our own doubts, and keep both the dangers and the doubts always uppermost in our thoughts. Such a struggle against the dictates of common prudence would little help our usefulness to one another, or that peace of mind which Christ so often promised to His followers, and so freely bestowed upon them.

According to the proper import of the words, on the other hand, this bidding takes off the pressure of the future and requires us to seek a high and mighty principle which may bear up under all cares by lifting them up to God. The rule of Christ is not one of senseless slumber, but of pious watchfulness. He never urges men to drown their cares, but to bear them. His precepts were not meant to force us down to the rank of brutes, but to lift us up among the angels, in His own likeness, unto the very glory of God. "Be ye therefore perfect" was His literal command. "Be ye therefore perfect, even as your Father which is in heaven is perfect." It is not the design of Christ's religion to check our thoughts, but to control them; it does not throw away our powers, but guides them in the wisest way towards the best ends. It begins and ends with one great principle, the root and substance of the rule now before us, the very spirit and strength of that rule, and that principle is *trust in God.* Such trust alone can ease the anxieties of the day, and carry the burdens of the morrow. The temper maintained by this principle is that of reliance upon God—full, open, cheerful, fixed reliance upon God. Such confidence in a Father's love and power makes all troubles and pains alike, and finds in the promises of Divine succor relief from the dangers of our own weakness and blindness. This temper of mind is the secret of all true contentment, and the buoyant upholder of industry and faithfulness among men. It fits us to our condition, keeping always in mind both our wants and our abilities. The whole avail of life for our own good depends upon this rule. It rests upon our relations to God, and these relations are the source of our whole being, our powers, our fortunes, our hopes. Trusting in the Almighty is leaving ourselves in the hands of Infinite Love, and Wisdom, and Power. It is the highest duty of the creature to the Creator, drawing all other duties in its train, and reaching the least desires or the humblest acts of him that aims to display it. Such is the range of that plain rule of Christ, "Take no thought for the morrow."

II. For the better appreciation of this rule, we shall now consider what is condemned by it. This condemnation assumes a double form. It is directed both against those habits which violate this rule virtually, and against those habits which, although not themselves violations, are yet inconsistent with its observance.

In the first place, indifference to the morrow breaks our Saviour's rule. He is not enjoining upon us to live as if another day could not be; it is enough that we live as if it might not be. The morrow, He says, shall bear its own cares. This is what we are to think. Take no thought, bring on you no care, undertake no trial which belongs to the future. We have enough to do now, in preparing for labors and sorrows to come. Christ would not have us to forget this; He makes this the ground for something beyond it, and because we are, and ought to be aware of difficulties awaiting us, bids us leave those difficulties to their own time, and take no thought for the morrow. We break this Divine command, whenever we hide from ourselves the thought that the morrow must come with its dangers and evils, and ought to find us watching. Who could ever keep this rule better than the Heavenly Master that taught it? Yet how was His soul straitened in looking out for the bloody baptism which in Him must be accomplished! How soon did His thoughts run on from the fate of His forerunner, to His own sufferings on the morrow! How carefully did He declare to His disciples the scourging, and wounds, and death, which should come between their present fellowship and His future ascension! Had He no thought of the morrow, when He brake the bread before His Apostles, and gave it unto them, saying: "This is My body which is given for you; this do in remembrance of Me?" Had He no thought of the morrow, when watching for it alone in blood and agony, He cried: "Father, let this cup pass from me?" Let His example teach His precepts. Take no thought for the morrow, which does not agree with this model for our thoughts, "Sufficient unto the day is the evil thereof." What better rebuke than this for the idle, the spendthrift, the prodigal? Every day shall be laden with its own sufferings; why should they heap up future sufferings by throwing off the thought of death, by wasting the advantages of to-day by indifference to the morrow?

2. This leads us to observe, in the second place, that the rule laid down by our Lord is meant expressly to condemn the neglect of present duty. It is drawn from the principle which our Lord uttered just before it. Knowing how often men overwhelm themselves with the cares of the present life, and how often things of eternal value are lost in their eagerness to provide for temporal wants; knowing that men were too apt to confine the whole future to the morrow, our blessed Lord taught us to repress our care for earthly things, to hold them in less esteem, to expect them only in the way of duty. "Seek ye first," were His words of wisdom, "seek ye first the kingdom of God, and His righteousness; and all these things shall be added unto you." And because this attention to our present, our ever-pressing duty was the first great principle of a religious life, the only source of the Divine blessing, He subjoins the command, "Take *therefore* no thought for the morrow." For we ought to take this thought, that the neglect of to-day increases the dangers, and duties, and pains of the morrow. The present time with its powers, its chances, and its duties, is all that we can call our own. God has allowed us this, He may never give us the morrow, or else send it to us, if we neglect our present duty, as a stumbling block, a burden, and a curse. We ought, moreover, to take this thought to ourselves, that as God grants us no less time than we need, so He

gives us no more than we can use to advantage. A long life is short enough to prepare for an eternity, to lay up rewards, to ripen ourselves for the presence of saints, of angels and archangels, and of God Himself. No repentance can ever make amends for a day wasted. The sin may be forgiven but the loss remains. The advantage, the eternal profit, the heavenly rewards of this life must remain less by the worth of a day than they might have been. And when we think for what an infinity of bliss our few and evil days are fitting us, we can better reckon the worth of a single day, and the need that in gaining the spiritual profits of to-day we should take no thought for the morrow. Let us also remember that God's promises are conditional, and always continue so till they are fulfilled. The whole course of the future depends upon present duties. Our faithful discharge of God's will now is the only means of a blessing hereafter. The future is a result of the past and the present managed by those secondary causes through which the Almighty acts. We are not placed here as living machines which must work out a certain fabric, or break. We are rather like the plant which must thrive by care, and must grow by the nourishment of to-day, or else be fruitless when the harvest comes. We are as a vineyard of the Lord's planting which must rejoice in the dew and the sunshine of each day and night, or be given over to cursing. We are like the grass which to-day is and to-morrow is cast into the oven. The voice of wisdom is, "Work while the day lasts. Take no thought for the morrow : for the morrow shall take thought for the things of itself." What was the answer of our Lord, when warned of the death awaiting Him? "Behold, I cast out devils, and I do cures to-day and to-morrow, and the third day I shall be perfected." He must finish the work given Him to do, He must do the lesser works of love to-day and to-morrow, and afterward fulfil the great work of death. . Present toil, present faithfulness was His perfect way. "To-day, if ye will hear His voice, harden not your heart."

3. But in the third place, this rule condemns the abuse of our present time to covetousness. The great pretext for this sin is our need of supplies against future wants. The rule of Christ roots out such a pretext, "Take no thought for the morrow." As it forbids us to postpone duties, so it requires us to anticipate mercy. Commandments and promises go together; God reveals the one that we may earn the other, "If thou wilt enter into life, keep the commandments." Our hope of a blessing to-morrow depends upon our trusting his word to-day. If we seek first His kingdom and His righteousness, earthly things shall be added unto us. Covetousness distrusts this promise, seeks first the earthly blessing, takes thought for the morrow, and the morrow only. Its aims reach not beyond the wants of time; its desires and strength are wasted in clinging to that which must soon fail, and in gaining beforehand what God promises to furnish in due time. The

life which our Lord requires is one of reliance upon Him, founded upon faith in His promises, performing always His will, looking for his blessing only upon honest, self-denying industry, — pure-minded and strong-hearted labor in our calling. Riches heaped up by going beyond this rule must rust upon our hands, must carry with them the curse of idolatry. Why should we bow down to the cruel Divinity of self-satisfied plenty, when the maker of all has eternal riches for them that bow down to Him? Why should we yield the affections of an immortal soul to the worship of what rewards with care and not with strength, and pay homage to the dust out of which we were made? This is not going on to heaven, but going back to earth. A man's life consisteth not in the abundance of things which he possesseth. These are only the garb of life; death shall strip it off; estates and gettings cannot go up with us to judgment; if they reach God's presence they must go before us on the pinions of charity, and written within and without, "Holiness unto the Lord." They must be given up in the self-denial of to-day; they must be replaced by the toils of to-day; they will appear, if ever, where golden censers carry the incense of perpetual prayer. Lift your thoughts, then, beyond the wants of this world; labor for the meat that endureth; learn with the holy Apostle both to abound and to suffer need; as to *covetousness*, let it not be once named among you, as becometh saints. So trust in God as to "take no thought for the morrow, for the morrow shall take thought for the things of itself."

IV. There is yet another spirit which falls under the rebuke of our Lord as inconsistent with the strong heart and the calm will which His rule requires and his grace forms, this is an uneasy distrustful spirit, harassing itself with fears of future ill. It is unmindful of our daily death, and fears *that* will come to-morrow which must come in some measure every day. It has forgotten the curse which always is uttered, which every where is borne, "Cursed is the ground for thy sake: in sorrow shalt thou eat of it all the days of thy life; in the sweat of thy face shalt thou eat bread till thou return unto the ground." It forgets how the blessing comes, which in its very course of triumph fulfills the curse, "Blessed are they that mourn, for they shall be comforted. Blessed are ye when men shall revile you and persecute you, and shall say all manner of evil against you falsely for my sake." "Take, therefore, no thought for the morrow. Sufficient unto the day is the evil thereof." Evil is our appointed lot; enough for each day's strength, enough for our true advantage. It is as easy to endure it to-morrow as to-day, for the same hand always helps us, that we should not be overcome of evil. As we pray for our daily bread, so we daily pray, Deliver us from evil. The suffering which shall profit us comes now, we know not whether we shall meet any greater till death itself comes. That is the only danger which we are sure will befall us. For this struggle with the king of terrors we must be preparing all our life, taking this preparation upon us as our daily duty, looking on death as a part of that evil which may come upon us this day, not leaving it for the unseen and uncertain morrow. So, while we live to die, we shall take no thought for the morrow, we shall make each day to answer for itself. There is no restless dread in such a life, but the patient following of that Lamb of God who offered Himself a daily sacrifice, looking unto the end of life as only the filling up of that death which He died daily. His life and His words are a perpetual rebuke of the care-worn and harassed Christian. Though a man of sorrows, He forgot not to be a pattern of zeal; with the cross before Him, He went about doing good. When He spake of our fears, He pointed us to the fouls of the air, which wait on Him that feedeth them; He bade us consider the lilies of the field, arrayed in the glory which no human wisdom could reach, but God Himself put upon them. And the counsel which he draws from such sights is this, Be ye not of doubtful mind, fear not, little flock. It is one of the inconsistencies of human nature that men will trust so much in the faithfulness of their fellow-men, knowing their fickleness and bias, while they distrust their Maker and Preserver, the changeless source of every gift which they enjoy. They will even lavish their affections on that which must die, and be afraid that His love may fail who liveth forever. They are unwilling to content themselves with God's present favor, and harass themselves with the chances of their failure in His service, and forfeiture of His mercy. But we have no right to take fears beforehand in such a way; it dishonors God and betrays ourselves. Our only way to guard against future ill is to watch and pray. This forestalls temptation, strengthens endurance, possesses the soul, keeps down our fears.

V. Lastly, this rule of Christ has direct reference to our steadfastness in Christian principles, holding up to rebuke, as a palpable inconsistency, our yielding these through dread of sufferings, or for the sake of worldly gain. Over some minds, the reproach and scorn of men, or the lash and the faggot of persecution, will hold an almost resistless power. Another man will cheerfully endure the contumely or cruelty of his enemy, but easily yield to the fascinations of station and the delusive offers of a flattering distinction in life. Both think too much of the morrow; both count too much upon its pleasures. It has none of its own to give. If we are permitted to find any in it, they are the rewards of mammon, the hire of another master. God has not promised them, nor given them, and His blessing cannot go with them. He that yields in either way must meet a fearful fulfillment of our Saviour's words, "Ye cannot serve God and Mammon." Clinging to His revealed will must lay us open to many reproaches, whether they come in open persecution or in the jeers and neglect of a hollow-hearted world. The way of Christ was the heavy journeying of one despised and rejected of men. What marvel if others follow, when the whole valley of affliction has been hallowed by His tears and His blood? If we enter not the valley with Christ, we are following the highway of the world. We must hold to the one or love the other; we must hate the blandishments of the world, or despise the reproach of Christ. "No man can serve two masters; therefore I say unto you," were the words of our blessed Lord, "therefore I say unto you, take no thought for your life, what ye shall eat or what ye shall drink. Is not the life more than meat?" Has not life some higher end than the satiating of appetite? Is not the present life, this very day, of more esteem than to be lost in pleasures, or wasted for naught? Think better of that which God has given you. If any harm must come from spending the day well, how much greater the risk in spending it ill! Why, then, should we shrink from the future dangers of a Christian life, when we turn back only to heighten our dangers, and heap up evil for the morrow? If we would bear the marks of the Lord Jesus, we must hold fast His testimony. He call us to suffer with Him. Whoso forsakes the ease and riches and endearments of earth for His sake, shall receive what is as cheering, and valuable and lovely in this life with persecutions. We must wear the crown of thorns and the robe of mockery. These are a part of our triumph; under them Christ lives in us; He is providing the future for us. We have no need to take thought for the morrow; we know that God is as able to help us then as to spare us now; we are rejoicing in the peace of God; we leave the morrow to Him, who alone has it to give and to prosper. The voice of warning cries, "Sufficient unto the day is the evil thereof." Heaven sends back the encouraging echo, "My grace is sufficient for thee." Had you rather have been St. Paul with the thorn or St. Paul at Lystra? Had you rather have denied Christ with St. Peter, or been chained with him in the dungeon? Had you rather have been in the visions of John, or in his baptism of blood? I had rather have tasted the pains of the martyr than looked on the scenes of the future; I had rather have groaned with the soul that cried from under the altar, than have stood with the angel breaking the seals. I had rather come out of tribulation into heaven than die among the praises of millions.

We fear that Demas took too much thought for the morrow; but St. Paul protests, "I die daily." No, we have no advice for the morrow. If you will beat down the fears and pleasures of the world, to-day take thought, earnest thought for repentance; if you will rejoice in the smile of the Almighty and the exultation of a heart at peace with God, defer not till the morrow; to-day lift the voice of prayer, and league yourself with your Maker. If you will vow your wealth, and your strength and your will to God, promise it not to-morrow, but to-day speak it in your heart. When the last ill of humanity is coming upon you, you will need the grace of to-day, and have no thought for the morrow.

XXXIII.

LIBERALITY REWARDED.

ISAIAH xxxii. 8.

"The liberal deviseth liberal things; and by liberal things shall he stand."

IT is almost superfluous to descant at this day upon the praises or the promises which belong to the character of liberality. This is one of those virtues which are quite cursed by every man's speaking well of them. The liberal man stands in the high places of public estimation. If the great wind of applause could move us out of churlish habits, the shout of our day over liberality would give resistless impulse. The nobleman of conscience, *the honest man*, and the eulogized aristocrat of Scripture, *the good man*, are quite superseded by the greater wonder of civilized selfishness, *the liberal man*. It is scarcely possible for any other species of goodness to pass current, unless it have along with its value of intrinsic weight the image and superscription of liberality. Upon the mathematical and logical principle that the greater includes the less, the liberal is supposed to embrace most of the necessary virtues, and the proverb of the day might read, "With all thy gettings, get liberality."

I would not announce any such millennial news as that envy and detraction and scandal were dead, and generosity was thriving because there were none of these foes to gnaw at it. The charm is not in the virtue, but in the name. True liberality is no sooner recognized than before. It is as disputable as ever whether the title has been earned, and almost every degree of this virtue may be sought and gained by a man without his acquiring the credit of the least degree. The name is the honor. The majesty is in the word, as some lawyers have thought was the case with the king. And our honoring of liberality consists not in giving it to every claimant, but in disputing every one's claim to so high a title.

The subject of the text is therefore in this sense peculiar, that while each one will claim its application to himself, he is less tempted to pass the topic over to his neighbor.

Granting, then, the most universal pretension to the blessings of the text, we have each of us a personal interest in increasing the amount of the promise.

I need not enter into an argument to make it evident that the special province of the gospel was to bring into repute and into conspicuous existence this virtue of liberality. God made Himself a model of it, devising offerings of His own free-will, —giving with the utmost delight,—profuse, measureless in His bounties,—and putting all the achievements of redemption at the beginning and of man's goodness throughout upon the score of God's liberality, because everything was inaugurated and completed by the grace of God. There is no liberality in man, but is a faint image and reflection of what first comes to us in the Infinite Model. Jesus, the Giver of Himself for the world, was but the well-beloved of God, the Son in whom Deity must be well-pleased, because He was in the flesh this impersonation of Divine Liberality. The Father seeing this intention and this effect, could not disown the image of Himself, and though the Son was flesh and blood, yet was He worthy of a name above every name, because He was the Incarnation of Liberality. And there has since been no model of human character which God would sanction that has not exhibited the mission of Jesus,—whose appointment of ministrations rests in the sentence, "Freely ye have received, freely give." Liberality was the *source*, it is the substance of Christianity,—Divine in its inception, for all "is the gift of God," and blessed in its action above all endowments, for "it is more blessed to give than to receive."

What, then, is involved in the promise appended to this quality? "By liberal things shall he stand."

The stability here predicted was in its first and feeblest sense verified in the reign of Hezekiah. Under his sway, the liberal disposition was restored from its obsolete state. The free-will offerings over and above legal tithes and taxes abounded under the hand of this reformed and penitent monarch.

Nay, the disposition to a liberal and pious use of his advantages, notwithstanding the hopeless tuition of his childhood and the profane example of his father, exhibited itself on his first accession to the throne. From his ninth to his twenty-fifth year he had shared the luxuries and felt the tainting wickedness of the royal palace. Public corruption, promoted and protected by the neglects of religion, rioted around him. No safeguard was reared around this heir of power, save the priceless blessing to him of a devout mother. Filially heeding her instructions, the piety of his youth ripened into the liberality of manhood. He ascended the throne at the blush of manly vigor to impart to the sceptre that authority of virtue and that charm of generosity which the childhood of obedience and the habit of religion had stored in his own soul. Scripture renders this description of his traits into the devout phrase, "He trusted in the Lord God of Israel; so that after him was none like him among all the kings of Judah, nor any that were before him."

"The reformation of religion, under Hezekiah, aimed at three purposes: the extinction of idolatry, the correction of the nation's morals, and the restoration of God's worship to the Divine model established under David." This was the bosom-object of "the liberal devising liberal things." This was the picture in the view of the prophet. And our interpretation must be drawn not only from the words themselves, but from the character of the man and the work of reformation which signalized his reign. To effect his liberal purposes, he began by an exhortation to the priests and Levites. Reformation must begin with the ministers of holy things, that it may effectually spread among the people. "The Levites, and such of the priests as were right-minded, obeyed with alacrity; the priests doing that which they only could do, in cleansing the Holy of Holies and the sanctuary; and the Levites acting as their ministers in the court of the Lord's house. This done, the king gathered the civil rulers, and sanctified himself with them in the sin and trespass offerings, which were typical of his death; without which there could be no remission of sin and no sanctification of the human heart. He then proceeded to restore the rites and ceremonies which the law required, and with exact solemnity to renew the magnificent temple-worship with instruments and vocal song, commanded by God, arranged by his prophets, Gad and Nathan, and established by David. In a word, he renewed the use of the Book of Psalms.

The blessed effects of this reformation were exhibited in the zeal with which the people flocked to the passover, and with which all who were there present, on their return to their several cities, broke in pieces the images, cut down the groves, and threw down and destroyed the high places and altars devoted to idolatrous worship. Nor was this all. The brazen serpent itself, which Moses had cast and erected, by God's command, as a symbol of love and mercy, and as a means, through faith, of curing disease and preventing death,—the sign which had been for more than seven centuries preserved, venerated as the work of their great lawgiver, and associated in the hearts of men, with the wonders wrought in the wilderness—even the brazen serpent itself was broken by the king's command, and called Nehushtan, a vile thing of copper, because it had been made the instrument of idolatry.

The reason for this extreme measure is obvious. In the degenerate condition of the people, what was originally an auxiliary in pure devotion, had become the support of foul idolatries. The symbolic worship of the serpent was the worship of the great enemy of God and man, of a being full of subtlety, deceit, and poison. Like the Manichees of the Christian era, the polluted Israelites made a Deity of wickedness itself. Idolatry was thus the root of all the public crimes that had defaced the kingdom. In its *mildest* form, idolatry degrades and vilifies the Incomprehensible and the Almighty; in its *most corrupt*, it panders to the worst vices of which man is capable. In proportion, therefore, as the people were reclaimed from their false worship, they became more and more virtuous, more and more prosperous, more and more zealous, more and more liberal and generous. The favor of God towards them was manifested by increased abundance; and plenty, honor and glory shed their united splendor over all classes of men in that happy kingdom. The source of the blessing that waited upon his liberal devisings is tersely given, "The Lord was with him; and he prospered whithersoever he went forth."

In this sample of history (and history is God's diagram), we read not only the description of the liberal, but the fulfillment of the prophetic promise, "by liberal things he shall stand."

Stability is the product of which liberality is the root. Ordinary calculation is reversed, and the subtractions of liberality are the real additions of strength. And this stability, which Providence had intended to illustrate in the person of the pious king, expands itself into its triple elements.

The liberal monarch was sustained by his service and sacrifices of free-will, in the stability of the cause which engaged his youthful zeal,—in the stability of his earthly fortune, in spite of its hazards, and in the stability of his peace under the apprehension of impending calamity and death.

There seemed, in the first place, to be a sort of preservative power in the generosity and self-devotion which characterized his youth. Although a man of infirmities, touched with the weakness as well as the greatness of manhood, and none the less a man for being a king, there was a stability imparted to the cause he espoused by the very fact that he was liberal in its behalf. The success and the perpetuity of the reformation grew out of the generosity that prompted it. What had he on his own side at the outset, except the precepts of a wise mother and the dictates of a cultured conscience? Religion itself in all its sanctities of station, of custom, of precedent was against him. With a meaning formidable to common courage, wickedness was in high places. The doors of the Temple were shut, the sanctuary was defiled. Idolatry grouped its disgusting images around the sacred symbol of ancient piety. In contempt of these disadvantages, his well-disciplined youth prepared him for the sacrifice of every interest to the work of reforming the decayed religion of his people. There was no pause for some tide of favor,—no waiting till the current was set and then floating upon its surge,—no devising of measures to spare himself and throw others into the task and the peril. His first step was vigorous. And by the very force with which his first act of royalty trod upon temptation, he secured the promise that his heart's desire should stand. The reformation reign became the brilliant episode of Jewish history. It was one prolonged career of prosperity. The heart that devised liberally was preserved in strength. And the king whose piety thus consecrated his plans never beheld them defeated or forsaken.

My brethren, we affirm this to be but the type of the promise that always waits at the door of liberal devices. "God is not unfaithful that He will forget your works and labor that proceedeth of love." He cannot forget a man who leans upon the arm of His Providence. He cannot be faithless to a man who makes it the first point with his conscience to be a giver like God. I need not wander into royal homes for examples. It is written along the whole page of Providence. "There is that scattereth, and yet increaseth." The generous impulses that enlist a man in a good cause, lead him into the more hearty love of the cause. From being liberal, he becomes cordial. By the effort which unselfish motives prompted, he acquires an interest in the goodness of the cause. He loves what he had at first only approved. And in the reward which no eye can see, but his own heart can feel, he finds an assurance that by "liberal things he shall stand." Whether that liberality be the open hand of the bountiful giver, or the wide heart of charitable construction upon other's faults, or the generous utterance of sentiments narrowed by no prejudice, it has Providence for its ally; and the cause it cherishes shall remain the cause of its delight. How many of those whose Christian perseverance has brought them near to the prize of a ripened piety, first drew their hearts towards the excellence of the Christian's hope as they laid their offerings of liberality upon the altar? The man who has closed his heart against the promptings of liberality, has foreclosed his hope of heaven. True piety will be starved out where the impulses of generosity will not survive. The multiplying and coldly calculating breast of parsimony may throb in the delusion of its narrow, and unfeeling religion,—but how dwells the love of God in that heart which has thus cast off the love of our brother? Philanthropy is not so much the child as the twin-sister of piety. Angels that minister with all their gifts to the heirs of salvation, cannot welcome to their ministry the man whose gifts always flow in upon himself. Faith in Providence is the foundation of faith in Christ, and when the heart has shut up its liberality, as if God could not provide and would not reward, faith, though its dead leaves flutter amid the breathings of the spirit, faith is dead. The man of true hope is he that deviseth liberal things.

The stability which rewarded the liberality of Hezekiah, extended to his earthly fortune. The treasures of his kingdom grew with their consecration to the service of God. And the throne which his free bounty, his generous thought of the people's benefit had honored, was secured to him in peace through the hazards of more than a quarter of a century. The Assyrian, bloated with conquest, came up to threaten the integrity of his kingdom,—but God put a bridle in his jaw and a hook in his nose, and the entrenchments of liberality were left unmolested. In later years, the king was brought upon the bed of sickness to the verge of death. But even here the recompense of his liberality forsook him not. The respite and the rescue came from heaven, and the receding shadow on the dial at once told that no human power had been equal to this cure, and symbolized the prolongation of his days as the recession of death's shadow upon the dial of mortality. My brethren, there is something of the same promise wrapt in the first commandment with promise. Filial piety, as a virtue distinct in itself, stands under the blessing of lengthened days. Its tributes of honor are but a laudable form of that liberality which deviseth for the proper objects of our thought liberal things. History is but the repeated act of

Providence confirming this promise of an earthly stability.

I am no champion of any such theory of present reward or retribution as would reckon the virtues of men by the measure of their worldly prosperity. The mercy that corrects is often more painful than the long-suffering which forbears to smite. But when we regard the contented mind as wealth above all price,—when we consider how much better than affluence of possession is the enjoyment of a thankful spirit,—when we weigh the losses and disappointments of earth against the comforts of soul and the increased firmness of every grace after trial,—when we estimate the comparative value of a perishable prosperity and a sense of elements in ourselves superior to all vicissitudes, we can grasp the promise that by liberal things,—forestalling the changes and chances of life, and locating our wealth in the rich emotions of the generous hearts,—we shall stand.

But there was a consummation of results in the tranquil termination to which this monarch's life was brought. Although warned of the calamities that should befall his rebellious and ungodly people, a blessed calm was spread over his later years. "Is it not good," he submissively asks, "if peace and truth be in my days?" Whatever frown of heaven might impend over the prospects of the kingdom, his personal experience was tranquillity to the last. The Providence that stamped its triumph upon the care-worn brow beneath a crown, illustrates the blessing which waits upon the obscurer walks of piety. Peace is the great gift—the wonderful gift of God,—God's peculiar gift,—and peace is the allotment which heaven pays to its favorite, the liberal devising liberal things. No fever of avarice burns within his veins. No grudging passion curdles his blood. No fear of Providence stares upon his conscience. The sacrifices of his life were made on hope,—and hope, like the tender mother, casts her sheltering mantle over the chilled and shivering limbs of her dying child.

> "Sure the last end
> Of the good man is peace. How calm his exit!
> Night dews fall not more calmly on the ground,
> Nor weary worn-out winds expire so soft."

XXXIV.

MOTHERS AND BROTHERS.

St. Matt. xii. 49.

"And he stretched forth his hand toward his disciples, and said, Behold my mother and my brethren!"

IT is the province as it is the custom of one who rises above the level of common thoughts, to speak in phrases which are enigmatic. His higher point of view justifies a higher style of expression. Partly from the disqualification of the unprepared mind to receive the sentiment, and partly from the danger of intrusting truths among those who are sure to suffer by their abuse of them, the phrase of our Lord assumed the enigmatic character of parable or apothegm.

Let me not be understood to say that it was any mark of greatness, or was any aim of Christ, to affect profundity, or to cover up sense in obscure and equivocal words. My meaning rather is that the desire to be useful in our language, and to make our words carry their weight of sense, obliges us to intimate, by allusion, what would not be accepted in its fulness, and to reserve, for those whom it may profit, the riper explanation of subtle truth. Jesus spake with authority—He taught by parables—He showed wisdom which His learned adversaries could not dispute, and yet the common people heard Him gladly.

There was some exhibition of this act (if we may so term it) in the instruction which He derived from the interference of His mother and His brethren with His discharge of His high functions. They were slow to perceive the office that was devolved upon Him. Though He had seized upon His destiny from early childhood, there seems to have been no clear appreciation, even on the part of His mother, of the work that lay upon Him. His tarry in the temple, when twelve years of age, asking and answering so strangely and so wisely, was a part of that Father's business, which He recognized as His task. And afterwards, when many a glimpse and pondering had convinced Mary of the wonder of miracle that lay at His command, and she attempted to precipitate this display of His office, there was something of rebuke in His reply—"Woman, what have I to do with thee?"—as if it were impossible that she or any other mortal could divine the office He had to fulfill, or could assign the times and places for the manifestation of His glory. Something of the same haste on the part of His mother and kindred, and something of the same chiding for their interruption of His office, appear in the incident connected with our text.

It seems, from St. Mark's account of events, that the zeal and the wonder-working of our Lord had drawn throngs around Him, and had occupied Him so intently that neither Himself nor His kindred could observe their domestic rules. "And when His friends heard of it, they went out to lay hold on Him; for they said, He is beside himself."

The history proceeds to tell us what malicious advantage was taken of this remark from His friends, and what scorn the Pharisees cast upon Him as a child of phrensy and a tool of the devil. And now, when, with persevering pursuit of His office, He seeks again the crowd of hearers, and rallies again around Him the disciples of His system, a mother's timidity and the distrust of kindred again recall Him from His work. Misconstruing His destiny, they arrested His work. Deeming the duties of domestic affection to be the paramount obligations of life, they hindered Him in His office. And measuring the ties of relationship only in the direction of consanguinity, they gave Him occasion to teach the higher source of kindred and affection. "He stretched forth his hand toward his disciples, and said, Behold my mother and my brethren! For whosoever shall do the will of my Father which is in heaven, the same is my brother, and sister, and mother."

In these incidents, there are three main topics on which our thoughts must dwell—the disposition of the kindred of Christ; the regard which He really had for His mother and brethren, and the deeper ground of attachment which His words reveal.

In the disposition of the mother of Jesus and of His brethren, there is evinced the natural tendency of our most innocent and our purest earthly affections to overpower and outwrestle the efforts of a holy wisdom. They quite unawares carnalize our nature. While we think them lawful emotions, and act upon them without a suspicion, they bring us into collision with the work of Christ. Who supposes that the mother of Jesus had forgotten His strange relation to her, or His supernatural endowment? Who supposes that the ecstatic dreams with which she watched His infancy, or the pale awe with which she looked upon His childhood, had gone from her mind? Could she have forgotten that angels were foretelling His greatness, and that the Heavenly Father had always waited upon His steps? But even piety and wonder and faith bent before the violence of a mother's affection.

She joins with her kindred in their blind interference with His charities. She remonstrates with the authority of her maternal relation against His zeal and self-sacrifice. She puts her love in the place of duty, and, true to the spontaneous impulse of a woman, she can see no higher mission than the gushings of natural affection.

Now, if our Saviour had only viewed this disposition from the mother's side, there would have been everything to commend in it. It was natural; and who can blame what is so genuine? It was the fulness of affection; and what so next to Divine as a mother's love? It was the unselfish thought of peril on *His* part; and what quickens heaven in us like this acting unselfishly? It was the suggestion of friends and the result of counsel; for his brethren were with her in the appeal.

We say, then, that our Saviour would have seemed to spurn all this goodness, and to throw contempt upon her affection, had He replied with unqualified reproof. Not so. He rather brings into more unmistaken prominence the fact that human affection prompted the interference. The love of a mother and the attachment of brethren are thrust by Him into the most conspicuous honor. It was as if He had said, "I tell you there is vast power and there is depth beneath depth in this might and magnanimity of affection. There is a world of love in the soul of man, and none but God has anything like it. The heartstrings are cords that heaven uses for its melodies. Hear it, ye disciples, my love has no image on earth to represent it, but those constraining, overpowering, all-subduing emotions which tie human souls together as mother and brethren. Behold my mother and my brethren!"

The serene dignity of His reply consisted in its reservation of this honor to the love that actuated His kindred, while He exposed the blindness that lay upon their spiritual understanding.

In thus charging with defects of grace that mother of Jesus, whom some misnamed Catholics have extolled beyond the Redeemer, I must fortify myself with the testimonies of antiquity, which all profess to respect. Theophylact taxes her, in this act, "with vain-glory and guilt in endeavoring to draw Jesus from teaching the Word;" Tertullian pronounces her guilty of "incredulity," and St.

Chrysostom accuses her of "vain-glory, infirmity and madness."

Under the shelter of these three ancients, I may employ milder terms of crimination. I only say that they failed to reach the height of spiritual understanding, and that, by an eclipse of soul, the higher sources of affinity were obscured from their view. Their disposition was to put their religion into the fervor of natural affections, instead of bringing the affections under the guardianship of religion. They forgot the order of things, and placed the earthly relation first, as if God's being and God's authority came in as a sort of auxiliary to the affections of this life.

Need I say that the true order is hereby reversed, and the true proportion of our duties first, and then of our character, destroyed? There is a kind of goodness that rests in just this posture. It is domestic kindness, it is the love of relations, it is the heart of tender friendship, it is the godliness of the brethren of Jesus; and it is well. But it is not sufficient. The great goodness is wanting. God is the first claimant. The chief love that benefits us is the love of God. And the sum of all charms is in the glorious greatest and best of beings. In His Word He calls Himself, in His Providence He shows Himself a *jealous* God. The putting anything above Him, or anything before Him, is the mortal sin. He withers that which we incline to substitute for Him. He makes the heart sore with its eagerness for other attractions. Or, what is still more terrible, He withdraws Himself and leaves us to our idolatries when we are bent upon refusing His love. And this is the harmonizing which we make of the two declarations, "that God is love," and that He is "a jealous God." It is His claim, and our blessedness, that there should be nothing nearer to us than Him. And Christ, in His work of salvation, stands to us in the place of God, drawing us by Himself towards His Father, and transmuting all our affections of faith into the love of God. For He it is that challengeth this right in our souls, "Who so loveth father or mother more than me, is not worthy of me."

The subject thus conducts us to the second topic offered by the text—the regard of Christ for His mother and His brethren. We say, then, at the outset, that the language in the text, so far from intending to disparage His earthly attachments, implies that they were ardent, enduring, intense and unconcealed. He puts the appearance of fervor and firmness upon them. He uses them to image forth a love and an affiance which could not so well be the object of sight. How could that which was itself ambiguous or reserved be the representative of what is plain and prominent? For the sake of showing to the faith of all generations the explicitness and the reality of His affection to His disciples always and everywhere, He compares it to that which was distinct and glowing in His life—the love of His mother—the love of them that were by nature the nearest.

Now, without expanding the entire revelation on

this point, it is enough to observe that our blessed Saviour Himself, in patterning perfection, did receive into especial closeness and ardor of affection, some of those who were brought into earthly relations with Him. We read of the disciple whom Jesus loved—of the love which He had for Lazarus and his sister, and on account of which a miracle of interposition was expected. We observe a special intimacy of our Saviour with the beloved John. And we see that this bosom-friend of Christ, who leaned upon his breast in the hour of confidence and of suspense, was the dying friend of the Saviour, to whom, with filial affection, He committed the mother at the cross, and whom He commended as a son to the love of that mother. In all respects, then, Jesus had no fear of hazarding his benevolence and his width of affection for mankind by concentrating His human sympathies upon a special friend. There is, on the other hand, a systematic effort in the gospels to give clearness and intensity to these His personal affections. They were the marked indications of His human tenderness—they were the weakness (if rough manliness may so term them) of His heart—they were the sources of His cares, His tears, and the earthly solace of His final agony.

I take it, then, that our Lord was conscious of the delicacy and exquisiteness of His own affections for His mother and His brethren—conscious of the undisguised candor that exhibited this affection—conscious of its part in the culture of a proper human character, when "He stretched forth his hand toward his disciples, and said, Behold my mother and my brethren!"

There must be, therefore, some deeper ground of attachment than our natural relation, which could thus bring the wide diversities of mankind up into a species of kindred with Christ.

This new source of relations is the third topic which the text reveals.

There was really no novelty in this discovery of deeper sentiments in our nature. It was among the earliest statutes for man. It was, indeed, a sort of need with which he was created. His soul was constructed upon the plan of adaptation to new relations. The first symbol of Christ's love for His church was the man's heart that could leave the father and mother and cleave to the wife. The relation was still earthly, but it showed the capacities for enrichment that belongs to the human soul. I know not if I have uttered this with enough precision. The soul of man is endowed, in its creation, with the power of framing to itself relations which involve the exercise of its warmest affections, and which were no part of its natural ties.

And I say that the heavenly relation into which the love of God brings us is paralleled, because it was symbolized from the beginning by this conjugal affection. The doing of the will of God, the actual placing of ourselves in relation with that Blessed Perfection, is appointed to put us into a new family, and that God's own, God's blessed, and to bring out a still nobler development of our nature. It makes us kindred with the Infinite Being. It calls out affections which mock at death. It gives us sympathy with the greatest of our kind; nay, it passes humanity, and we are of angels' lineage, *sons of God* they call us, akin with Christ, of that family which knows no death, for its name is immortality. O honorable name! which is above every name! which is the kindred of Him that hath immortality! Birthright incomprehensible! Brotherhood immaculate! What lineage of greatness can compare with this household name, this title of endearment, which the King of kings applies to the least of them that love His Father—"Whomsoever shall do the will of God, the same is my brother, and my sister, and mother."

My brethren, I have no desire to parade the plain, though important truths which stand upon the surface of this theme. They must have arrested our thoughts as we surveyed this text. We cannot escape observing the practical and the comforting assurance given here, that our Saviour looks with the most unfeigned and the most intense interest upon all His disciples. Though He perceives their infirmities, though He reads the intricate lessons of corruption beneath our professions of piety, though He sees the lingering frailties of humanity, though He knows that the blood of earth touches the heart which His blood has cleansed, yet He receives that warm desire of discipleship as the appeal of consanguinity to His own breast. We tell with shame of our depravity, but He hides the shame under His bending compassions, and says, "My brother!" We mourn in our calamity, as if it were sorrowful to be mortal and to be human; but He stands before us as the man of sorrows and acquainted with grief, and says, It is only the cross of love, my sister and my mother.

There are, however, two grand instructions hidden beneath the surface of this text. They are not capable of being amplified within our limits. I can only suggest them, praying God to make the suggestion a root of reflection.

The first suggestion is that the love of relations and friends is the school in which are disciplined for the widest charity and the highest, even the heavenly society. There is some kind of resemblance between the virtue that here abides under earthly relations, steadfast, gentle, submissive, prompt in duty, alert in feeling — some resemblance between the kindly and faithful keeping of earth's brotherhoods, and the happy participation in heaven's affections. That philanthropy which always leaps out of its own relations, and burns only for the far off charity—which passes by the neighbor in his moans, and reaches a strained pulse for the distant Hindoo — which is grand upon a wide scale, and contracted as the scale is narrowed —that philanthropy which must reorganize society and have rudiments to love, or it has no hope and no heart for the work — that philanthropy which has no gentleness and no heartiness at home and in its own kindred—that philanthropy, though it *bleed* to serve its fancy, though it give its body to be burned, is not charity, is not patiently do ng the will of God, and has no share in that h r.d which points from the heart that loved its kindred with the voice, "Behold my mother and my brethren!"

There is a universe of philosophy wrapt in the homely maxim, "Charity begins at home."

The second instruction to be suggested is the dependence of love upon practice. We are used to speak of it as a feeling. And we are too likely to think of it as the same, and no more. And, as a consequence, we are apt to flatter ourselves that the more the feeling the greater the love—that our Christian character is only genuine as it takes this form of strong feeling; nay, that the beginning and the substance of Christianity is to be possessed with these forces of feeling. But this is all false philosophy, and a contradiction of Christ. He puts the element of love in the fact of practice. It is the doing of God's will which draws out His title of brother. He disowns the reality of the imaginative sentiment, and He has no idea that true love can exist or grow in us except as it lives in practice.

My brethren, this is the attraction which charms God—this is the winning way that touches the heart of Christ. To come in the practice of our duties—to come as those that are too loving to ask any other privilege but that of serving God—this is that warfare which besieges heaven and takes mercy itself captive.

XXXV.

PURITY.

ST. JAMES iii. 17.

"The wisdom that is from above is first pure, then peaceable, gentle, and easy to be entreated, full of mercy and good fruits, without partiality, and without hypocrisy."

THERE are two methods proposed to the choice of men, by which wisdom can be acquired. One is the slow, and painful, and endless method of experience, learning our errors by suffering for them, and increasing our confidence in truth, by observing that it is salutary and irreversible. The shorter, the easier, and the more compendious method of conveying wisdom is by impartation, enabling us to know at once what others have reached by long and arduous experience, and enriching us not with the problematical and timid conclusions of half-tested truth, but with sure and reliable results. Faith is the direct road to this latter fountain of wisdom. Faith in men conducts us to their oracular announcements of what has been found by them to be wise. But man's scope of certain knowledge is so limited, that when we touch the verities of eternity, or need some guidance through new difficulties and into other worlds, or even appreciate the mysterious relation between our own secret being, and the Being that searches our inward thoughts, faith assumes a new form, rises into grander power, becomes the guardian faculty of the soul, receiving from an infallible source, and imparting to our frailty "the wisdom that is from above."

Holy Scripture in its mention of *wisdom* seems to be vibrating between the practical and the dogmatic sense. Wisdom often puts on personal attributes, and addresses our attention as a Chief Counsellor in the designs of God, when He first conceived the fabric of the Universe, or when He arranges the marvels of redemption. And then it appears in its more earthly and narrower sense as meaning no more than the well-balanced order of our human faculties. There is but one key to this strange confusion of scriptural ideas. The Christ of grace is the explanation of the enigma of Scripture. He that was the wisdom of God, He that growing here as a child in human wisdom was the Everlasting Counsellor. He that was with God "when He prepared the heavens, and was daily His delight," and yet coming from above, "His delights were with the sons of men," has alone bridged the chasm which lies between that consciousness in Scripture of the personality of wisdom, and that consciousness in man of his ability to possess wisdom.

And this very tendency of wisdom to bring down the heavenly into the practical principles of a human life is what gives such a direction to the

Apostle's language. "The wisdom that is from above is" evinced in qualities which every human soul can understand and acquire.

The subject before us, then, is no ideal and romantic phantasm. It is a substantial and practical combination of virtues, assuming the precise order which is here represented. And the reality of this supreme wisdom in us displays itself so as to justify the description, "the wisdom that is from above is *first pure*."

Our plainest avenue into the resources of this Scripture is by the two inquiries: What is implied in this quality of *purity?* And for what reasons is it assigned the *first* place among the characteristics of a genuine wisdom?

In attempting to fix our gaze upon an object of so much delicacy and sensitiveness as *purity*, we must not forget that our finer perceptions are called into demand. The blurred and blinded eye of the sensualist can scarcely discern these beautiful lineaments. The jaundiced eye of jealousy and spite finds purity itself spotted with blemishes which have their origin only in the diseased eye of the observer. Dismiss this grossness, and guard the eye of your soul with the veil of humility while you look upon this faultless model—purity. What is it philosophically? What is it in effect? It defines itself to the mind's eye as distinguished from mixture and from pollution.

The gold that has one atom of the baser alloy is not pure. You must disengage it from that which mixes with it, and blends with its substance or you may have the rich compound but you have not purity. Whatever in our habits intercepts our clear view of the Holy God, whatever obscures our transparency of heart, whatever mixes with our motives so as to leave the least doubt or confusion as to our sincerity, is the ruin of purity. To lose this clearness and perfectness of soul it is not necessary that we should be a lump of malice, it is only necessary that we should give inlet to a debased and sordid element.

Why, the wise man of the world perceived this distinction between purity and admixture. Even a chance fly turns the sweet odors to offence, "So doth a little folly him that is in reputation for wisdom and honor." But where unmixed clearness and perfectness of God's gifts would be exhibited there is an effort to emphasize their disengagements from all alloy. "The words of the Lord are pure words, as silver tried in a furnace of earth, purified seven times."

Purity is also to be distinguished from pollution. That which carries no corruption in its substance, which holds no impurity in solution, may yet be defiled by stains and contagions. The pure waters of the fountain may gather turbidness from the channels into which they flow. The diamond that bears no flaw may be coated with the material that destroys its lustre. The soul stained with the conscience of guilt is blotted and impure. In deprecation of this pollution, the wise man utters his counsel, "Let thy garments be always white;" and the Apostle instructs his son, "Keep thyself pure," for he, conscious of conniving at no man's ruin, could protest, "I am pure from the blood of all men."

Alas, for our lame and wayward nature! Who is pure, if this be our standard? Who never permits one baser element to mingle with the singleness of his heart's devotion? Where is the tenant in this body of corruption, who has never permitted a spot to deface the record that God reads?

Among the accusations of my fellow-mortals, my outward innocence may echo its challenge; but to the vision of that Purity which chargeth the angels with folly and writeth bitter complaints against man,

"The Spirit, in His power divine,
  Would cast my vaunting soul to earth,
Expose the foulness of its sin,
  And show the vileness of its worth."

No, it is not in man to cleanse his own heart, or to lift it up before his God and say, "There is no fleck of sin upon this mirror of Thy perfections." Rather need I cry "Create in me a clean heart."

Yes, it must be a creation. It must be not that first breath on whose blank page I have written such characters of shame; it must be the new begetting which the Spirit of God produces, moving upon the chaos and confusion of this universe within. Then shall God pass His blessed oblivion upon my sins; then shall the blood of the Lamb purify those tainted tides that have throbbed through my heart; and purified, from the source of undefiled purity, shall become to me the new inheritance, the earnest of those pure and brilliant things that live where sin and death are known no more.

And what are the effects of this imparted purification? Let us barely hover over them for a moment, and epitomize the description.

Purity, thus our possession by grace, will take the sceptre from polluted nature, and begin the exercise of its sovereignty over our thoughts. They rambled in forbidden lawlessness; they resented the control which refused them secret indulgence; they snapped the chains of conscience, and hurried the soul through scenes of filth, under the dark shadows of malignity, into the smeared and defiling caverns of foul imaginations, while our resistance was but the feeble, sickly hesitation of a willing victim. The new creation empowers the thoughts to banish these corrupting intruders, or, at least, to fling them behind our back with a disgust which resembles the indignant contempt of the Undefiled One, "Get thee behind me, Satan."

Within the screens of secrecy, into the laboratory of the soul we penetrate. Here desire takes its shape; here the will wields its rod of authority; and in this council-chamber is it decided whether the hidden idolatries of a lustful heart, or the sweet perfumes of pure desire, shall meet the footsteps of our visiting God. He stands before the door, and the test-question with which He searches us concerns these secret desires. Do we behold

His face in worship? Do we hasten to greet His approaches with a warm desire to be purified and welcome? Do we crush with a holy vengeance upon ourselves those tantalizing desires that reach out for what the hand dares not touch? Then has the sweet angel of purity killed the serpent in our hearts; then has the new life filled us with the new love; then has the baptism of purity cleansed the secret home of our desires, and made it a sanctuary that invites pure angels and their purer God.

But it is purity in a world of contamination, the lily among the thorns, and in its tremulous and precarious form resembling the sensitive plant. It fears the breath that fans it, trembles at the eye of God, shrinks at the shadow of danger, and hides itself from the temptation that might soil its integrity. If there be not in our soul this sensitiveness, fearing to be sullied and shunning contact with everything that blemishes our service of God, then is our purity but the cold marble statue that stood unblushing amid the orgies of debauching Paganism, and not the living, trembling exotic that shudders in this clime of sin and waits for a congenial paradise.

We recognize the entrancing and cherubic ideal. We concede that this grace of purity is the enviable and spotless radiance which befits the heavenly world, and gleams before the most faultless human soul as a pattern towards which we elevate our hopes, and far from which our infected nature drags its gross propensities.

Why, then, should this exalted perfection be

placed in the very forefront of our virtues? Why should it be assigned the leadership in the army of our aspirations? Why should the wisdom from above be *first pure*, when its ultimate and remotest achievement is to put on incorruption? My brethren, there is a profound philosophy in this very arrangement. It is intended to imply the origin and source of our religious life. It is not a power originating in our depraved and sullied nature. Its fountain is Purity Immaculate. It gushes from the throne of God. He imparts, or we never partake. No human breast has contrived the grace that animates and purifies. No teeming wit of man has expelled those defiling imaginations, and washed the conscience of its uncleanness and guilt. The power that now creates is from the same Being who said, "Let there be light, and there was light." "Every good gift and every perfect gift is from above, and cometh down from the Father of lights." All that restores, all that lays the foundations of new life must be sought at His hands. It is first among the treasures of His perfection, and then among the bestowments of His pity, and therefore it is first pure.

This prominence of purity refers us also to the elements out of which all the beauties of the Christian character are to spring. They cannot be grafted upon any stock of falsehood. Some semblances of the angelic, and some short-lived blossoms of the saintly may cling to a branch whose root and sap is falsehood. But the living, perennial, fragrant charms of a life wise for eternity must bloom upon the thriving stock of truth. The first essential for any life that has alliance with Nature and Providence is truth. And the only assurance that we can have of permanence to our principles and stability to our virtues is sound and uncorrupted truth as the basis of our mental structure. It is fruitless outlay of our care when we have not immovable principles for our foundation. Human infirmity weakens more than half our best work. The first inquiry of all genuine wisdom is for foundations that cannot be shaken. The first de mand of a soul is truth. The first element of wisdom is doctrine undefiled. And therefore St. Peter speaks with the same philosophy as St. James, "Ye have purified your souls in obeying the truth."

There is a third and most impressive reason for assigning to purity the first place in the order of virtue. That reason is involved in the startling fact that impurity is the most fatal adversary which heavenly wisdom is required in this world to encounter.

Take this in its broadest sense, and dispute will not be offered. If impurity consists in the unbridled license of sensual thoughts; if it betrays itself in unrestrained and wanton desires; if it entertains no hatred for the enormities of lust, and no dread of the pestilence that poisons the soul; then is it the inveterate enemy in imagination, in word, in society, of everything that helps to ennoble or to sanctify our nature.

But we leave this wide field of observation, and

descend into the nearer particulars of life, and we allege that impurity clogs the very approaches of salvation, and sways the world with a deadly supremacy. One of the first essays for reclaiming the sordid and the abject is the lesson of cleanliness. The sanitary wisdom of communities strikes first at the death-bearing heaps of filth. The audacities of shameless impurity must yield to the outraged decencies of life, or society feels itself to be wallowing in the sickly symptoms of dissolution.

It is the hope under most of the temptations of life that time will unmask them, and the wearied soul will flee to better delights as it feels the hollowness of those it has pursued. But impurity is one of those strong delusions that never relax their bondage till we are helpless to retrieve our lot. It fascinates when we would resist. It plunges us into filthy thoughts because we attempt to wrestle with it. It suggests the most revolting suspicions of all that is pure and undefiled around us. It stings us into compliance with its degrading demands when we are robust, vigorous, and active. It steals upon our weak and morbid moments. Learning and culture will not shelter us from its gay and painted pollutions. The Solomon that explores every recess of knowledge cannot guard his own heart against this corruption. It turns the courts of royalty into voluptuous dens, smothers churches in its loathsome scandals, loads the calendar of crime with perjuries and brutalities, kindles fire-brands that desolate our homes, flings a jewelled robe over the rotten mockeries of propriety, and makes the very sanctities of religion contemptible when cloaking these carcasses of moral pollution.

Impurity is the secret destroyer that devours the souls of millions. This it is that drags the young Christian into the mire of treachery to his vows. It is impurity, is it not, that renders all our virtues so timid and cowardly; that makes us irresolute, artful, and evasive; that puts great barriers of impossibility between our defiled conscience and the sweet dreams of innocence; that unnerves our better purposes and compels us to trample down the bitter accusations of memory, the candid rebukes of repentance; that makes such multitudes of seemly and generous men afraid to wear the aspect of religion, ashamed of an appearance which their inward indulgence belies, conscious of a secret torture which apathy alone can alleviate, and willing to carry into the presence of Infinite Purity a defilement which dares not even pray for forgiveness. I believe it, my brethren, and I utter it with all the sorrow of one that sheds the tear of despair, there is no sin so inveterately corrupting as impurity, none that so teases the conscience, blinds the eye, nurses the heart for cruelty, enfeebles the better powers of our nature, frightens the angels from their watch and ward around us, deadens the sense of heaven, separates us from the companionship of Jesus, and leaves us drifting wrecks upon these billows, deserted by the Holy Ghost.

When Thyatira wore this stain upon her brow,

there was no remedy but great tribulation. "I will kill her children with death, and all the churches shall know that I am He which searcheth the reins and hearts; and I will give unto every one of you according to your works."

XXXVI.

PRACTICE VERSUS PROFESSION.

St. Matthew x. 33.

"Whosoever shall deny me before men, him will I also deny before my Father which is in heaven."

THERE is a help to the exposition of these words in the fact, that they were intended for the safe-keeping of those who were sent into the midst of danger. They are fastened to a prediction of suffering and hazard. They were designed by their burdens of interdict, to weigh against great temptation. Their force was laid as a buckler over the breasts of men, who were despatched upon an expedition among wolves, and these the more to be feared because they were not only cruel but crafty, not only ready to devour, but concealing their remorseless jaws under sheep's clothing. In such a desperate mission, silence must often be the best exhortation, preserving while it proclaimed not innocence. Escape from the mouths of such incorrigible subjects, for their efforts might often be the dictate of prudence. Yet there were concessions to these devourers of souls, which might save the flesh of the messenger at the expense of his innocence. Against these timidities and surrenders, Christ assigns a limit for their prudence. They might have a care for their bodies, and flee out of danger, but nothing must be permitted to lay a wound upon the soul. They might covert all they could by being harmless, but they must know that nothing ever should be gained by being faithless. They might discreetly shun too close a contact with every one that wore the wool of innocence, and stole for hunger into the flock, but no amount of deception and treachery on the part of others, no conversion of the whole flock into disguised wolves could palliate their defection, or screen them from the fangs of misery, if they denied Christ.

Evidently, the danger that was to beset them, and the crime that was so denounced in this penal statute of grace, was an unreality of character. It was the wearing of innocence in the face, and of a wolfish appetite beneath it. It was the appearance of biting the grass, while the jaws sought for flesh and blood. In a word, it was the assuming of that character which they were sent to convert. They were in danger of keeping their outside pretension on, while they adopted the maxims, copied the actions, nursed the appetites, and betrayed the dispositions of unbelief and ungodliness. Other men might make their denial of Christ in sceptical judgments, or in profane and derisive language, other men might deny Him by refusing to profess an open and entire allegiance. But this danger lay in another direction. They might deny Him, even when they professed to be His disciples and His champions. Their denial was a practical contradiction of their pretension. Denial in their case would be trebly aggravated.

It would be, first, the most solemn denial of Christ. It would be, second, the most treacherous and deceitful denial of Him. It would be, in the third place, the most mischievous and pernicious denial of Christ.

This practical denial, coupled with a pretence of allegiance, is the most solemn way of offending. It passes out of the region of a man's judgment, where his scepticism may be sheltered, and may have some covert from blame. It passes beyond the mere utterances of the tongue, which may be hasty and ill-considered and revoked in the shame that follows. It is a crime not only begotten in the heart, and nursed by the passions, but authorized and caressed and approved by our perseverance in the action, for it is to be noted that we are not speaking of some sudden and surprised act of denial, some chance defeat of our better habit and our firm resolution. I am speaking of a character that a man has taken and kept, of practical, and acted, and continued wickedness which a man is all the while cloaking and dissembling with a show of piety. It is, we say, the most solemn of all denials, because it is denial carried into practice. It is the utmost that a man can do to testify what he really believes and really means to act upon. It shows not so much the violence of temptation, as the determination of his heart. It is the putting of all emphasis upon an evil life, and saying the most plainly and the most boldly that whatever religion may be worth, it is not worth following. When a man takes oath, he puts himself upon solemnity, and calls God to witness that he speaks the whole truth from his heart. And so when a man puts wickedness into the fibre of his actions, and lives as a denier of the spiritual law, and then calls God to witness by his pretence of religion, there is a solemnity in his denial, which can only be visited upon him in justice, when amid the solemnities of final judgment, God is called to witness, and Christ denies this worker of iniquity.

This denial of Christ is a practice that stamps a falsehood on our profession, in the most treacherous and deceitful of denials. With the name of Christ upon their lips, and the honor of that name at stake in their lives, they are but betraying Him with a kiss. There is something extraordinary and hopeless in this way of sinning with a smooth face. To hear some such professors of religion utter their panegyrics on self-denial and spiritual purity and brotherly kindness, and their philippics against pride and dissipation, you might suppose that Christ had given them a special commission to paint a virtue and to daub a vice. But, alas! the superhuman melts away when you look below the tongue. They are no more than they call themselves, *professors* of religion. I do not like the phrase, to make the best of it. It has too much the sound of putting the religion in the profession, instead of making the religion such as to profess itself. But for them there is no apter designation.

They put their whole character into the business of professing religion. And were it not for seeming to deal in invective rather than the gospel, I should take a melancholy pleasure in holding up to view, and to our detestation, this counterfeit of a Christian. Such a man, lifting up his right hand to bear the testimony of a saint, and clinging with his left to the frauds of a sinner, grasping now the mercy-seat of God, and now the instruments of inhumanity, holding up his right hand to swear by the faith of a Christian, and with his left dealing far and wide the oaths of resentment and rage, "He feedeth on ashes: a deceived heart hath turned him aside, that he cannot deliver his soul, nor say, Is there not a lie in my right hand?"

Unto most men, the gospel is the beseeching invitation, "*Come* and *welcome*." Over the waters of tossing care, and over the crowds of earthly passion, the voice of Jesus trembles as the soothing breeze upon the fevered brow, "Come, come unto me." But the same voice deepens into forebodings of *woe*, woe unto hypocrites, and shall swell at last into accents of indignation, as the treacherous suppliant pleads his profession in palliation of his practices, "I never knew you, depart from me all ye workers of iniquity.'

This contradiction of our profession in our practice is the most mischievous and pernicious denial of Christ. The subtle cavil of the scorner is known to be the protection of his career; the bitter jest of the profane is seen to issue from the wishes and prejudices of his own heart; and scepticism, however triumphant in argument, concedes itself to be ignorant of the moral power of faith. But when a Christian man has learned the art of holding at the same time his religion and his sins, he becomes a quoted precedent for every scorner, jester and sceptic. Upon him, as the premiss, hangs the mischievous inference that religion is no element of our true character. It is argued, out of his example, that God has pronounced no wedlock between piety and virtue. The suspicion which his sins have excited lies against the religion he pretends. He brandishes the keys of heaven only to show how confidently a man can hold these, and yet neither go in himself, nor suffer them that are entering to go in. When he prays, and prays the more that he may sin, the more the world shrinks into the sullen conclusion that our prayers make us none the better; when the dormant emotions of religion awake, and hurry him into acts of piety to hide away his sins, the world scorns a religion that thus indulges instead of expelling sin. Entangled in the snares of a corrupt nature, there is no remedy and no escape for him, but in the thorough reconstruction of his character. If he persist in his disguises, mischief spreads around him; if he abandon all restraint and all appearances, mischief strews his path; if he brave the odium of the world, and claim that there is no incongruity in his pretension and his practice, mischief exults in his confession, and on his testimony drags iniquity up to the elevation of impunity, because he has dragged religion down to the degradation of an empty pretencc.

Can there be a more direct denial of Christ than this fastening of his name upon our evil practices? Is there any blasphemy, any desertion, that so emphatically disowns him—so openly and unqualifiedly contradicts not only His words, but His office, His very nature? When a ruffian insults us, we can bear it, for his act is the proof of his own indecency; when an enemy maligns us, we can yet hope to touch his honor; when a friend deserts us, and a pledged companion breaks his vows, we can reason with him, we can pity his weakness, or we can confess the just occasion for his offence; but when a man protests that he is my friend, and then chases me with falsehoods and aspersions and hostility—when he alleges that I consent to the terms of such friendship, when he claims that I have given occasion for all his treachery, and am pleased with his vileness, and am honored by his false professions, there is no alternative left but to deny the charge by denying him. I may bear with a friend's infirmity, I must listen to his apologies; but nothing can bind me to disown my own nature and deny the very virtue which makes me worthy of friendship. So holiness is the synonym for Christ; innocence was His nature; a purity that sprang out of His heart enveloped His life; He came to save us from our sins; the banishment of sin, and not the exculpation of the sinner, was the end and aim of His work; He loved us, not for our sins, but for His own longing to see us holy.

With what possible complacency, then, can he endure the contradiction of his gospel, the libel upon his life, the treachery to his very pity, which would convert Him into the origin, and patron and flatterer of our evil lives? No, disguise it, extenuate it, prevaricate as we may, Christ was the friend of man's repentance, and not of his iniquities. Whosoever by a practice nullifying his profession, whosoever shall so deny Christ before men, him will Christ deny before His Father in heaven.

But our thoughts are finally directed to the penalty which is suspended over the guilty denier of his Saviour.

My brethren, we covet not the faculty of delineating the miseries of the outcast, or giving vivid reality to the gloom and terrors of hell. Conscience will in this respect assert its own accusing office, and signify by its reproof the greater shame and the greater agony which must at last overwhelm both body and soul.

Let us, however, in few words allude to the extent of the calamity involved in our denial before God, the searcher of our hearts, before the multitudinous array of angel witnesses, before the assembled universe. There can be no doubt that our rejection by the Saviour Himself in that last awful day, is the ultimate punishment which he intends to denounce.

Let us recollect, however, that this conclusion of judgment is not a work outside and separate from the system of grace. The government of man by Christ tends continually to this end, and leads by direct processes to this last judgment. It is not out of the course of grace, but its crisis; it is not a perishing of Christ's mercy, but a consummation of it, and what has not been begun before cannot begin there, what is enacted there will be but the completion of that which has had its course. It is so with our rejection by Christ in the day of judgment. It will be but the final and irrevocable consummation of a denial that has already been exhibited and transacted by Christ.

He has an office under grace, which He is perpetually exercising for man. He stands before the Father as the living representation of our race; with His broken body He pleads for sinners; with His wounded brow He appeals to the covenant of mercy. "Behold, I am the victim," He says; "I am taking this tempted sinner under my care and guidance, suffer me to reason with him; let me speak to his conscience by the mouth of my ambassadors; let me put my spirit upon him, and anoint him for my servant; I will be his security till grace has done its utmost; Spare my people, spare for my blood's sake the penitent, the struggling, the unwitting enemy of God." And the gifts and graces freely shed upon rebellious man attest the efficacy of this Great Intercessor's unwearied prayer for man.

But here is the man that turns the grace of God into sin, that tastes the gift and owns the heaven-sent supply, and yet creates out of this mercy only an argument to harden himself in sin. Christ cannot own him as a being untried by grace; Christ cannot plead for him as a servant endeavoring to keep his fidelity; Christ cannot pray for grace where grace is useless, grace is denied. No; the very compassions of a Saviour are rejected, the spirit of God is refused admission, grace is willfully, knowingly, deliberately made of no effect, and even an intercessor has no appeal to make, no voice on his behalf to utter, except to deny that such a pretended servant and favorite has any lot among the righteous. It is decreed before the Father, "Ephraim is joined to his idols, let him alone." Compunctions do not come, shame comes not, the end of the dream comes not, the renewing Spirit comes not, God's approving voice comes not.

He sleeps,—sleeps in his infatuation, sleeps with his false dream of safety, sleeps on the ribs of a volcano; sleeps till the last judgment morn opens to his appalled vision, the record of every accusing sin, with no Christ to stand between him and the accusation.

You knew that I was your Saviour, yet you *sinned;* you knew that I gave you grace to live righteously, yet you sinned; you knew that I snatched you out of the miseries of guilt, yet you sinned; you knew that I pleaded for you, to give you help in being holy, yet you sinned; you knew that I must desert those who refused obedience, yet you sinned. Behold, ye angels; behold, ye risen dead, here is the paltry gain, here is the empty, hollow pleasure that tempted an immortal spirit to deny the King of Glory and put Him to an open shame.

Behold, ye witnessing angels, here is the wicked soul that claimed to be mine, claimed to be the delegate of my will.

Did ye eat and drink in my presence? did I teach in your streets? I tell you, I know you not, whence ye are.

When we feel us cold and drear,
We have now some friendly ear
To alleviate our fear.

Who a pitying ear will bend,
If the Judge be not our friend
In our everlasting end?

XXXVII.

YOUNG MEN STRANGERS.

EXODUS xxii. 21.

"Thou shalt neither vex a stranger, nor oppress him."

THE Jews were of opinion that this commandment was especially imperative, because it was repeated no less than twenty-one times in the Books of the Law. As a prohibition, it was of peculiar obligation upon them, on account of its defining the limit to which their separation from strangers could extend. But as implying a course of conduct directly the reverse of the acts prohibited, its obligation is upon Christian principles increased. They were required to refrain from molesting the stranger. Their system of religion was national and exclusive. Their rights came by lineage. The bond of blood was their highest source of privilege. Kindred by flesh were their only brethren. And their law was built, not upon the common rights of all men as equals, but upon the special favors enjoyed by their nation. Their toleration of strangers was in commemoration of their sojourn as strangers in the land of Egypt. It was in compliance with their condition of separation from the rest of mankind, that the taunting or oppression of strangers was laid under inhibition.

Christian brotherhood recognizes, indeed, especial claims in the household of faith; but it limits its charity by no demarcations of blood. Its great love is for the soul, and that, by its immortality and its excellency, embraces all the inferior distinctions of the body. The principle of generosity which thus entered into the Jewish system as a restraint, becomes, in the Christian system, an impulse and a law. The stranger was an object of protection by special provision; he is now an object of care and interest by special obligation.

There are, perhaps, as many indications of the active philanthropy now required in our book of Christian precepts, as the twenty-one indications of prohibition discovered by the Jews. Whatever their number may be, there is distinct demand of the duty.

How often do Apostles rescue from the oblivion of human selfishness, that virtue of patriarchal times and of angelic blessing, hospitality. How often do they draw the distinction between the luxury of a revel, and the simplicity of social generosity. How often do they read us through the circle of kindness to men, until the Christian law is summed up in the twin precepts to love the brotherhood and honor all men. And that we might have no suspicion that strangers were left unprotected by the abrogation of Jewish statutes, our Saviour republished the law, and made it to stand till judgment-day, and threw a pall of warning over it, intimating that, when He took the seat of a judge, one article of indictment would be that He, in the person of one of the least of His brethren, came as a stranger, and we entertained Him not.

The sick and the naked and the hungry are no more the representatives of Christ than the stranger. His doctrine runs, at least, as high as heathen morals.

It were unjust to treat with scorn the stranger.

> "For all the poor that are,
> And all the strangers, are the care of Jove."

In estimating, therefore, the nature of the offices thus required of us, we are not to suppose that the stranger will ever cease to be the object of Christian kindness. Christ will continue to come in that form, and every man will be judged according to his demeanor towards this ambassador of God. Nor are we to imagine that the convivial table of profusion is the entertainment which Christ is seeking. He comes in the character which a stranger symbolizes, unsheltered, exposed to wrong and deception, forming yet his estimate of life and his habits, cut off, in great measure, from the natural safeguards of a home, and depending upon the offices of others for his escape from circumstances of peril or pain.

It is not denied that the progress of civilization has modified essentially the duties of hospitality. Nor can it be doubted that a corresponding progress in the art of imposture and the effrontery of refined address has widened the breach of separation between men, and banished promiscuous hospitality from regions of Christian light and Christian crimes. It is more difficult to discriminate, than when character was kept out of the polishing-lathe of the world. The crime that has violated the sacredness of hospitality, has compelled it to erect its own safeguards. Throw men even now into the circumstances that once surrounded primitive society, and you will see the same virtue reproduced in the same forms. It is not dead, because it has lost its ancient form. The same spirit that prompted a simple hospitality, bends the features of refinement towards those who stand in the place of strangers.

Let us take, for instance, the class of young men who are thrown, by the present arrangements of society and necessities of life, upon the resources of kindness which Christian feeling renders to strangers. Our larger commercial cities abound with this class of most interesting objects for Christian care. And our inland towns must, in their measure, contain the same elements. The mere effect of our institutions promotes the growth of this class. Young men are seldom, in this country, contented with the space where their parents' fortune has located them. They partake of that which is the huge social vice of our times—aspiration. They long for what fashion and an arrogant voice calls a higher level. If the quiet walks of retirement have been the school of their boyhood, they must urge their way into the theatre of crowded enterprise. If the advantages of wealth and plenty have satiated their boyhood and been dissipated in amusement, they will hanker for positions of display, and plunge into some metropolis of refined dissipation. Whatever the taste, whether for business or for gayety, the town and the city attracts to itself armies of young men. In their position of novel employment, they are, in all respects, strangers. Acquaintances may surround them, and society may be opened to them, but they are classed by the influences to which they are subjected, and so far as any conservative control is concerned, they stand in the position of strangers. Home! that charmed circle of hallowed influences! is deserted by them. They may have a roof, they may have the eyes of kindred upon them, but their ambition is to break away from the restraints of domestic power. They are not without God in the world, but they are the next thing to it, because in heart and will they are without a home. They have thrown themselves upon the bosom of fortune, hopeful and bold and determined, and the bosom of quiet affection tying us to contentment and prudence and modesty, and care of ourselves on account of others, is purposely and proudly deserted. The first struggle costs pain, but the unhardened nature soon complies, and the soul, whose whole education has been due to the tender vigilance of home, thinks that it is the happy life of independence to work out manliness apart from home. The bywords and the cant phrases and the swollen vernacular of this new homeless life are learned, and it is natural to talk in this dialect as smoothly as a Mormon in his unknown tongue. The young man makes himself, thus, by his very energy and force, a stranger in the land. He is astray from those inclosures which confined his boyhood.

This change is not the whole. He has not only lost the guardianship of natural affections, but he has cut the strands of influence that once guided him, and is in the way of new influences to direct or to fetter his character. Were he launched among the shoals and reefs of society as an experienced navigator, we should have little apprehension of his danger. But, unfortunately, he undertakes to manage the helm of an immortal destiny at the precise period when his imagination is most easily lured by appearances, while his judgment is least fortified by experience. He knows neither the world nor himself. A thousand suggestions of conceit now entangle his steps, which, in maturer life, he would trample in the dust. His danger lurks for him. If he shuns many perils, he may be lost in the last. Associates that mean no harm, and associates of deeper craft will betray him. He cannot select his company, for he has not the skill; and when he begins to define his circle, it is already drawn for him by others' tastes and others' interests. The wassail-bowl sparkles here. The painted smile of lust bewitches there. The gaming-table spreads its mystic charms. Laziness chains him to the bed of

Sunday neglect. The strut of foppery engages his emulous mimicry. Carousal promises to soothe the weariness of labor. Frivolous reading tempts his vacant mind. And if in dull and hard resistance to the solicitations of profligacy, and the natural vivacity of youth, he spurns the temptation of the prodigal, then comes from the darkened side of his nature a temptation lighted by no blessing of God, the passion to be rich. Meshes of evil encompass the young man. His safety he thinks to lie in his spirit of nobleness and independence; but age teaches him that it lay in his principles and in the defence of God.

Little does that young man, modestly assuming the tasks of life — little does he dream of the trembling anxiety that quivers upon the heart-strings of a father. Little does he dream of that agony of prayer with which a mother implores the protecting arm of God to shield him. In his situation of exposure (unconscious exposure), with the deceits and the ambushes of a strange land around him, with a danger at every step of which he knows nothing by experience, he is, in his unprotected and hazardous condition, as a stranger in our streets.

But his peculiar claim upon our interest does not terminate even here. When we pass to consider his relation to that most important transaction of life, our religious duty, we have reason to regard the young man as emphatically under the misfortune of a stranger. To our religious duty we are fastened by nothing so much as by habit.

Excitement will last as the dew lasts, till the sun is up, but habit is like the river that, in the heat of noontide, sends up the vapors that make its own supply. Habit is lost in the restive change which the young man seeks. Whether among the influences of home, or in the isolation of a strange society, the young man, loosening the bonds of boyhood, is too likely, and is quite certain, if his principles have been weakly formed, to disrobe himself of his religious habits. With this proneness, let him be, at the same time, among strangers; let him lose the law of the fireside which summoned all, both young and old, to the sanctuary of God; let his merry hours be so many, or his passions so strong, that he cannot bear sober discourse; let him hear the profane tongue and the censorious misanthrope and the ignorant scoffer charging upon religion itself the abuse of it which men exhibit; let him count the many of his own age overcome of temptation, and the few that are wise for eternity; let him come to see that wealth neglects God and talent carps at the wisdom of God, and fashion only makes a convenience of religion; let him lose that persuasive power of holiness which is found in seeing its daily triumph over the vexations of the household and its patient earnestness through the practical difficulties of life, in silent, meek, unostentatious retirement; let him miss the sympathy without which one cannot receive and enjoy and digest the great truths and the magnificent hopes of religion, and what term so exactly expresses the religious loneliness of the young man as that which imports a species of banishment mingled with a degree of danger—a stranger in a strange land.

Here, then, my brethren, is an object that not only needs, but, under sanctions of our own eternal gain or loss, demands a Christian interest. We owe it to society that these strangers, which form a portion of every community, should be attracted to the house of God, and encouraged in every good deed which their conscience approves. We owe it to them that they should be made to act a part in the work of religion. The thronged haunts of debauchery, and the withering frown of God upon our religious efforts, and the swelling multitude of men that live respectably and honestly, and yet live as if religion was a fable and Christ a preacher of false alarms—these are the fruits of a system which began by neglecting the child, and blossomed in leaving the stranger to perish.

Is the fault in the clergy? Then were they blind leaders of the blind. But I do not admit the accusation. Christian society has been in error. It has looked at the ripened power of the world, instead of the buds that might be nourished. It has been behind its work, and attempted to prop the weak things, when it should have aimed at the sources of power, and laid up future strength by preserving and sanctifying these. When Cataline was designing his monstrous mischief, he did not tamper with senators and bribe a decaying power in the realm. He won, and he instigated, and he owned the young men of the city, and the pillars of the empire were in his hands.

My Christian friends, I have taken this class of strangers in society as but an instance to indicate how the duty of care and Christian watch over strangers still continues.

There are other classes in society that stand in similar circumstances of peril and dependence. There are the humble poor—of little account in the statistics of the fashionable world, but noble by the patent of heaven, and received before angels as kings and priests unto God—there are brethren who ask not to trespass upon your intimacy, but claim your countenance of complaisant humility as you hope to look upon that poor man who reigns in heaven—there are wanderers from distant shores, who would seek here the same altar that fed their forefathers with the bread of life, and claim no nearer approach to you than to kneel with you beneath God's roof—there are widowed Christians and needy children that plead the trepidation of a stranger's heart in excuse of their exile from privileges of the soul.

Think not that the minister of God is alone or chiefly interested in this duty to strangers. Every conscience confesses that the punishment will be wide as the offence. Prophecy lifts its finger of threatening, and points to the woes of the past and the dismal horizon of the future. In the past looms up the scene of a land that had devoured strangers, and, in the sequel, strangers devoured it. Prophecy traces upon its scroll the fearful denunciation, "I will send a famine in the land, not a famine of bread, nor a thirst for water, but of hearing the words of the Lord. And they shall wander from sea to sea, and from the north even to the east; they shall run to and fro to seek the word of the Lord, and shall not find it."

And what is that veil which now covers the heart of Israel but the judgment upon a people vexing and oppressing strangers? And what is the dispersed race, once covenanted in Canaan, but a living witness sent around the earth to show what they would not themselves believe, that the oppression of the stranger would bring a whirlwind to "scatter them among all nations whom they knew not?"

XXXVIII.

GREAT FAITH—THE CENTURION.

ST. MATT. viii. 10.

"When Jesus heard it, he marvelled, and said to them that followed, Verily, I say unto you, I have not found so great faith, no, not in Israel."

THE Gospels appointed for the Epiphany Sundays are arranged upon a plan that will disclose itself to any careful observer. They are in fact successive Epiphanies, or manifestations of the Redeemer's glory. They begin with his wisdom and understanding as a child, the juvenile symptoms of the wonder that lay in his person, and they touch upon those miracles which were for the most part manifestations of his glory, conducting us through the manifestation of His Providence, leaving the wheat and tares to grow together until the harvest, and terminating with the manifestations of His grandeur and majesty, when He shall come to judge the quick and the dead.

In the gospel for this day, two of our Saviour's miracles are presented. In the account of the second of these, occurs His recognition of the spirit and disposition, which gave occasion to the exercise of His beneficent Omnipotence. The disposition and character of the man for whose sake the miracle was performed,—the psychological structure and the whole bent of feeling in this man,—what distinguished him and made him the magnet to draw out divine virtue for his benefit,—this is, so far as we are concerned, the lesson and point of the history. As a manifestation of the Christ, there is another leading intention in it. From this miracle it appears that He was able to speak the word only and the sufferer should be healed,—that there was no real occasion for His contact with the object or His view of the object that needed His power, although there was here, as on other occasions, a waiting for the proper disposition and application on the part of some person concerned.

Yet as antecedent to this distant exercise of His healing might, and as preparatory to the shining forth of His Divinity, was the requisite of such faith as He had not found in Israel. Even before Christ can disclose His energy, man must be in a fitness to receive it. Before the glory can be manifested, there must be a soul of faith to attract the glory. It is not suffering that challenges this intervention of the Godhead,—it is not the extremity of the sickness or the hardship of the case or the mere effluence of pity, that causes God to act and manifest Himself; so much as it is the manner in which Christ is supplicated, and the spirit that prompts the petition to Him, and the character of the man who begs for the aid. Thus the benevolence of our Redeemer is relieved of that impulsive, precipitate, indiscriminating appearance which attaches to almost all of human goodness. It is not an emotion merely,—not a mere habit of being touched with the sight and sound of sorrow. It is discerning, wise, sagacious pity,—full of heart and full of judgment, quick to perceive a merit wherever it exists, and too great for the little slurs of prejudice and partiality.

Looking beyond these qualifications of the act of Christ, we are directed to the qualifications of the centurion, who drew from the Divine Witness the panegyric, "I have not found so great faith, no, not in Israel."

To apprehend the force of this commendation, we must survey the incidents that gave rise to it.

By comparing the accounts of this miracle as given by the two Evangelists, it seems that an officer of the foreign corps which ruled the Jewish Province, had broken from the heathen and polytheistic bonds of his education. He was one of that class which Providence had raised up in every metropolis of civilization. Abjuring the name and mythic religion of their fathers, they sought of the Hebrew Jehovah, that better truth, and that nearer approach to life which might reach them in the courts of the proselyte. At Rome, at Tarsus, at Antioch,—in every region where the wandering Jew had come in commercial contact with the refined Gentile, proselytes had confessed the glimmer of hope to themselves that was shining through the types and figures of the Temple. They were everywhere the waiting spirits that hailed the word of life. Adherents of the Judaism they had espoused, they were easily won to the higher philosophy that came in the preaching of faith. This centurion was one of these waiting proselytes. He had thrown the fervor of an honest zeal into the religion he embraced. Conscious as he seems to have been of its deficiencies, and ready as he seems to recognize a more profound system, he yet devotes himself in his providential position to the furtherance of religious measures. By birth a heathen, he is by generosity the builder of a synagogue. The servant of this centurion lay at his house palsied and ready to die. Messengers are dispatched to Jesus, invoking his aid. The messengers fulfill their errand with an added urgency, suggesting of their own mind that his favor to the Jews—his regard for their religion—ought to recommend him. But the centurion's sense of his own unworthiness and of Christ's greatness, disdained such intercession. He will not ask for the Redeemer to come beneath his roof. There is no need that the Master of all forces should condescend. "Speak the word only," is his entreaty; and as if to map out the impressions of his own thoughts, he likens the power of Jesus in the supernatural world to his own command amid the discipline of the camp. It was the mere conception of a soldier,—whose idea of authority was framed upon the model of peremptory command. In his mind, the higher the rank the less the condescension allowable. It was anomalous in his view of superiority that the greater should come down to serve the less. There was nothing in his tuition to authorize an application for the personal presence of Christ under his roof. He was a man under authority, by no means the chief and by no means irresponsible, and yet it was his wont to say, Do this, and it was done. Evidently his appeal to Christ was full of the conviction that every power that could reach his servant's misery was at the command of this Redeemer. He pictured the Miraculous Teacher as a Supreme Governor among the hidden agents of Divine power. There was no reservation of uncertainty or skepticism. His whole manner was the exhibition of complete and unreserved confidence in Christ. Abandoning all such pleas of merit, as that he was a proselyte, and that he had an honorable name among all classes, and that he had built a synagogue, and that he was seeking a mercy for another and not for himself,—abandoning all such arts of recommendation, he uncovers a heart full of trust in the power of Jesus and therefore empty of pride in himself. To see a heathen man, and a soldier, and a bearer of authority, thus carried into the earnestness of humble, child-like, honest importunity for his servant, was a scene at which Jesus marvelled. He detected the real source of this character. He knew out of what such a man was made. He could penetrate the virtues that lay on the surface, and tell what was the leading principle that shaped such a man into such a character. And drawing the true wisdom from the fact, He says to them that follow Him, "I have not found so great faith, no, not in Israel."

Now the real difficulty of this history is in that

effect upon the mind of Christ, which is described as His marvelling. The expression implies a surprise and a wonder,—as if something had crossed His view which was both unknown and unexpected. But how can surprise and wonder to this degree be predicated of One who knew what was in man, and could foresee as well as discern the thoughts of the heart. And how shall we dare to outforce Scripture itself, and assert that the scene was no occasion of marvel to Jesus in His Divine nature, but was so described as affecting his humanity,—how can we so untie the knot without coming in peril of the Nestorian heresy, or breaking Christ into two personalities?

I take it, therefore, to be obvious that there was an exceeding excellence of character in this centurion, and that the supernatural was joined with his natural traits and had produced in him a disposition that transcended common virtue and natural goodness. The marvel of Jesus was but the recognition of this Divine power at work upon his soul, —the knowledge of which Christ had of something more than man in the character this centurion had attained. It was not the higher traits of human nature that surprised the discernment of Jesus. It was the discovery of a character which was to Christ the token of God's work upon the soul, and God's indwelling there. The miraculous was manifest to Jesus in that centurion's heart, and He marvelled before man could see that there was occasion. So that from every point of view, we are directed to the traits of this centurion as the real origin of the healing miracle. Now we do not say that this man of faith had been overpowered of God, and had merged his human traits into a supernatural character. We only allege that the greatest miracle, as Jesus looked upon things, was such a man. His eye beheld more wonders in that which God wrought upon the centurion's soul, than in that which God wrought upon the paralytic's body. The surprising and transcendant act in Jesus's estimation, was God's forming a heathen sinner into such a believer. That was to the eye of Christ the primary and the overtopping wonder. Nothing that could be done to men's bodies was so wonderful. Nothing that was asked at His hands was so grand and august and magnificent. No, the strengthening of those failing limbs,—the reviving of that palsied frame was as nothing in comparison with the life and throb that had come into the soul of a heathen and a sinner. There was healing indeed. There was life from the dead,—and life the more sublime because it was moral and spiritual,—and life the more wonderful, because it was immortality that had been dead. Oh, greatest of miracles, mightiest of wonders,—the soul of man inhabited of God, the dead in trespasses made alive by faith!

And here is the centre towards which all the rays of glory in this miracle converge. They were all intended only to make sure and to make conspicuous the fact that God's great miracle was His work upon the soul of sinful man. My brethren, let the theme touch our own sympathies. There is nothing greater to be transacted in heaven or earth, —in time or eternity, than this which God would every day transact in our souls. Would you have a miracle? Would you have a sign from heaven? Behold a greater marvel, when grace forms the sinner. No word of Jesus lifting the palsied sufferer from his woe,—no trump of archangel waking the lifeless body from its silent grave,—is so mighty, so marvellous, so fit to sweep the convictions of men into obedience, as the wonder of grace shaping the soul into so great faith.

But what was it that evinced this greatness of faith, this excellence passed upon the soul of the centurion? The history reveals many adjuncts and embellishments of faith, many a trait that made the man illustrious and praiseworthy and in favor with his generation. There was some gleam of this kindly disposition in the favor which he showed to the Jews, and in the piety that erected the synagogue. There was a brighter way in the humility and modesty of the man. But as we draw our conclusions from Scripture and not from conjecture, the inspired hand points us to two especial constituents of character which justified the encomium of Christ.

His great faith was evinced most distinctly in his love for man. There was a sense of the high and great capacities of our nature which drew towards acts of exceeding kindness, humanity and nobleness. So our Saviour treats him. So He evidently regarded the faith of this centurion. "As thou hast believed, so be it done unto thee." But how done unto him, except as he had made the suffering of the servant his own, and absorbed himself in the feeling of humanity?

The sufferer that roused all the sympathy of this centurion, was his servant, such as at that day it was unusual even to treat with humanity, and Cicero was obliged to excuse himself to his friends because he grieved at the death of such in his household. But this centurion counted this man as himself, and had no thought that Christ would scruple to send His healing power into that subaltern rank of life. And when we consider that this applicant was a soldier, and accustomed to the separations of class and rank, the simplicity and the fervor of his humane feelings are the more to be remarked.

My brethren, it is "faith" that binds this world together,—faith in the capacity of man for something better than an everlasting round of sin and vanity and sorrow. And I very much doubt whether the blessed Jesus looks with any complacency upon those great pretensions to faith that are devoid of lively humanity,—that think much of their own rectitude in life and doctrine and look down upon the mass of men. That was the kind of mind which Israel at that day applauded and produced.

The other constituent of greatness in this soul was his sense of authority. He deemed it the mark of a Saviour to be not only good and gracious, tender and pitiful, but carrying the power of command. He believed that Jesus wrought by messengers and ministers and servants, and this faith was uppermost in his thoughts and in his speech,—and elicited the approval of the master, "I have not found so great faith, no, not in Israel."

XXXIX.

THE FAITHFUL RECTOR.*

PROV. X. 7.

"The memory of the just is blessed."

TO recognize the merits and recollect the favors of personal benefactors is a duty indispensable to any character claiming the ordinary measures of virtue. Public benefactors whose sacrifices were conspicuous and whose contributions to the public good were eminent, should be cherished in the memory of men and recorded upon the tablets of an imperishable gratitude. Civilization has everywhere erected its monumental lithographs of this sentiment, or inscribed its sculptured testimony to this sacred claim. The highest culture of our race in Christian sanctity has not discountenanced nor repealed this edict of the human heart as its gratitude emerges from barbaric stupor. Obelisks solidified against oblivion the ornate eulogies of a cultured age. The rude cromlech in Wales, and Devonshire, and the continent attests that Druidical religion consecrated the memory of heroes.

* This and the following were preached in commemoration of Rev. Dr. Andrews, fourteen years rector of Christ Church, Binghamton. J. G. W.

The history carved upon the rock in Nineveh, and illustrated with brilliant pigments upon the corridors of Luxor and Thebes, or inscribed with lavish art upon triumphal arches exhibits the effort to perpetuate the honor of signal deeds and the worthies who performed them. Events survive in their effects, but names pass into silence. Gratitude assumes the form of justice, when embellishing the record and prolonging the praise of those who have deserved better than to be forgotten. Such is the perverseness of our nature that many excellencies must wait for posthumous honor. Bacon has expanded the idea in these words, "The name of good men, after envy is extinguished (which cropped the blossom of their fame while they were alive) presently shoots up and flourisheth; and their praises daily increase in strength and vigor." It was accordingly the proverb of the wise man, who had penetrated to the core of human experience, that "the memory of the just is blessed," or as the Septuagint gives it with still greater exactness, "The memory of the just is with encomiums." Nor does that voice of wisdom pause with this echo of Providence, but duplicates the hope of the righteous by denouncing the curse of time against splendid sin, "So I saw the wicked buried, who had come and gone from the place of the holy, and they were forgotten in the city where they had *so* done."

A memory growing in sacredness is but the legitimate sequel of a life that was growing in holiness. And if all nations that were bold in character or polished in acquirements have provided for enduring testimony to that which was most glorious in their estimate, we are not surprised at the same principle in Christianity accumulating praise upon the memory of sacred functions meritoriously discharged, and of exalted purposes intrepidly pursued. Inspired teachers could not remit this to the sure impulses of our Christian gratitude or sagacity. They inculcated it as a part of our practical religion. And they placed it in no obscure part of our spiritual structure, but made it a kind of cement between two courses, putting contentment on one side, and steadfastness on the other, while between them is this injunction, the natural bond between patient trust in God and patient stability in His doctrine. "Remember them which have the rule over you, who have spoken unto you the word of God, whose faith follow, considering the end of their conversation: Jesus Christ the same yesterday, and to-day, and for ever."

Nor is there less force in this precept because it concerns both the living and the departed teacher. It is only the more impressive when it links in the same clasp of regard the present pastor who needs our emotions of affection and respect, and the rewarded tenant of Paradise who needs no more than that his example and his recompence should be our incentives to follow him into rest.

To sanctify the memory is the grand office of the gospel. This treasuring and preserving faculty is the chief token of our immortality. It is this that carries the present into the future, into eternity.

To save the memory from torpor and from torture is eminently man's salvation. And Christ's work is omnipotently our salvation, because it compasses both these effects, giving us eternal life that implies no extinction of memory, and making that life to grow out of pardon, out of sins forgiven, forgotten, washed away, so that memory might be felicity, might be *rest*. It was congruous with His whole work of salvation, therefore, to pronounce the great object and benefit of the Spirit's coming to be that "He should bring all things to our remembrance." A dispensation of the flesh might be satisfied with giving us enjoyment, and rolling us perpetually from world to world of pleasure. But a dispensation of the Spirit is not represented by this mere succession of novelties, this forgetting one and finding another delight. It animates and cherishes the memory, and it stimulates our trust in God not by the dream of what we expect, but by the transporting sense of what has been conferred. The All-Wise Redeemer of our nature fitted His gospel to its end when He appointed the highest act of worship to be the showing forth our devotion "in remembrance" of Him, and made it the test of well-adjusted virtues, that they were ready to crystallize themselves into this mode of commemorating and honoring the Greatest of Benefactors.

I need not ramble among the vestiges of exhausted empires, I need not clamber among the ruins of Athens and Karnac, I need not kindle my torch of exploration to decipher the epitaphs of the catacombs. Let me but enter the sanctuary of the

Christian's resort, and the altar which bespeaks alike his duty and his privilege reminds me that no elevation of man exalts him above the obligation to preserve the name and the praise of the world's benefactors. And if no chiselled marble reproves the forgetfulness of man, and obscurity veils on earth what shall be as the sun in the heavens, yet is there a record which flames before the eyes of angels, and of which the Psalmist spoke, "The righteous shall be in everlasting remembrance."

We thus array before our minds our justification in the grateful tribute of honor to the worthy departed. Vindication of our act in this specific instance is superfluous. The vestry of this parish have merely given expression to the public sentiment which they represent. The paltriest measures of worldly calculation would deem it due to fourteen years of half-requited services that some appreciation of the generous and self-devoting spirit should survive the gifted labor. But the high admiration of a congregation that once basked amid the glow of a fervid eloquence, and was elated with the consciousness of feeding upon the product of extraordinary talent, cannot content itself with merely rendering sculptured praise for the ministry of wisdom and salvation. Higher motives swell our hearts, and more reverential regard engraves itself upon our record. The Divine commission which He bore, the gracious trust of the gospel which He dispensed, the Heavenly Master whom He served, the sublime model which His words pourtrayed, and the all-enduring patience to which His life through infirmity and injury aspired, these elevating topics cluster in halo around His memory, and snatch our souls from grovelling thoughts. We interpret symbol and syllable under this solemnizing dictation. The tablet itself announces to us, and will declare from generation to generation, that honor is due to the faithful witness for the faith once delivered to the saints.

> "Nam te voluit Rex Magnus Olympi
> Talibus auspiciis exhortem ducere honorem."—ÆN. v. 533-4.

The voiceless dead thus speaks again. The testimony of His death prolongs the proclamation of His life. It is in fitting consonance with this record of His Pastorate, that the inscription which is personal has been placed upon the four-leaved figure commanding the centre of the tablet. The four contiguous circles so blending symbolize the glorious gospel, committed to us by four evangelists, designed for diffusion in the four quarters of the globe, represented by the four living beings before the throne, and first typified by the four emblematic banners that conducted the Israel of the olden redemption. The same symbolism reappears in the surmounting cross. It is the summit of our rejoicing, and the signal of our hope. Death throws a dark shadow upon it, but neither neutralizes nor debases it. The cross of our Lord Jesus Christ is our glory, and we place it above every other emblem of our faith, nor thus as if some detached object belonging not to the lines of our humanity, but as gathering into itself from either side both portions of our nature, atoning for Jew and Gentile, reconciling the heavenly and the earthly, appealing to the righteous and the ungodly, and summing up both in one. And whether we view it in one or other of its three aspects, the Trinity of the Godhead is concerned in every aspect and the triplicity of our nature is regarded by it at all times, whether we are considering the love of God manifested in the crown of the cross, or the saintly examples of patience which its right hand presents, or the sympathy with the sinner which its left hand holds forth to the penitent.

Lest the doctrine so compressed in symbol should be misinterpreted, we bring out in bold relief as a part of the solid substance of our system, so prominent that it cannot be pared down, and so vitally important that it projects between the cross and its preacher, the I. H. S., the sermon in stone, which assigns this to be our hope that the salvation derived from the cross, becomes personally our own, by our living, genuine union with Christ. Human history completes itself in three brief chapters, a birth, a life, a death, and all of life a mere parenthesis between eternities. But grace indites history by its own method, and shuddering not at death deems it no interruption of that life which passes from pain to peace, from toil to rest. Perhaps some messenger of grace may convey tidings to that reposing soul. We must record as modestly as his own keen sensibilities would have dictated. No fulsome eulogy insults the humility of the enraptured soul. Human praise, and human blame are equally impotent where the approbation of God is joy eternal. "It is required in stewards, it is demanded of these dispensers of the mysteries of God, that a man be found faithful," and we record all that the book of remembrance will exact, fidelity to the master, fidelity to the conscience, fidelity to the flock. Far beyond looms the day of reward. The Sun of Righteousness ushers in this golden radiance. The blood-stained cross vindicates its purpose. Brilliant, untouched by one dark line, blood-bought, and therefore precious is that inheritance which lies beyond the veil. We behold it only by faith. But the hope does salute our vision. That we cannot dismiss. It is deep-rooted in the promises of God, and we put it at the base of all our consolations, it is emphasized by the utterance of the Everlasting Lamb, the Light of the New Jerusalem, the Sun of the Universe, and like golden flashes of the eternal morn it gleams upon the eye.

So much of doctrine inculcated by symbol do we attach to our memorial of the faithful departed. These lessons will live on for our descendants and for stranger's sons, the stereotyped instructions of his faith and of our delight to honor it and him. Under the Divine protection these walls will shelter centuries of men, and these marble tongues will speak when our frail tenements are forgotten dust.

"Be it so!
Enough, if something from our hands have power
To live, and act, and serve the future hour;
And if, as toward the silent tomb we go,
Through love, through hope, and faith's transcendent dower,
We feel that we are greater than we know."

WORDSWORTH'S POEMS OF IMAG., iii. 270.

What, then, is the tradition that is to be transmitted as our recognition of the work Providentially performed by that honored servant of God?

The answer involves some review of the career and the traits of that eminent Christian minister. We will not undertake the detail of events in which he mingled. That becomes the Biographer. That may illumine the chronicles of the Church. We are rather occupied with the general impression produced by his character, or with the peculiarities which help us to appreciate his qualities.

There are two elements which always enter into the constitution of individual character, and which must qualify our judgment of its merits. These important constitutions are first the natural endowments, what might be called the original forces of the person, and secondly the circumstances that occur to soothe his powers.

Neither natural gifts, nor surrounding circumstances altogether make the man. They only show him forth. The real manufacture is in the amount of increase which his own effort gives to the natural gift, and to the accidental advantage.

Among those native energies which our reverend friend possessed, we are not to omit a warm affectionateness of disposition, and innate integrity of heart. The combination of these traits produces a candour and fervour of manner, which does not always escape criticism, although it carries power. Such early buddings out of strong soil must take the risk of frosty blasts. They hasten to maturities of feeling and of conviction towards which the slow world has scarcely turned. In outstripping much that is good, much that is wise, they incur the censure of being precipitate and over-heated. That is only their occasional danger. Ordinarily they display a character which endears friends, and grapples them with hooks of steel. They feel the ardors of undissembled friendship, and they impart the same. Their honest purpose extenuates their infirmities, and the glow of their nature rebukes the chilly reserve that purchases safety at the expense of a torpid and unfeeling heart.

It was such material that furnished the leading champions of our new-born gospel. Peter in his vehemence, Paul in his unquenchable zeal, were chosen to their chieftainship because they had too much of heartiness and too much of magnetic glow in their nature to be cool calculating machines. It was not painful to them to be in the lead if their solitude was only the incident of their integrity. Dispassionate and phlegmatic reasoners might exclaim in pitying tone—"Much learning doth make thee mad;" but wisdom that is to madness close allied would reply—"I speak the words of truth and soberness." We may be justified in terming this compound of sobriety and warmth, a kind of natural enthusiasm. In half-enlightened and shallow souls it is rashness and temerity, and with them it makes ruinous leaders and mischievous followers. But give to this natural enthusiasm the power of experience, and the advantages of discipline and the momentum of robust intellect, and you have the fortitude of an Athanasius, the probity of a Washington, alacrity in good that emulates Gabriel, and sincerity in zeal that imitates Paul. Men may spurn its bodily presence as weak; they may decry its speech as contemptible; but they cannot dispute its magnetic attraction, they cannot refute its argument of affection. I speak of our venerable and lamented brother as one whose acquaintance was more limited than your own, as one familiar with only the later phases of his last tremulous months. But I surely did not mistake him. Such enthusiasm amid the apathies of decline could not have blossomed in the frosts of age unless it had permeated every fibre of his life. Petty peevishness may be the moss that grows upon the remains of an amiable life. But deep disgusts and sturdy indignation are the later throbs of a heart which has been exuberant in its affections and ardent without dissimulation.

Nature was not niggardly towards him, for nature intended him for honorable achievements. He was appointed to the office of a burning torch, rather than the shining iceberg. His mission in life was to warm and attract and conduct souls eager for something that would encourage them towards the wisest and the best, and not to startle by cold splendors their unloving exclamations of wonder. His natural endowments and his providential duties were thus brought into harmony, and grand forces grew up under his hand, and in their Christian results, far as they were beyond his humble hopes, he found occasions for thanksgiving, and we meet the ample blessing. Great gifts to man dwell in crumbling habitations. Strong powers bring great dangers. The mighty sway of the heart is not compensated by propórtionate strength in all the faculties, and the gifted man with his resistless emotions must sometimes be the roused volcano. The ashes of his weakness must somewhere appear. It may be in the surprises of grief; it may be in the impetuosities of indulgent affection ; it may be in the consternation of unexpected disappointment and defeat; it may be in the dreaded decrepitude of exhausted age. Whatever they may be, they simply warn us what earthen vessels hold these destined stars.

Perhaps there is no shock that so unstrings the the fortitude of our nature as that which convulses and overwhelms advancing age when we find nature itself withdrawing gifts and snatching away the powers which are most treasured. When imagination drops the weary wing,—when memory is treacherous to him that caressed her,—when the eloquent tongue is beggared into feeble tones,—when the hungering affections must hover around silent graves, and infirmities must hide themselves in unfriended retirement,—then nature at last seems to be deserting her favorite, and the portals of another world alone disclose the restoration and replenishment of our impoverished hopes. Natures once affectionate, and once beautiful in their sincerity, retire then by instinct more and more to the pure shelters of domestic peace. They nestle where the affections last decay, and where infirmity is only the more sacred.

Blessed are they who, like our greatly gifted leader in these trusts from Christ can repose amid the tranquillities of a home which filial tenderness made every day brilliant with affection, and Christian zeal made a daily residence for the Spirit of God.

The sequel of his fate illustrates our description of his nature. It was not strange that a life so intense in its affections should droop when the greatest sorrow came, and repressed vigor refused support, and that desolated, disheartened nature should quiver and sink breathless into the arms of everlasting love.

A nature that found so much of royalty in wearing the crown of patience, and revelled so luxuriously in the affluence of its affections, might echo those unambitious lines which the humble curate of Loweswater left inscribed upon his Parish Register—

> "Let him that would, ascend the tottering seat
> Of courtly grandeur, and become as great
> As are his mounting wishes; but for me
> Let sweet repose and rest my portion be."

XL.

THE FAITHFUL RECTOR.—II.

PROVERBS x. 7.

"The memory of the just is blessed."

IN our former view of the personal traits and career of "the faithful rector," whose honor on these walls is to your honor, we governed ourselves by the consideration that any wise estimate of character must involve two entirely distinct subjects. We accordingly occupied ourselves with that which is first essential to an accurate measurement of character, the natural endowments, the original forces of the person, his gifts of intellect and of feeling. But as when we speak of one's mind and heart, we cannot always draw a nice line between what is due to nature and what comes by acquirements and laborious use of nature's gifts, so we put the whole result into one view, and we regard the excellencies of mind and the developments of disposition as one entire credit to the man. You may call it nature's bounty to him, or his own acquisition, but his it is, and he praises the God who gave and the God who helped, calling it all divine, while we honor the man for the result. In that respect we recognized in our reverend friend many occasions for highest praise. We felt that God had greatly blessed this community in the long residence and the useful activities of a man so rarely gifted and so capable of giving brilliant display in the way of intellect, and oratory and learning. We admitted that there was a new claim to the gratitude of this Parish for one who could not merely shine when splendor was needed, but was also warm and fervent in his feelings, and sent glows of ardor into other hearts, and wielded this power the better and the more permanently because it was so obviously in him sincere, undisguised, undissembled. And yet the halo which others could perceive encircling the traits of this reverend servant of God was that which was all unobserved and unknown to him, the radiant beauty of unaffected humility. These eminent qualities would not have commanded the admiration of all at any moment of his career, when the question of his personal character was raised. We are not always in the mood to render just or generous judgment towards those living among our own envies, ambitions, desires and competitions; our own gratification, or our own emoluments, may be the vaster elements in our judgment, and we will judge of men more by our own ideal of what we dream to be admirable, than by a fair estimation of those gifts and powers which they do possess.

There is, however, a second method of shaping in our own view the real proportions and constituents of personal character. We dismiss our first mode of regarding the long-admired and severely-tried instructer and guide of this Parish, and we address ourselves to what we proposed as the second method of reaching a judgment that would be true to the facts, and more likely to present the peculiar traits of the distinguished man. This requires us to recognize the circumstances that hung close around his life, and in him as in all other strong and gifted men, materially affects the exhibitions of power at least, and perhaps the mental and moral powers themselves.

The first of these important circumstances is the fact of his habituation to study, and to discipline, and to the cultivation of the mind by contact with ripe and great intellects from his earliest days. Perhaps we do not all apprehend the force of this fact. We are rather disposed to conclude that if one eventually goes through a certain round of studies, he learns and masters just that prescribed amount, and it matters little at what age he travels through the subjects. This is not the place for discussing schemes of education, and I will, therefore, refrain from a controversy on the subject of precocity. Suffice it to say, whether we pronounce him to have been precocious or not, we deem some of his most remarkable qualities to have been the natural effect of early industry in scholarly tasks, and early association with men of pure and careful culture. From his birth at Ipswich, Mass., July 26th, 1792, to his graduation in high honor at Harvard in 1810, was an interval of but eighteen years.

It was thoroughly improved, and it set his mind in its most pliable and impressible period among influences, that made learned pursuits a delight, and the classic tone of language and illustration always natural and pleasurable to him. Eight years of unremitted study ensued upon his college course. It conducted him first as a student at law, and then as a practitioner, and afterwards, under the impulses of religious conviction, as a theological student to the twenty-sixth year of his life, when he was licensed to preach, and despatched as a missionary of the Presbyterian Board to itinerate through Midland and Western New York. We thus observe that he ran up to mature manhood, familiar with study, occupied with themes that tasked his mental powers, and that came with a succession the best calculated to interest his faculties, and to train his powers to their utmost. His boyhood put the then prominent power of memory to its best use. With such equipments of scholarship as fortify us against narrow notions on the one side and against conceit on the other, he pushed into those questions of social order, of property, rights, and of evidence, which are embraced in the study of law. But the law was his school-master to bring him to Christ. It was with him as with many minds, the prompt conclusion of conscience, that mere law is not sufficient for man, but redeeming, sanctifying, comforting power must reach him ; not displacing law, but saving him by a new heart, with the law of Christ as the focal power. There is no difficulty in tracing the effects of these circumstances upon the cultivation of our deceased friend. Early years devoted to liberal studies leave an impress of delicacy and elegance upon the mind, which will appear in all its productions. They create a dis-relish for those blunter efforts, and for those gaudy and sonorous forms of speech which captivate the less educated, and in that respect early discipline in study places the scholar at a disadvantage with the masses of men. He begins to live from his youth upon a different plan of taste and of imagination to that occupied by minds not given to scholarship. What seems to him simple and most appropriate and most forcible, falls upon minds unprepared to enjoy its terseness or its classic allusions, and is obscure, tame, feeble, distasteful, even while strongest and clearest. And this would have been the result in our eminent brother's attempts to bring his furnished mind into contact with the community that waited for his Christian guidance. But other circumstances modified the result; let us bring these into view.

The leading influence to modify mere scholarship was his early application to a subject so practical as the law. It deals, indeed, with abstract principles, and has its abstrusities; but these must immediately come into practical detail, they must meet the world as it is. They cannot go dreaming about an ideal man and an imaginary goodness; the theory of law is good for nothing except as it applies to the every day habits and the ordinary sentiments of society. It was, therefore, fortunate for our friend, with his acuteness of nature, that he turned the very enthusiasm of his youth into that school of law where he learned so thoroughly not only how good and finished men feel and speak, but how the great mass of society are influenced, and what disguises mask so much of human nature. His natural sagacity became under this tuition a kind of insight that penetrated man's motives, and looked keenly through them, while they supposed all their secret purposes muffled up and undiscovered.

Without this rare combination of power to please the scholar and power to penetrate the schemes of ordinary men, he could not have achieved that signal success which enabled him to command the confidence of elements the most dissimilar and contradictory. His educated taste would have delighted in the choicest topics and the most faultless treatment of them; but his legal training, especially in his creditable efforts as a practitioner, showed him that the human heart was not touched by these exact and silvery sounds. And when it became his calling and his hope to *save* men, he found that he must leave the heights of Parnassus and rush into the smoke and the mire where they abode. And yet those who witnessed his struggles to rescue friends and neighbors from the darkness and filth of their sins, will attest that he always appeared as one who could not forget the exquisite diction of the scholar, or the sharp phrases of the penetrative mind, or the beautiful imagery of a superior intelligence. The most of us are content to thank

God that we are saved at all, and to leave to the season of heavenly rewards our attainment of knowledge and of faculty in some near approach to such more gifted men.

We recognize the law, as the agent of the Spirit of God, to produce that great change in his life's purposes which directed his first manly thoughts to the ministry of the gospel. But the influence of this legal pursuit lasted into another remarkable change. The mercy of God was preparing him by these processes for a powerful instrument towards the vindication of God's Church. We in our impatience at God's slow plans, in our haste to leap over God's preparations, would have thrust this brilliant young scholar into the full trust of the Church's ministry. To us this would have seemed the grander triumph of the truth, and the most convincing testimony to our Episcopal ministry. But God's ways were circuitous, and as we judge them, less startling. Eight years of experience in the Presbyterian ministry were needed to mature that judgment and to test that conclusion which at last brought him to Bishop Hobart for orders. He had previously ministered in a Presbyterian Society at Norwich, in Chenango Co., but was now undergoing the transition of his Christian relations, while giving the benefit of his ripe scholarship to the Oxford Academy as Principal. And in this revolution of his Christian attachments, the same controlling causes were at work which we have already observed forming the texture of his character. Had he devoted himself to theologic study without the preparations of the law, I extremely doubt whether he would ever have repaired to the Episcopal ministry. But the laws of human evidence well explored by him, and but little appreciated by the mere theologian, conducted his mind logically to the position which our Church maintains, that the Apostolic ministry was Episcopal, that the Bishop's office as superior among ministers is perpetual, and that Christ has never given man the right to make a new Church instead of that the Saviour gave them. The mind employed on subjects of law may not by that be the better fitted for examining or discussing doctrinal feuds which depend upon spiritual insight and upon a lively conscience, but the historical argument for the form and authority of the Church as an organized system, is especially conclusive to one who has learned the laws of human testimony.

Yet the law so swayed the mind of our reverend friend that the fashion of Presbyterian doctrines in his day repelled and converted him. The persuasion of his early education and his first adhesion was the betraying the interior action of two contending principles. It was the old dogmatic orthodoxy, and the new system of Revivals, that were warring in the body, and afterwards stood contentiously apart, as old school and new school. There was a tendency towards the practical and the sober in Dr. Andrews' views of religion, which made both systems repugnant. His legal mind could not acquiesce in those schemes of mechanical excitement which travestied the majesty of Christian emotion. His inclination through the law to test all doctrines by their practical conclusions could not submit to the dry, hard system of absolute decrees which stiff Calvinists were proclaiming as the marrow of the gospel. From every side of his nature he was thus impelled to seek his repose and his work, where his faith could rest, and his conscience could apply his energy, in the bosom of the church that showed to him the Apostolic features.

Under the ministry which now demanded his glad sacrifices, his labors were manifold and singularly successful.

Christ church, Sherburne, owes its origin to him. St. Andrew's, New Berlin, was the scene of three years' ministrations. After two years rectorship in Hudson, and another two years at New Berlin, he entered upon the charge of the parish in 1836. A man of narrower experience or less courage would have faltered, amid the difficulties that confronted his rectorate here. Disaster speedily fell upon the most promising of earthly fortunes, and upon him was visited all the querulousness which attends this state of public affairs. He bore it bravely, in self-denial, with meagre returns for his labors, and many a discouragement. But patience prevailed. And life ran on past its zenith, until the wearied and disheartened spirit, sixty years a pilgrim, begged the privilege of leaning upon its staff and blessing those it could no longer lead.

Time brings its revenges, eternity brings its rewards. He saw the one, he will be satisfied with the other. Even now, the tribute to his surpassing powers swells upon the ear, and on these walls will linger the proof that no human stratagem can defy the decree of God, "the memory of the just is blessed." How much he endured, and how praiseworthy efforts he was capable of making, I have known but partially; there are those among us who could rehearse the praise and the indignation in bolder language than I use.

Before our grateful remembrance of such an eminent light in this Parish, there rises a model which should attract the imitation of those who can now survey his merits. He was a pattern of modest and unostentatious excellence, never pushing his own claims, retreating from the opportunities of distinction, shunning the acts that stir men's applause, and rather tempting their criticism than tarnishing his self-respect by flattering their weakness. I need not tell you how rare is such a character among those whose temptation is to aim at popularity.

He was a model of firmness in abiding by his convictions. With all his rapidity of thought and readiness of expression there was no haste in adopting a conclusion, but when it was a principle that must be maintained, there was no shrinking from the demand. It summoned him to fling aside the ambitions of youth, and he obeyed. It tore him from his traditional attachments, and required him to espouse a religion which was then traduced as lifeless, formal, and effeminate; but he clasped his Bible to his heart, and proclaiming that the voice of God in that word was too distinct to be doubted, he put the cross upon his shoulder and marched among our forlorn few.

He was a model of faith in the love and power of our adorable Jesus. All theories must be brought by him to this standard. Do they let forth the all-sufficient salvation in the grace of Christ. The abstract and ingenious system of doctrines, that might have pleased his intellect, was tempted beneath his resolution to seek and follow that system which proposed to save men by Jesus, and not by philosophy. There was a recoil in his mind, like the heavings of a volcano that would not be pent up, whenever the scheme, however plausible, or however popular, obscured or hazarded the loveliness of Jesus and His grace.

This was the key-note to all the sweetnesses of devotion in this great man's heart. He sought the Church, and loved the Church, and suffered for it, because the love of Christ constrained him. And he grew into greater and greater distrust of all those sentiments which are paraded as pious, but assume the supremacy which is due to Jesus and His love. Can we say it of ourselves? Is there any shadow of such a substantial virtue in us, with our self-seeking, our self-planning, our aiming at a religion that shall be easy and flattering, and the very flimsiest mockery of a cross? Hear the grand echo from the old Apostle, and from the life that tracked his footsteps, "As we were allowed of God to be put in trust with the gospel, even so we speak; not as pleasing men, but God which trieth our hearts."

ADDRESS,

Delivered at the Dedication of Seneca Lodge, No. 113, Waterloo, June 24th, 1867.

M. W. STEPHEN H. JOHNSON, G. M.

M. W. G. M., rendering to us the favor of your personal presence, giving the interest of your dignified character and the sanction of your high authority to this occasion, lend me the' protection of your patience, while, in the name of this gratified assembly, and especially of these brothers submitting to your gavel, I tender you our unqualified thanks, and while in the name of a present and a future humanity. I congratulate the brethren of this Lodge upon the honorable auspices that attend this new era of their beneficent work.

The salutations of a similar honor are cheerfully accorded to you,* M. W. B., as once invested with that exalted power, and as always illustrious to them that appreciate genuine merit, by the amenity of your unassuming manners, by the pellucid elegance of your modest diction, by your proficiency in Masonic lore, by your thorough command of our traditional, and profound jurisprudence, by the fraternal spirit that prompts and pervades your

* Hon. John L. Lewis of Penn Yan, P. G. M.

counsels, by the sanctity of the desolate sorrow that has broken your fatherly heart, and by your meek resignation to the mysterious chastening of our heavenly Father, and by that purity of character, which like the Koh-i-noor, rarely produced by the Almighty architect, drinks the light of heaven to reflect it in dazzling beauties, a treasure which potentates covet, and no ignoble man can possess.

It would be an impertinent solicitation, were I to employ my honorable position in urging you, W. M. of this zealous Lodge, or your brother-associates in this well achieved enterprise, to hail with thankfulness and delight this day of coronation for your cherished plans. I rather avail myself of this permission to be the utterer of your own sentiments in soliciting you to regard me as heartily joining in your acclaims, sharing in your pleasure, and throbbing with your hopes. Your spontaneous demonstrations of brotherly regard, will not permit me to entertain for a moment the feeling that I am in any respect a stranger. Your own suffusion with the mild influences of our unselfish fraternity so pervades your demeanor, suggesting the brotherly word, warming the grip, and kindling the features, that I can only be one of you in this hour when all of you are enlisted for all mankind, but especially for the brethren. The leer of indifference, the cruel criticism of a foe, how can I fear it, when you are the rampart that shelters my feebleness.

And you, my friends, that without ungenerous prejudices have assembled to blend your sympathies with those who do not address you as fraternizing in Masonic privilege, though honoring you in other relations, many of them sacred and impressive, have I to beg your congratulations? No, your very presence attests a readiness to commend the good intentions and applaud the glad success which render this day festive.

You rejoice as citizens. You share in the triumph gained for humane and noble objects. If you feel not the pulsations of the fraternity, you do exult in the advancement and elevation of our race which every movement of the fraternity proposes. No paltry narrowness limits your sympathies, but you hail the testimony that another provision has been made to transmit the claims of faith, hope, and charity unto generations that are yet unborn.

And you, fair representatives of heaven's last best gift to man, we congratulate ourselves that you are here to grace and beautify the scene, sweet ornaments of Paradise, the only comfort that guilty man could carry out of Eden, for here does it well beseem you to be present where the sanctities of religion welcome the tokens of restored brotherhood, and where the great social engine for woman's rescue from oppression and injury, the Masonic institution remonstrates against the masculine cruelties of rude and unenlightened society.

Our theory of human excellence is based upon the principle that the best patterns which are not more than human, must be somewhere defective. As some philosopher has phrased it, "There is no superior man without some grain of folly; but this folly, like that of the cross, is the divine part of reason. This mysterious power Socrates called his demon." We accordingly represent the possibilities of virtue in a circle that approximates perfection as its centre, but on no side touches it. And two remarkable exemplars are erected by us into prominence. To one of these we dedicate this festal day in our Masonic calendar, among our authorized traditions we commemorate as one of the eminent patrons of Freemasonry, that conspicuous beacon in the darkness of the past, that unquenchable exemplar of faithful rebuke, the vindicator of moral precepts and the harbinger of resurrection-light. What perversion of character can result from a system which preserves and honors such traditions? None, but the formation of dispositions prone to sternness against vice. The exclusive study of that bold model might render some imitators too inflexible and sturdy. We have therefore another model of uprightness in the Apostolic John, fervent and affectionate, eagle-winged in his sublime contemplations, but saturated in every emotion with the spirit of love. While we, as Christian Masons, in a land that adores the immaculate High Priest of our salvation, pursue the round of our varied duties, these are the samples of austere bravery on the one side, and of mild suavity on the other, on which the Masonic eye is taught to rest with complacency. Brothers, in this traditional light! Have I disclosed anything foreign to the actual spirit and purpose of our Fraternity? Friends and witnesses! is there anything in this captivating theory which you reject because the practical result so contradicts it? Do you spurn me as a pedler of ideals, when my wares should be reality and fact? Be patient, then, and be trustworthy, while I impart to you under injunction of the utmost caution how you use it, one of the most vital and peculiar secrets of Freemasonry, which is, it proposes no *argument* for its own *vindication.* If you will keep so much of the secret well, you deserve to have more of it. I trust you for your honest look, and will tell you another secret: Freemasonry has no secret in its keeping which every good man ought not to know, none but such as every good man craves and is eager to learn. Ah, you are playing Delilah with me, you are coaxing all the mysteries out of my bosom, you are flattering me with your attention, until I can keep back nothing of my strength. So now I must tear off the last veil, and unbosom the terrible mystery of all. Freemasonry has no secret sheltered under its ceremonies and disguises, but such as it is willing every good man should possess if he only has it *lawfully.*

But herein is the graveness of public allegation to our discredit. The point of difficulty is this, that any system intrinsically good, and actually aiming at the benefit of man, should assume the appearance and submit to the imputation of being secret, pledged to keep in the dark, and apeing the airs of importance by sitting with closed doors and being fearfully mysterious. I am on the same side with the fault-finders. I cannot find the material in the old, grand, venerable structure of Masonry, which is so transcendently mysterious as to be a better truth because it is a secret one.

I am one of those iconoclasts that denounce this mode of putting special sacredness on images which are no holier than man. Who is there that goes in for demolishing all these secret trades, exposing all these hidden arts, and letting the noble public have the first right to everything? Let him raise his rallying cry. I may join his party. But it must be thorough reform, pausing at nothing, and throwing everybody's mystery open to my virtuous curiosity, or I will have none of it.

First, we must revolutionize this whole secret system of love-letters, and the forlorn swain, aching to empty his heart into tender syllables, shall no more fill the poetic corner of the newspaper with his anonymous ditty, or buy the use of two lines in a city daily for his enigmatic initials about the young lady who winked at the corner, or dropped a glove at the church-door. These mysterious puzzles must come out into honest daylight like published banns. That perfumed love-letter must be contraband, and be confiscated for publication. Those iniquities of tender correspondence must be printed and pasted on the lamp-posts, lest unsuitable matches should disturb the discreet, or vile elopements shock society. We must have these furtive devotions of young enthusiasts, like the prayers of old Pharisees at the corners of the streets, and that at the unwitching hours of broad-day. In one word, we will explode this whole mystery of love-making, and have a new era without whispers, and pressures of the hand, and secret conspiracies of fidelity to each other.

We propose to systematize this business, and to issue policies of love-insurance, but the risk will involve strict conditions. The memorandum will specify there shall be no sparks in the kitchen, no matches in the parlor, no secret fires in young hearts. Frizzle-headed Patrick from Far-down shall not hitch his chair within three feet of simpering Bridget from Killarney, and no love-promise shall be proved unless two parties swear to it, one of whom shall be an old maid that has not refused three good offers, and the other a male minor with a single stamp in his pocket, who was courageous enough to propose without stammering. All hail the day of mysteries unveiled! What bankruptcy will it bring to gossips! What fabulous values to the stock of them that make love with frost-bitten affections!

But setting all badinage aside. Is there not something rather unnatural in this crusade against retirement? Is it not war against the Creator, this attempt to break down all confidential relations, all the blessed charities of life which let not the left hand know what the right hand doeth?

Why, that epitome of common sense, the common law, pronounces a man's house to be his castle. Is it merely in the sense of its being his shelter from bailiffs? Or is it his domestic lodge, where a heavenly secrecy protects and delights all that nestle within that charmed circle? It is there his virtues grow, his weaknesses are helped, his weariness refreshed, his selfishness banished, and the sinews of his goodness and his fortitude braced up for new wrestles with the hardships of life. A home that is less than this is a chafing chain upon the heart. But the greater proportion of its virtue rests in the conceded fact that here we have confidence, the hallowed veil of mystery that defies intrusion, and the endearments of parent and child, of brethren sacred to each other, and of wedlock that keeps a solemn vow.

Break this magic spell of privacy, and what remains of the sacredness of home, sweet home? If you wish to dissolve society into mere puddles of pollution, begin your deluge of desecration by unbinding the restraints of secrecy upon domestic confidence. Loosened ligaments of home attachment are but the synonym for loose morals. My proposition involves no sheltering of private vices, no treasuring of iniquitous secrets. But it does contemplate that play of the feelings, that surrender of everything to the kind affections, without which the strong virtues grow crabbed and whimsical and harsh, and even the philanthropic sentiments degenerate into a milk and water affectation.

We will rise, however, to a still more elevated plane of observation, ascend with me the heights of Zion, and there discover that man carried up into the more sacred exercises of his immortality never becomes exempt from the law which imposes certain restrictions of seclusion and privacy and implicit confidence upon his better virtues.

What part of our character so deserves and demands positive, and public, and undisguised testimonies of its reality and power, as our religion. Smothered and secreted, it smoulders and expires. If it be not our light before men, it is darkness everywhere. Its vitality is its openness, its manifestation in every act, its translation out of the heart into the language of unambiguous deeds.

But what is that religion worth, however palpable it shows, which has not tenfold more of inward secret power, of interior hunger for righteousness, of unrevealed thirst for light and truth, of private communing with its Eternal Source, of a whole volume of inward experience whereof the outward demonstration is but one leaf. It has a vast interior life which none but the All-searching Eye reads. It has prayers which vibrates only in the ear of God, hopes and fears which may not be talked of, revelations which it cannot tell, and raptures which no earthly language can describe. To unbosom it all to our fellow-mortals is to ruin its purity. The very attempt to uncover these secret proceedings of the soul is fraught with danger. Hypocrisy falsely clothes what we thus pretend to unclothe. The taking away the veil is the violation of its sacredness. A religion that pretends to talk itself all out is a religion that terminates in talk. *Honesty* needs no *cloak*, it is the *face* that speaks the better because unveiled. But *modesty* dismantled is modesty no more.

Yes, with reverence be it spoken, the Almighty would cease to be the All-gracious, were it not His system of giving Light to His Universe by keeping secret reservations for them that keep faith with Him. The light that sparkles from pole to pole of His creation is the light that sheds its midway glory between the east and west, luminous with this sentence, "The secret of the Lord is with them that fear him, and He will shew them His covenant."

Is it so with the awful verities that Heaven has lent to man? And must that stupendous argument of man's value, his religious life, hide the vaster and the more sacred portion of itself in secret palpitations which the Almighty hand alone can quell? And does the derision of mankind hiss at the absurdity which would unveil the pleasant affections of domestic life alarmed at the mention of intrusion? Such is the fabric of nature, and such the will of Him that breathed it into being, and throbs in all its pulses.

But when you have the traditions of virtue, and the incitements to science, and the exercise of the fraternal spirit, all these fused into a brotherhood, binding the ages together, insisting that not mere human blood, but the will to elevate and improve our common humanity, creates a stronger tie than the melting bond of a common mortality, when men recognizing this duty to help each other in surmounting the difficulties of virtue agree upon symbols that shall speak to all races, languages and times the same admonitions and the same hopes, is there to be no household confidence, no sacred privacy that shall mark this symbolic instruction as a privilege, and as a trust, not flung away upon crowds of contemptuous and profane, but reserved for those who will be pledged to maintain and to honor it? The man that would be better than he is, the man that would help his brother be wiser and better, the man that dares fetter himself with the obligation to make this life more heavenly, and this human nature less selfish, less sordid, less narrow and inhuman, that man, and that man *only*, is fit to be a free and accepted Mason. Anything else caricatures our craft. The false man, the vicious man, the selfish, grasping, sneaking fraction of a whole sound manhood may wear our apron, but he does not work at our trade. He must be large-hearted, or there is not room in his bosom for our virtuous secret. He must be willing to trust his brothers, or they will fear to trust him. A man of whom the best is that part of him which every one can see, is very suspicious material for a theory of virtue which especially values what is not seen.

All perfect globes have an outside and an inside. Every great system of truth has its exoteric and its esoteric doctrines. We have been standing on the surface of our fraternity-theory looking outward. The outside observer says that the rind of our theory is secrecy, and that when this is peeled off there is little pulp left, and that little may be worthless.

Now, with your permission, brethren, I will reverse my position, and summon to your recollection the inward principles of the craft. Let me bespeak your pardon if I forget that there are uninitiated present while we presume upon this exposure of Freemasonry. Think not that I dream of letting more light into our institution. It has an obstinate way of forbidding that.

My object is rather to do the work of the facetious Hibernian, when digging a hole through the wall of the over-dark cellar. "Well, Patrick, my good fellow, and so you are for getting a little more of this blessed light down there," said the passing neighbor. "And is it the blessed light that ye say," replied Pat, "and sure, I am after making a hole to let the *dark* out." Precisely my purpose, I am for letting the dark out. And this consists in viewing our Masonic system as a social bond. It does not exist for the individual except as a member of its social body. The individual alone cannot preserve it. Combination and consent are the elements of its vitality, the essentials of its existence.

How does this society take form? All human societies, that stand by law and expect perpetuation, must assume one of three forms, or put them in combination, the monarchical, the oligarchic, or the democratic. My impression is that no perfect organization of human society can subsist without blending the three.

How is it with our Fraternity? Freemasonry is eminently, unequivocally, inevitably monarchical. Be not startled at this declaration. Its monarch is the word of God. Without this it dissolves, it perishes. It asks no *outward* light, because this gift of God to man is its *inward*, sufficient, unquenchable light. And while the natural gifts are all it assumes to hold in its custody, it avows the supernatural to be the true light of man, and thus conducts him to the portals of religion, that entering there he may find the good and perfect gift which the monarch of the Lodge has commanded him to seek.

Empires stand by their submission to force. Nations focalize themselves in the will of an autocrat. Governments crystallize themselves into solidity by acknowledging the sovereignty of a constitution. But we stand from age to age by the awe of the Divine word. In this our symbolism centralizes. The *knowledge* that outvies and underlies all knowledge is the word from God. All light that reflects from the Universe centres in this original of light. The initial lesson of a world's Genesis, as of Masonic creation, is "God said, let there be light." The possibility and the potency of all light to all the faculties is in God's word.

Every system that contains wisdom clusters around a central idea. The appearances of the system may vary, but it remains substantially and vitally the same while the central focal idea continues in its place of honor and power. That dominant invariable idea in Freemasonry is the indefeasible sovereignty of God's word. That is not the sun of our system, but *more* than the sun, even the power that stations and enlightens the sun, the beginning of all creation, both of life and of a living fraternity. The immense compass of all the powers that Freemasonry carries through the generations of men gravitates towards the Word. Remove this from its inviolate supremacy over our beliefs and over our actions, and there comes the crash and ruin of our system.

Tear out the heart from its focal centre, and where is the galvanism that can make the body live?

Smite with scorn the living venerable constitution by which your nation survives, and who but a crazy dreamer would expect the healthful functions of freedom, or the perpetuity of uncorrupted patriotism? No, certain ideas and certain facts are not only elemental but vital. And in our Masonic system this is the irreversible necessity, the throne and the altar are one, and that throne occupied by the word of God. Brothers! is there any genuine monarch visible among us but that Divine Guide, at the beginning of our career spreading its pages to teach us fraternity, and unfolding its leaves of light when the dark grave grasps our mortality.

And yet when you touch the details of administration, and of direction and authority, you immediately find the wisdom of our brotherhood vesting these powers in a few. We admit the principle that the best should rule, amenable to no constituency, checked by no conspiracy of cabal or of multitude, controlled only by the law and the landmark. We have tried this principle for ages, and we have found it bringing all work to the plummet and the square. With us, the best is not the most learned, nor the most devout, nor the man most applauded of the crowd, but he that gives his best energies with most zeal and with greatest effect to the production of harmony, fervor, and stability in our work. So long as authority vests in such men they represent those ancient and venerable aristocrats, the time-sanctioned landmarks of the craft which must not be removed, bounding all ambitions, outliving all fluctuations, like God's landmarks, the *ever*lasting mountains, the *never*-wasting seas.

But the *charm* of the Brotherhood is that, "We meet upon the level." *Equality* writes its magic word upon every one that enters our door. The monarch upon our throne is our crown of glory; the best men in the best places are our sources of order and strength; but the *sweet attraction* that like a mellow atmosphere, bathes the brotherhood in continued delights, is the principle that banishes all the factitious distinctions of life, all the upstart conceits and arrogances of the world, and places upon one level, the millionaire and the laborer, the king and the peasant, Solomon and the just illumined craftsman.

How it blends the contrasted conditions of life!

"*Mollia duris, sine pondere habentia pondus.*"

Back to your kennels, ye snarling haters of mankind! The Lodge hushes your discord.

Back to your hopeless darkness, ye retailers of doubts and scepticisms, and atheistic chaff! The Lodge bars its precincts of holy light against you.

And ye, that cannot brook equality with your brother, because toil hardens his hands, or because the pale hue of mental stress is upon his studious brow, this is your rebuke, "We meet upon the level."

"Shine, brother, in thy place, and be content;
The stars pre-eminent in magnitude,
And they that from the zenith dart their beams,
Visible though they be to half the earth,
Though half a sphere be conscious of their brightness,
Are yet of no diviner origin,
No purer essence, than the one that burns,
Like an untended watch-fire, on the ridge
Of some dark mountain; or than those which seem
Humbly to hang, like twinkling winter lamps,
Among the branches of the leafless trees;
All are the undying offspring of one Sire;

> Then, to the measure of the light vouchsafed,
> Shine, brother! in thy place, and be content."

Brothers that have felt the illumining and warming rays of Masonic light, have I misrepresented our theory?

Is there any feature in my picture of our social system, which I have overdrawn?

You justify it, you pronounce it correct. You join with me, then, in declaring that such is the theoretical compend of the three principles in human government in whose honor we this day raise the banner of our fervent allegiance.

Such is the fraternity in furtherance of whose purposes a structure furnished with appropriate symbols, garnished with admirable art, and ambitious of beauty that may perpetually hint the beauties of a glorious high throne from the beginning, is this day dedicated to three objects under the one name Freemasonry—the enthroning of God's Word, the assertion of law and order, and the promotion of equality among all by degrading none.

Every thing that is virtuous in man rises up to join in this acclaim. All the nobility that is in us falls into the procession of triumph on this coronation day. The best part of our nature feels itself represented in this jubilee of our immortality. We have built least for ourselves, most for the future. We have mingled, neighbor and stranger, rejoicing sharers in this new structure, and congratulating friends from other precincts, we have mingled as *brothers*, erecting here our pillar of testimony that man belongs to other elements and other destinies of which this earthly scene can furnish only the *symbols*. But man belongs for the present to this life and to its demands. Masonry binds him to these present duties and these present needs. But the cord that signifies obligation is of two strands, the one, virtue's history in the past, the other, immortality's bond with the future. We scorn the fanaticism of progress that breaks the tie of reverence for the past. We crush the addled egg of stagnation that promises no glorious, heroic, enchanting future. Brotherhood to come,—the desire of all nations waiting at the door,—liberty and light, light and liberty, the mother and the son, yet to visit the darkened habitations of emancipated man. Labor nowhere to be defrauded, and misfortune everywhere to be befriended; these are the gleaming beacons towards which we steer our unintimidated, undiscouraged hopes.

But we have ordeals to pass. This voyage of progress is not on placid seas. Human life holds terrible elements and horrid jealousies. Our system wakens their fury. We provoke them by our mightiness, we tempt them by our infirmities. We rouse them innocently, and we justify them by our follies. We honor our fraternity, and jealousy panic-stricken flies to the combat. We discredit and betray our sacred theory, and indignation springs to its weapons of assault.

I am not amazed at this. The wonder would be that it should be otherwise. Few words will explain it.

Human society subsists under two necessary, inevitable, interminable sovereignties. They both concern the multitude as a mass, and the individual as like the mass a world in himself. The one sovereignty is earthly, but God-appointed, wielding its protection and its demand for the rights of person and of property, and may be termed the civil order. The other sovereignty is spiritual, and sublime, viewing the man always in relations to the supernatural and the Divine, and may be termed the ecclesiastical order. Both are sacred and inviolable, each in its sphere is blessed and each in its legitimate jurisdiction fortified by the right hand of our Creator. But what an unsolved problem, what a riddle that bewilders human perversity, to write for each sovereignty on rock that no proud waves can wash, "Thus far shalt thou go and no farther."

Between these wrestling sovereignties supporting both, encroaching upon neither, aiming to be not civil order, but its ally and strength; not ecclesiastical order, but its adherent and subordinate, stands our mysterious fraternity, distrusted by both, buffeted anon by one and by the other, but never nursing one passion of resentment, scarcely daring one syllable of retort, and while the forms of justice hound and manacle its adherents, it steadily inculcates faithful citizenship, while the frightened champions of orthodoxy defame and denounce, it calmly whispers "put your trust in God, and patiently follow him that 'points to heaven and leads the way.'" By the honest timidity of the one, by the conscientious jealousy of the other, we are the sufferers. For every ordeal we are the better. It is virtue that grows brighter in its calamities. We may groan and writhe again, but we never shall perish until man has adjusted himself in equal and indissoluble perfection as the citizen and as the saint, and in the architecture of the stupendous and eternal Lodge, where no symbol is needed, where they need no candle, neither light of the sun, where the burning scimitars of the cherubim shall guard the everlasting gates. Providence shall need us no more.

Such is the social system in whose honor we this day raise the banner of our fervent allegiance. Such is the fraternity in furtherance of whose purposes, a structure is this day dedicated to the enthroning of God's word, the assertion of law and order, and the promotion of equality among all by degrading none.

Can we silence the testimony of our praise? Can we leave uncommended this result of a zeal that has so fitly expressed itself to the eye, and in its laudable purposes shows a valid title to the tribute of our hearty praise?

The temple which the wisest of kings projected, and the genius of gifted Hirams planned, was built from secret arch to the lily work of elaborated capitals, with the choicest of materials and the outlay of the utmost skill. It symbolizes the structure of profoundest faith at the foundation, and of exquisite finish in every virtue which we must prepare for God's glory to inhabit.

The work you this day dedicate may shelter generations that will have forgotten the names of the builders. But the moral structure we each of us shall rear, is the home that each of us must finish in a few brief days, and then occupy forever.

www.ingramcontent.com/pod-product-compliance
Lightning Source LLC
LaVergne TN
LVHW020927110826
845150LV00004B/791

* 9 7 8 1 4 2 5 5 5 3 9 1 3 *